Ben Goldstein
Ceri Jones

The **BIG** Picture

2nd edition

A2 ELEMENTARY Student's Book British English

www.richmondelt.com/thebigpicture

CONTENTS UNITS 1–4

1 One world

1.1 A WARM WELCOME p6
- G to be
- V countries and nationalities
- " word stress

1.2 ME AND MY WORLD p8
- G possessive adjectives and possessive 's
- V personal possessions
- " /ɪ/ and /iː/ sounds
- ✓ talking about yourself

1.3 WHERE IN THE WORLD p10
- 🔧 before you read
- V useful adjectives
- ⇄ work in a group

1.4 MEETING AND GREETING p12
- 📹 saying hello
- FL greetings and introductions
- " sentence stress
- ✎ filling in forms

2 My life

2.1 BOOMERANG KIDS p16
- G present simple (I, you, we, they)
- V verb collocations
- " do you /djuː/

2.2 ALTERNATIVES p18
- G present simple (he, she, it)
- V families
- " -s ending
- ✓ completing a short text; writing a message

2.3 A VIRTUAL FRIEND p20
- G question words
- 🔧 listen for specific information
- " question intonation
- ⇄ talk about specific information

2.4 THAT'S INTERESTING! p22
- 📹 Nadiya's family
- FL small talk
- " showing interest
- ✎ a personal profile

3 Days of our lives

3.1 TIME ZONES p26
- G adverbs and expressions of frequency
- V daily routine verbs
- " sentence stress

3.2 TAKE IT EASY p28
- G modifiers
- V free-time activities
- " emphasizing modifiers
- ✓ listening to a long conversation

3.3 HAPPY BIRTHDAY p30
- V months and ordinals
- 🔧 understand ideas in paragraphs
- ⇄ write about specific information

3.4 LET'S CELEBRATE p32
- 📹 a special day
- FL making suggestions
- " sounding enthusiastic
- ✎ a blog post

4 Home life

4.1 A ROOF OVER YOUR HEAD p36
- G there is/are
- V houses and rooms
- " short answers

4.2 A HOME FROM HOME p38
- G prepositions of place
- V furniture
- ✓ reading three short texts

4.3 THE UNDERGROUND CITY p40
- V places in a town
- 🔧 listen for main ideas
- ⇄ take notes

4.4 AN UNUSUAL HOME p42
- 📹 life on the road
- FL directions
- " sentence stress
- ✎ asking for information

CONTENTS UNITS 5–8

5 Shopping around

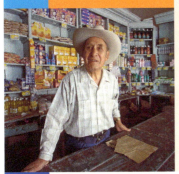

5.1 THE END OF THE MALL p46
- G can/can't
- V shopping
- 🗣 sentence stress

5.2 LOOKING GOOD p48
- G present continuous
- V clothes and accessories
- 🗣 -ing /ɪŋ/ sound
- ✓ answering questions about a conversation

5.3 ON THE STREET p50
- G present simple and continuous
- 🔧 find information in a text
- ⇄ work together

5.4 CAN I TRY IT ON? p52
- 📹 our clothes
- FL shopping expressions
- 🗣 Yes/No questions
- ✎ describing a photo

6 The great outdoors

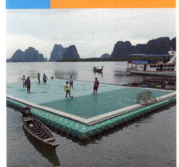

6.1 HOW DO YOU KEEP FIT? p56
- G like, love, hate + noun/-ing form
- V sports and leisure
- 🗣 likes and dislikes

6.2 A VERY SPECIAL PLACE p58
- G object pronouns
- V the countryside
- ✓ discussing a topic

6.3 WHATEVER THE WEATHER p60
- V the weather
- 🔧 identify opinions
- ⇄ explain diagrams

6.4 CAN I LEAVE A MESSAGE? p62
- 📹 storm chasers
- FL telephone language
- 🗣 sounding friendly
- ✎ messaging

7 On the move

7.1 BEFORE AND AFTER p66
- G past simple of be, there was/were
- V holiday phrases
- 🗣 short answers

7.2 MICROADVENTURES p68
- G past simple regular verbs
- V past time expressions
- 🗣 -ed endings
- ✓ reading a long article

7.3 COMMUTERS' TALES p70
- V transport
- 🔧 read in detail
- ⇄ simplify a text

7.4 GETTING AROUND p72
- 📹 crazy rides
- FL using public transport
- 🗣 question intonation
- ✎ an informal email

8 In the news

8.1 I MADE THE NEWS p76
- G past simple irregular verbs
- V life stages
- 🗣 past simple irregular verbs

8.2 CULTURE NEWS p78
- G verb + to + infinitive
- V entertainment
- 🗣 schwa sound
- ✓ completing a factual text

8.3 EYEWITNESS ACCOUNTS p80
- G sequencers
- 🔧 listen for facts and figures
- ⇄ talk about a text

8.4 I DON'T BELIEVE IT! p82
- 📹 Sophie's goals
- FL responding to news
- 🗣 echo questions
- ✎ a biography

3

CONTENTS UNITS 9–12

9 Food matters

9.1 BREAKFAST TIME p86
- G countable and uncountable nouns
- V food
- 🗣 consonant clusters

9.2 A HEALTHY DIET? p88
- G quantifiers
- V describing food
- 🗣 /uː/ and /ʌ/ sounds
- ✓ understanding details in short dialogues

9.3 LOVE FOOD, HATE WASTE p90
- G should
- 🔧 guess the meaning of words
- 🗣 should and shouldn't
- ⇄ help a friend

9.4 WHAT'S ON THE MENU? p 92
- 📹 soul food
- FL eating out
- 🗣 sentence stress
- ✎ a review

10 Technology

10.1 TECHNOLOGY TIMELINE p96
- G comparatives
- V electronic devices
- 🗣 pronouncing -er

10.2 CONNECTING PEOPLE p98
- G going to
- V communication verbs
- 🗣 going to /ɡənə/
- ✓ understanding short texts

10.3 ROBOT SUITS p100
- V parts of the body
- 🔧 identify reasons
- ⇄ write about a text

10.4 DO YOU FANCY GOING FOR A RUN? p102
- 📹 bionic boots
- FL invitations
- 🗣 positive and negative intonation
- ✎ an online post

11 A working life

11.1 MY SPACE p106
- G (don't) have to
- V school subjects
- 🗣 word stress

11.2 THE HAPPIEST PROFESSION p108
- G superlatives
- V jobs
- 🗣 the /ðə/ and /ðiː/
- ✓ listening and completing notes; understanding the general idea of conversations

11.3 THE CHANGING WORKPLACE p110
- G will for predictions
- 🔧 scan a text
- ⇄ explain in your own words

11.4 DREAM JOB p112
- 📹 comic book writer
- FL offers and requests
- 🗣 sounding helpful
- ✎ a formal email

12 Live life to the full

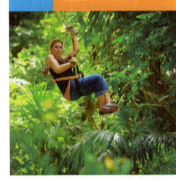

12.1 TRY SOMETHING NEW p116
- G present perfect
- V feelings and emotions
- 🗣 weak form of have

12.2 EXTREME ADVENTURES p118
- G present perfect and past simple
- V measurements
- 🗣 irregular past participles
- ✓ writing a short story

12.3 FACE YOUR FEARS p120
- G tense review
- 🔧 listen in detail
- ⇄ discuss concepts

12.4 COULD YOU RECOMMEND A HOTEL? p122
- 📹 sleeping in the sky
- FL recommendations
- 🗣 emphasis in recommendations
- ✎ an information leaflet

One world

1

Grammar G
to be
possessive adjectives and possessive 's

Vocabulary V
countries and nationalities
personal possessions
useful adjectives

Functional language FL
greetings and introductions

Skill
before you read

Video
saying hello

Writing
filling in forms

Exams
talking about yourself

The big picture: a message from space

1 Look at the picture. In pairs, guess the answers to the questions.
  1 Who are the people?
  2 Where are they from?
  3 Where are they?
  4 Who are they talking to?
  5 What are they saying?

2 🔊 1.1 Listen and check your answers.

3 In pairs, discuss the questions.
  1 Who do you say hello and goodbye to every day?
  2 What do you say?
  I say hello to my mother every day. I say 'Hola Mamá!'

5

1.1 A WARM WELCOME

G to be
V countries and nationalities

Vocabulary

1 Look at the picture. Match the continents with the words in the box.

> Africa   Asia   Europe   North America
> Oceania   South America

2 a Look at the Vocabulary box. Write the continents in the correct places.

   b Complete the nationalities with *-an*, *-ese* or *-ish*.

   c Add two more countries to each continent.

V countries and nationalities

Continent	Country	Nationality
(1)	Egypt Morocco Senegal	Egypti.......... Morocc.......... Senegal..........
(2)	Brazil Colombia Peru	Brazili.......... Colombi.......... Peruvi..........
(3)	Canada Mexico	Canadi.......... Mexic..........
(4)	China India Japan Turkey Thailand	Chin.......... Indi.......... Japan.......... Turk.......... Thai..........
(5)	France Germany Poland Spain	French Germ.......... Pol.......... Span..........
(6)	Australia	Australi..........

🔊 **1.2** Listen, check and repeat.

3 a 🔊 **1.3** « word stress » Listen and repeat the countries and nationalities. Notice how the underlined syllables are stressed.

   1 Mo<u>ro</u>cco   Mo<u>ro</u>ccan
   2 <u>Chi</u>na   Chi<u>nese</u>
   3 <u>Tur</u>key   <u>Tur</u>kish

   b 🔊 **1.4** In pairs, say the words and underline the stress. Listen, check and repeat.

   1 Japan   Japanese
   2 Poland   Polish
   3 Peru   Peruvian

Listening

4 🔊 **1.5** Listen to the conversation and answer the questions.

   1 Where are the people?
   2 What nationality is the man?
   3 What nationality is his wife?
   4 What nationality is the woman?
   5 Where are her parents from?

Grammar

5 🔊 1.5 Complete the conversation with the words in the box. Listen again and check.

am	are	aren't	I'm	is	isn't
it's	not	she's	they're		

A Welcome, please come in. (1) .... this your first visit to Morocco?
B Yes, it is. (2) .... a beautiful country. (3) .... very happy to be here. (4) .... you Moroccan?
A No, I'm (5) ...., actually. I'm Egyptian, but my wife's Moroccan. (6) .... from Rabat, but she (7) .... here at the moment. And you, are you American?
B Yes, I (8) ...., but my parents (9) .... (10) .... from Poland.
A Your parents are Polish? That's interesting! Please, have a cup of tea and a cake.
B Thank you.

6 Look at the conversation again. Tick (✓) when we usually use contractions (*they're*, *isn't*, etc.) or full forms (*they are*, *is not*, etc.).

		Contraction	Full form
1	Positive sentences	☐	☐
2	Negative sentences	☐	☐
3	Yes/No questions	☐	☐
4	Positive short answers	☐	☐
5	Negative short answers	☐	☐

G to be

+	I'm Italian.	We're Brazilian.	It's Turkish.
−	I'm not Moroccan.	They aren't French.	She isn't Egyptian.
?		Are you British?	Is he from Poland?
Y/N	Yes, I am. No, I'm not.	Yes, we are. No, we aren't.	Yes, she is. No, she isn't.

→ Grammar reference: page 132

7 In pairs, repeat the conversation in exercise 5, changing the countries and nationalities.

8 a 🔊 1.6 Choose the correct form of *to be* to complete the text below. Listen and check.

b 🔊 1.7 Look at the pictures. In pairs, discuss where the people and things are from. Listen and check.

Where's the coffee from? Is it from Spain?
No, it isn't. I think it's Italian.

All over the world, a big smile (1) *'re / 's* a great welcome, but (2) *'s / is* that enough? Well, no it (3) *is / isn't* – not always. In many countries, it (4) *'m / 's* also important to offer a drink or something to eat. For example, in Morocco it (5) *'s / isn't* usually mint tea and cakes – they (6) *'re / 's* small, sweet and very good. And drinks and cakes (7) *am not / aren't* the only way to give a warm welcome. Where (8) *am / are* these people and things from?

Speaking

9 What is a typical welcome like in your country?

10 Tick (✓) the questions you usually ask when you meet someone for the first time.

1 How are you? ☐
2 How old are you? ☐
3 Where are you from? ☐
4 What's your job? ☐
5 What's your name? ☐
6 What's your phone number? ☐

11 a In groups of three, take turns welcoming each other to your home. Imagine you're from different countries.

b Tell the class about your visitors.

This is Juan and this is Carmen. They're students.
Carmen's Spanish. Juan isn't Spanish. He's from Colombia.

1.2 ME AND MY WORLD

G possessive adjectives and 's
V personal possessions

Vocabulary

1 Match the words in the box with the pictures.

V **personal possessions**

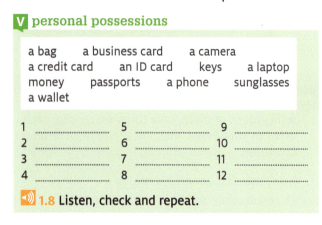

a bag   a business card   a camera
a credit card   an ID card   keys   a laptop
money   passports   a phone   sunglasses
a wallet

1 ......   5 ......   9 ......
2 ......   6 ......   10 ......
3 ......   7 ......   11 ......
4 ......   8 ......   12 ......

🔊 **1.8** Listen, check and repeat.

2 In pairs, say how many of the things you have with you today.

Listening

3 Look at the pictures again. Answer the questions about José.
1 What's his full name?
2 What nationality is he?
3 How old is he?
4 What's his address?
5 What's his job?
6 What's his phone number?

4 🔊 **1.9** Listen to José. Which personal possessions does he talk about?

🔍 notice

Use **this/that** for singular. Use **these/those** for plural.
Use **this/these** for something near you.
Use **that/those** for something not near you.

5 🔊 1.9 Listen again and complete the text with the correct words.

Hi, I'm José Luís. I live in ⁽¹⁾............... with my wife, but my job's in the USA. Our house is near the border and I cross it every day. Of course, you need to show your documents, so they're always in my ⁽²⁾............... Look, this is my Mexican ⁽³⁾............... And these are my passports – this is my ⁽⁴⁾............... passport and that's my Mexican one. My father's from the USA and he works in San Diego. I'm a lawyer at his company. This is my ⁽⁵⁾............... Its information is useful because the border police sometimes want to see it. They ask me about my father's work. They ask me about my mother and her family. They ask about the ⁽⁶⁾............... in my ⁽⁷⁾............... 'Is this your phone?', 'Are those your ⁽⁸⁾...............?' The police officers ask about everything … but it's their job. I guess they're the same all over the world!

6 When do you show your ID card or passport? Do the police ask a lot of questions in your country?

Grammar

7 a Look at the highlighted words in the text. In pairs, find who or what the people and things relate to.

'My wife' relates to José Luís.

b Match the possessive adjectives in the box with the subject pronouns.

| her | his | its | my | our |
| their | your | | | |

1 I ....
2 you ....
3 he ....
4 she ....
5 it ....
6 we ....
7 they ....

8 Look at the words in **bold** in the phrases from the text. Which means *of my father*? .... Which means *my father is*? ....

1 **my father's** from the USA
2 **my father's** work

G possessive adjectives and possessive 's

my	I'm French, but **my** wife is Colombian.
your	You're in class 3. This is **your** teacher.
his	He's late because **his** watch is broken.
her	She isn't here, but these are **her** glasses.
its	It's a beautiful country. **Its** beaches are great.
our	We're Indian. These are **our** passports.
their	They work in LA. Are those **their** business cards?
's	That's **Monica's car** = the car belongs to Monica

→ Grammar reference: page 132

9 🔊 1.10 ❝ /ɪ/ and /iː/ sounds ❞ Listen to the words. Notice the difference between the sounds /ɪ/ and /iː/. Listen again and repeat.

1 kiss /ɪ/   2 keys /iː/

10 🔊 1.11 Say the words in the box and put them in the correct columns. Listen, check and repeat.

| he | his | its | me | she | these | this | we |

/ɪ/	/iː/

11 Look at the picture. Where are the people? What are they doing?

12 a 🔊 1.12 Listen to the conversation. Say if the things belong to Marco (M), Lucy (L), both of them (B) or neither of them (N).

1 passport ....   4 watch ....
2 bag ....   5 laptop ....
3 phone ....   6 glasses ....

b In pairs, check your answers.

That's Lucy's passport.
No, it isn't. It's Marco's passport.

Speaking

13 In groups of three, choose three of your things and put them on the table. Invite a student from another group to your table. Ask and answer questions about the objects.

Is this your phone?
Yes, it is. It's my phone.
Are these Maria's glasses?
Yes, they're her glasses.

✅ Exam practice: page 156

1.3 WHERE IN THE WORLD?

before you read
useful adjectives

Reading

1 In pairs, ask and answer the questions.
  1 Do you like coffee?
  2 When do you drink coffee?
  3 Are there many cafés in your town?
  4 Do you have a favourite café? If so, what's it like?

> **before you read**
> Before you read a text, look at all the other information to help you understand it.
> • Look at the pictures, the title, the presentation, etc.
> • Ask yourself questions: *What kind of text is this? Who is the writer? What is it about?*

2 a Read the Skill box. Look at the pictures, the title and the headings. Guess the answers to the questions.
  1 Where is the writer from?
     a France   b Australia   c Brazil
  2 What kind of text is it?
     a a formal report   b a newspaper article
     c a personal blog post
  3 What is the topic of the text?
     a a very small café   b Brazilian cafés are different
     c our world is international

  b Read the text and check your answers.

3 Read the text again. Complete the table with things that are Brazilian or from other countries.

Brazil	Other countries

An Australian in **Brazil**

Home   About   Blog   Search

Posted: Wednesday 14 July

It's a small world

I'm in São Paulo in a little café near my apartment. It's a traditional café on the corner of a small side street. In the evening it's crowded and noisy, but at the moment it's quiet and empty. I'm the only person at the bar. I look around. The pictures on the wall are local scenes. The news on the radio is local news. Everything is very Brazilian … or is it?

The waiter speaks to me in English. Her English is perfect. I ask her where she's from. 'Dublin, in Ireland,' she says. Another waiter is from Spain and their boss is from Argentina. 'You're a long way from home,' I say. 'Yes,' she says, 'I am, but I love it here! It feels like home.'

I agree. This is a great place, and everyone is very friendly. The waiter gives me a menu. There's Brazilian coffee, of course, but there are also coffees from three different continents – South America, Asia and Africa! And it's not only the coffees that are from around the world. The snacks are French and Belgian, the sandwiches are from the USA and Cuba, the pizza is Italian. It's a Brazilian café, but the menu is totally international.

And it isn't just the café. It's the people, it's their clothes, it's the music. It's everything around me! I'm in Brazil, but I could be anywhere!

Is this so unusual? Not really. In fact, it's quite normal in our modern world. Think about it. Our movies are American, our technology is Asian, our food is from all over the world!

This café is a reflection of our lives. We really do live in a global world … is that such a terrible thing? What do you think?

Hot drinks

Coffees:
Blue Mountain 🇯🇲
Java 🇮🇩
Colombian 🇨🇴
Santos 🇧🇷
Ruiru 11 🇰🇪
Robusta 🇻🇳

Teas:
Gunpowder green 🇨🇳
Assam 🇮🇳
Sencha 🇯🇵

Snacks

Sweet:
Crêpes 🇫🇷
Waffles 🇧🇪
Brigadeiro 🇧🇷
Alfajores 🇦🇷
Bolinho de Chuva 🇧🇷

Savoury:
Coxinhas 🇧🇷
Philly cheesesteak sandwich 🇺🇸
Medianoche sandwich 🇨🇺
Pizza slice 🇮🇹

4 Complete the text with countries so it's true for you. In pairs, compare your answers.

Your phone is from ....
Your shoes are from ....
Your bag is from ....
Your watch is from ....
Your music is from ....
Your car is from ....
Your lunch is from ....
Your favourite film is from ....

5 Do you think we live in a global world? Are you happy about it?

Vocabulary

6 a <u>Underline</u> all the adjectives in the text in exercise 2.

b Match the adjectives with their opposites in the Vocabulary box.

V useful adjectives

1 quiet	a crowded
2 large	b traditional
3 local	c international
4 modern	d terrible
5 empty	e noisy
6 great	f unusual
7 normal	g little

🔊 **1.15** Listen, check and repeat.

🔍 notice

Adjectives come before a noun or after the verb *to be*.
This is **good** coffee. This coffee is **good**.
They don't change with plural nouns.
These are **good** cakes. NOT ~~These are goods cakes.~~

7 Complete the sentences with adjectives from the Vocabulary box. In pairs, compare your answers.
1 I'm from a .... town.
2 My flat is on a .... street.
3 It's in a .... neighbourhood.
4 The shops in my neighbourhood are ....

Writing

8 Read the captions. Then match them with the pictures.

1 This is my favourite street. It's old and very quiet. It's full of traditional little shops and the local people are very friendly!
♡ 16 likes

2 This is my new home. It's a busy, modern neighbourhood with shops and restaurants from all round the world. I love it!
♡ 9 likes

3 This is my favourite Italian restaurant. It's never empty because the food is great and the waiters are very nice.
♡ 18 likes

9 In pairs, find a picture of a place that you like. Write a caption for it. Use as many adjectives as you can.

⇄ **Mediation task:** All students, page 125

1.4 MEETING AND GREETING
FL greetings and introductions
🎥 saying hello

The big picture: saying hello

1 In pairs, match the words that mean 'hello' with the languages in the box. Do you know how to say 'hello' in any other languages?

| Arabic | Chinese | French | Italian |
| Japanese | Portuguese | Russian | Spanish |

2 **a** Look at the picture of some refugees. In pairs, guess the answers to the questions.
   1 Where are they from?
   2 Where are they going?
   3 How do they feel?

   b 🎥 1.1 Watch the video and check. How do the people in the town feel about the refugees?

3 In pairs, discuss the questions.
   1 Do any refugees live in your town?
   2 Are they welcome?
   3 Do you think it's important to say 'hello'?
   4 What other ways can you help refugees in a new town?

4 🎥 1.1 Watch the video again. Match the sentences with the people a–d.
   1 I'll welcome them with open arms.   ....
   2 Come in and say hello.   ....
   3 How do you say 'hello' in Syria?   ....
   4 When they said 'hello', I wasn't afraid then. ....

5 🎥 1.2 Watch Sophia and Dev talking about the video. Tick (✓) the ways they say you can help refugees.
   1 smile and say 'hello'   ☐
   2 give money   ☐
   3 say where the shops are ☐
   4 say how to use buses   ☐
   5 have a party   ☐
   6 teach English   ☐

6 **a** 🎥 1.2 Watch Sophia and Dev again. Do they know each other? How do you know?

   b Order the sentences.
   a ☐ Not bad.
   b ☐ Hi Dev!
   c ☐ Hey Sophia. How are you?
   d ☐ I'm good, thanks. And you?

Functional language

7 Look at the pictures. Where are the people? Are they meeting for the first time?

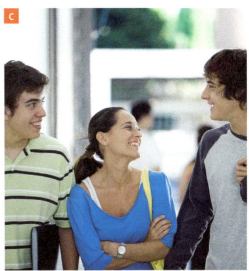

8 🔊 1.16 Listen to the conversations. Match them with the pictures.

1 ………   2 ………   3 ………

9 🔊 1.16 Listen again. Complete the conversations.

Conversation 1
A Excuse me, can I introduce you to Mr Smith? He's ⁽¹⁾……………… to the company. Mr Smith, ⁽²⁾……………… is Diana, she's the head of the department.
B Pleased to meet you, Diana. Please call me ⁽³⁾……………… .
C Nice to meet you, John. Is it ⁽⁴⁾……………… first time in Rio?
B Yes, it is. It's a beautiful city!

Conversation 2
A ⁽⁵⁾………………, let me introduce you to Pablo. Pablo, this is John, he's a ⁽⁶⁾……………… from university.
B Hi Pablo, nice to meet ⁽⁷⁾……………… .
C Hi John, ⁽⁸⁾……………… to meet you, too. How are you?
B I'm great. How about you?
C I'm fine, thanks.

Conversation 3
A Hey, Jack! How are ⁽⁹⁾……………… ?
B Hi Claire, not bad. And ⁽¹⁰⁾……………… ?
A Good, good. Are you on your break?
B Yes, I am. And you?
A No, I'm on the way home.
B OK, see you later.
A Goodbye.

FL   greetings and introductions

Introductions
Can I introduce you to …?
Let me introduce you to …
This is … He/She's …

Greetings
Hi … / Hey … / Hello …
Nice / Pleased / Great to meet you, (too).
See you later. / Goodbye.

How you are
How are you? / How are things?
Fine. / Great. / Good. / Not bad.
And you? / How about you?

10 🔊 1.17 🔊 **sentence stress** 🔊 Listen to the sentences. Notice how the underlined words are stressed. Listen again and repeat.

1 <u>Pleased</u> to <u>meet</u> you.
2 <u>Nice</u> to <u>meet</u> you, <u>too</u>.
3 <u>Let</u> me <u>introduce</u> you to <u>Pablo</u>.
4 I'm <u>great</u>. <u>How</u> about <u>you</u>?
5 <u>How</u> are <u>things</u>?
6 <u>See</u> you <u>later</u>.

Speaking

11 Practise acting out the conversations in exercise 9 using your own names. Try to stress the correct words.

12 In groups of four, imagine you are in a restaurant with a friend. You see a work colleague with someone you don't know. Practise another conversation.

REVIEW UNIT 1

Vocabulary
Countries and nationalities

1 a Write the name of:
   1 a country with a very famous capital city.
   2 a very cold country.
   3 a very hot country.
   4 a big country.
   5 a small country.

   b In pairs, compare your answers. Are the countries the same?

2 a Write the nationalities for all the countries in exercise 1.
   Italy → Italian

   b Underline the stressed syllable in both words.
   Italy   Italian

Personal possessions

3 a In pairs, look in your bags or pockets. Write the names of eight things you find. Are they singular or plural?

   b Tell your partner about the things you find using *this/that* or *these/those*.
   This is my wallet.   Those are my sunglasses.

Useful adjectives

4 a Write the letters in the correct order.
   1 tuiqe   *quiet*
   2 trgae   ....
   3 ytmep   ....
   4 ronaml   ....
   5 egral   ....
   6 noremd   ....

   b Write the opposites of the adjectives in 4a.

   c Choose four adjectives from 4a or 4b, and write short sentences.
   This is a quiet town.   This town is quiet.

Grammar
to be

5 Choose the correct form of *to be* to complete the sentences.
   1 It *'s / 'm* Paul.
   2 His surname *is / are* Stevens.
   3 He *'re / 's* from Cape Town.
   4 His telephone number *is / are* 7783451.
   5 No, he *aren't / isn't* married.

6 Write questions for the answers in exercise 5.
   What's his name?

7 Change the questions. Use *you/your* not *he/his*.
   What's your name?

8 In pairs, ask and answer the questions in exercise 7. Make a note of the answers.

9 Change pairs. Tell your new partner about your partner in exercise 8. Is any of the information the same for all of you?

Possessive adjectives and possessive *'s*

10 a 🔊 1.18 Complete the dialogue with the words in the box. Listen and check.

| her | its | my (x2) | 's | your (x3) |

   Cara Is that (1).............. bag, Paula?
   Paula No, it's Eva (2)............... They look the same but (3).............. bag is dark blue and mine is black.
   Cara And are those (4).............. keys?
   Paula Yes, they are. Sorry, I'll put them in (5).............. pocket. Oh wait, I can't find (6).............. mobile phone.
   Cara What does it look like?
   Paula (7).............. case is purple.
   Cara It's there on the chair, on top of (8).............. black bag!

   b In pairs, act out the dialogue. Use real objects.

Functional language
Greetings and introductions

11 Write the words in the correct order.
   1 later you see
   2 me introduce let you a friend to
   3 meet you to pleased
   4 are you how ?

12 a Complete the dialogues. Use the expressions in exercise 11.
   1 **A** Eva, this is Dani.
     B ....
   2 **A** I'm going home now.
     B OK, ...
   3 **A** ....
     B Fine, thanks. And you?
   4 **A** .... This is Sue.
     B Nice to meet you, Sue.

   b 🔊 1.19 Listen and check. Then stand up and introduce yourself to five people in your class.

🕐 Looking back

- Think of three things you can say about yourself.
- Think of two ways to say hello, two to say goodbye and two to say how you are.
- Which lesson or activity in this unit is your favourite? Why?

My life

2

Grammar G
present simple (*I, you, we, they*)
present simple (*he, she, it*)
question words

Vocabulary V
verb collocations
families

Functional language FL
small talk

Skill
listen for specific information

Video
Nadiya's family

Writing
a personal profile

Exams
completing a short text
writing a message

The big picture: a family on the move

1 Look at the picture. In pairs, guess the answers to the questions.
   1 Who are the people?
   2 Where are they from?
   3 What time of day is it? How do you know?
   4 Are they happy? Why/Why not?

   The family are probably in … because …
   I think they're happy because …

2 🔊 2.1 Listen to the family and check your answers.

3 In pairs, discuss the questions.
   1 Can you see families like this in your country? Why/Why not?
   2 How do people travel around where you live?
   3 Are you a happy person in the morning?

15

2.1 BOOMERANG KIDS

G present simple (I, you, we, they)
V verb collocations

Reading

1 Look at the picture and the title. What is the 'boomerang generation'? Read the introduction and check.

2 a Look at the reasons why people become 'boomerang kids'. Can you think of any more?
   a They lose their jobs.
   b They return from university.
   c They want to save money.

   b Read the rest of the text and match the reasons with the people.
   1 Manu ....   2 Laura ....   3 Carl ....

3 Do you know any 'boomerang kids'?

> 🔍 **notice**
>
> We use *be* + *a/an* to talk about what we do: *I'm a student*.
> We use *be* + number to talk about ages: *I'm 29*.

Vocabulary

4 Match the verbs in the box with the words to make phrases from the text.

V verb collocations

earn	find	have	leave	live
pay	share	study	want	work

1 .... in an office / as a waiter / hard
2 .... children / a good relationship
3 .... home
4 .... a job
5 .... money
6 .... alone / with my parents
7 .... at university / English
8 .... rent / the bills
9 .... a flat / a room
10 .... to buy a flat / to be a teacher

🔊 **2.2** Listen, check and repeat.

5 a Choose words to make the sentences true for young people in your country.
   Young people in my country …
   1 think it's *easy / difficult* to find a good job.
   2 leave home in their *20s / 30s*.
   3 have children in their *20s / 30s*.
   4 live *alone / with friends / with family*.
   5 earn *lots of / little* money.
   6 prefer to *buy a house / pay rent*.
   7 study at universities in *their cities / other cities*.
   8 have a *good / bad* relationship with their parents.

   b In pairs, compare your answers.

The boomerang generation

Young people who leave home but then go back to live with their parents are 'boomerang kids'. Today, we talk to three young people who are part of the 'boomerang generation' and we ask them four questions:

How old are you? *What do you do?*
Why do you live with your parents? *Do you like it there?*

Manu, Madrid
I'm 29. I work in an office in the city and I also work as a waiter at the weekend. I work hard and I earn money, but not much! I want to buy a flat and live alone, but houses in this city are very expensive. So now I live with my mother again. It's OK, most Spanish people leave home late, and they have children in their 30s.

Laura, Istanbul
I'm 25 and I share a flat with my friends, but now I need to go back home to live with my parents. Why? Because I don't have a job any more, and without money I can't pay the bills or pay rent. I like my parents' house and we have a good relationship, but I need to find a job … quickly!

Carl, Seattle
I'm 20 and I'm a student. I study at the University of California, but in the summer, I don't have a place to live, so now I'm back with my family. I don't like it. I share a room with my brother – he's 16. And most of my friends don't live near here. I study English and I want to be a teacher … but not in Seattle.

16

Grammar

6 Read the sentences from the text and underline the main verbs.
   1 Why do you live with your parents?
   2 I work in an office in the city.
   3 My friends don't live near here.
   4 I don't have a job any more.
   5 Do you like it there?
   6 We have a good relationship.

7 Answer the questions about the sentences in exercise 6.
   1 Which sentences are positive? .... negative? .... questions? ....
   2 Which word do we use with the main verb in negative sentences? ....
   3 Which word do we use with the main verb in questions? ....

G present simple (I, you, we, they)

+ I **share** a flat with friends.
   We **live** in the city centre.

− I **don't study** French.
   My parents **don't work**.

? **Do** your friends **pay** rent?
   Do you **have** children?

Y/N Yes, I **do**. / No, I **don't**.

→ Grammar reference: page 133

8 2.3 Complete the conversation between the interviewer (I) and Sian (S) with the correct forms of the verbs in brackets. Listen and check.

I Excuse me, what's your name?
S I'm Sian … Sian Lewis.
I Hi Sian. What (1) .... you ....? (do)
S I (2) .... as a waiter in a hotel restaurant … but I (3) .... to be an actor! (work, want)
I Really? (4) .... you .... in the movies, too? (work)
S No, I (5) .... … well, not yet! (not do)
I OK, and (6) .... you .... your job in the hotel? (like)
S Yes, I (7) .... It's great, but waiters (8) .... much money. (do, not earn)
I And where (9) .... you ...., Sian? (live)
S I (10) .... here in the city centre – near the hotel. (live)
I Who (11) .... you .... with? (live)
S I (12) .... a flat with two friends. (share)
I (13) .... you .... a good relationship? (have)
S Yes, we (14) ....! They (15) .... to be actors, too! (do, want)
I OK, well, good luck!

9 2.4 ❝ **do you** /djuː/ ❞ Listen to the interviewer's questions. How does he pronounce *do you*? Listen again and repeat.
   1 What **do you** do?
   2 **Do you** work in the movies, too?
   3 Where **do you** live?

Speaking

10 a In groups of four, ask and answer the questions. Write down any similarities you have with other people.

   What do you do?
   Where do you work/study?
   Do you like your job/course?
   Where do you live?
   Who do you live with?
   Do you have children?
   Do you have a good relationship?

   b Tell the class about any similarities you find.
   Julia and I work as teachers. We like our jobs!
   Oliver and Carol don't have children.

2.2 ALTERNATIVES

G present simple (*he, she, it*)
V families

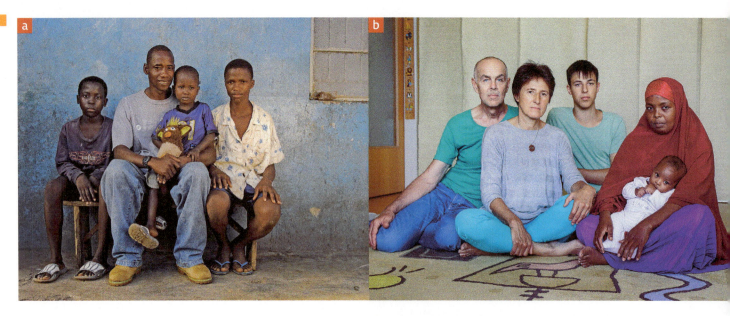

Vocabulary

1 Complete the table with the words in the box.

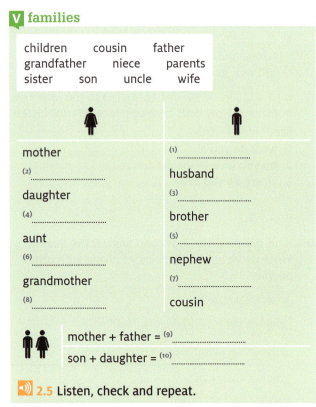

V **families**

children   cousin   father
grandfather   niece   parents
sister   son   uncle   wife

♀	♂
mother	(1) ....
(2)	husband
daughter	(3) ....
(4)	brother
aunt	(5) ....
(6)	nephew
grandmother	(7) ....
(8)	cousin

mother + father = (9) ....
son + daughter = (10) ....

🔊 2.5 Listen, check and repeat.

2 Complete the sentences with the correct words.
1 Your father's sister is your ....
2 Your mother's father is your ....
3 Your son is your brother's ....
4 Your brother's daughter is your ....
5 Your uncle's son is your ....
6 Your father is your cousin's ....

Listening

3 Look at the pictures. In pairs, guess the relationships between the people.

4 🔊 2.6 Match the phrases with the families. Listen and check.
1 A crowded house
2 A new home for a refugee
3 Help from a kind uncle
4 A family with an only child

5 🔊 2.6 Listen again and find Mohammed, Marianne, Corina and Li in the pictures.

Grammar

6 🔊 2.7 Choose the correct form of the verbs to complete the sentences. Listen and check. Match the sentences with the people in the pictures.
1 His father *work / works* in Qinghai.
2 At the weekend, he *teach / teaches* German.
3 He doesn't *have / has* a brother or sister.
4 She *study / studies* Medicine.
5 He *live / lives* with his two sons and his nephew.
6 Does she *like / likes* her big family?
7 She *go / goes* to university in the city.
8 She *want / wants* to help them.

7 Look at the sentences in exercise 6 again. Complete the rules with the words in the box.

negative sentences   positive sentences   questions

1 In .... with *he/she/it*, we add -s, -es or remove *y* and add -ies.
2 In .... with *he/she/it* we use *doesn't* and the infinitive.
3 In .... with *he/she/it* we use *does* and the infinitive.

18

G present simple (he, she, it)

+ Leyla **lives** in Austria.
  Her **son** cries at night.
  Marianne **watches** him.
− Mohammed **doesn't live** alone.
  His house **doesn't have** a garden.
? **Does** Corina **go** to university?
  Does she **want** to be a doctor?
Y/N Yes, she **does**. / No, she **doesn't**.

→ Grammar reference: page 133

8 2.8 Look at the family tree and complete the text with the correct forms of the verbs. Listen and check.

I'm Carol and I'm 22. I (1) _____ (study) at university in San Diego. I (2) _____ (have) two brothers. Peter is 18 and he's a student too, but he (3) _____ (live) at home with my parents in LA. Greg is 25 and he's a lawyer. His wife is Brazilian and they (4) _____ (live) in São Paulo. Lara (5) _____ (stay) at home and she (6) _____ (look) after their daughter, Ingrid – my niece! Carla is my mother and she's a teacher. She (7) _____ (teach) Science at a local school. My father Gordon is retired. He (8) _____ (not do) a lot now … well, he (9) _____ (watch) TV and (10) _____ (try) to learn Portuguese!

9 2.9 **-s ending** Listen to the sentences. Notice the pronunciation of the sounds in bold: /s/, /z/ and /ɪz/. Listen again and repeat.

1 She look**s** after their daughter. /s/
2 He live**s** at home. /z/
3 She teach**es** Science. /ɪz/

10 2.10 Say the words in the box and put them in the correct columns. Listen, check and repeat.

| fixes | makes | pays |
| shares | wants | watches |

/s/	/z/	/ɪz/

Speaking

11 Draw your own family tree. In pairs, ask and answer questions about the people.

Who's Barbara?
Barbara's my cousin. She lives in Bogotá and she works in an office.
Who does she live with?
She shares a flat with some friends.

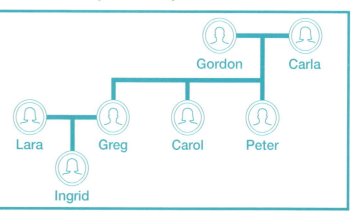

Exam practice: page 157

2.3 A VIRTUAL FRIEND

G question words
skill listen for specific information

Listening

1 Read the conversation on the phone. Who are Ben and Dana?

2 What does a virtual assistant do? Read the rest of the text and check.

3 Do you have a virtual assistant on your phone? What do you use it for?

4 🔊 **2.11** Listen to the conversation between Ben and Dana. Tick (✓) the things they talk about.
   1 the time ☐
   2 the weather ☐
   3 restaurants ☐
   4 their ages ☐
   5 nationalities ☐
   6 the traffic ☐
   7 birthdays ☐
   8 music ☐
   9 sport ☐

listen for specific information

Sometimes you have to listen for specific details.
- Think about the information you need to understand, e.g. is it a person, a place, a number?
- When people talk about the topic, pay attention carefully.
- Some words sound similar, for example *thirteen* and *thirty*, *Tuesday* and *Thursday*.

5 a Read the Skill box. Look at sentences 1–6 below. What information do you need to listen for?

b 🔊 **2.11** Listen to the conversation again. Choose the correct words to complete the sentences.
   1 The time is *7 a.m. / 11 a.m. / 7 p.m. / 11 p.m.*
   2 The weather tomorrow is *7 / 17 / 27 / 70* degrees and rain.
   3 It's Ben's *mother's / father's / sister's / brother's* birthday on Wednesday.
   4 Dana sends *white / pink / red / yellow* flowers.
   5 Dana is *American / Australian / British / Japanese*.
   6 Ben wants to listen to *pop / rock / classical / dance* music.

20

Grammar

6 🔊 **2.12** Complete the questions from the conversation with the question words in the box. Listen and check.

how many	how old	what	when
where	which	who	why

1 .... are you?
2 .... 's your birthday?
3 .... colour do you want?
4 .... are you from?
5 .... do you have a British voice?
6 .... voices do you have?
7 .... do you want to listen to?
8 .... 's your favourite singer?

7 Match the question words with what they ask about.

1 how old ....   a a number
2 when ....   b a time
3 which ....   c a reason
4 where ....   d a place
5 why ....   e an age
6 how many ....   f a thing
7 what ....   g a person
8 who ....   h a choice

G question words

How old are you?	I'm 32.
When do you start work?	I start work at 9.00.
Which animals do you like?	I like cats.
Where do you work?	I work in the city.
Why do you work at night?	Because I'm a doctor.
How many cousins do you have?	I have three cousins.
What do you want to eat?	I want pizza.
Who do you live with?	I live with my family.

→ Grammar reference: page 133

🔍 notice

Prepositions usually come at the end of questions.
What do you want to listen **to**?
Who do you live **with**?

8 🔊 **2.13** 💬 **question intonation** 💬 Listen to the questions. Notice how the intonation goes down at the end. Listen and repeat.

1 Which colour do you want?
2 When is your birthday?
3 Who's your favourite singer?

Writing

9 Read the conversation with a virtual assistant and complete the questions with the correct question words.

10 a Write three questions for each topic for your partner. Use as many question words as you can.

b Swap questions with your partner and write the answers.

🔄 **Mediation task:** Student A page 126, Student B page 128

2.4 THAT'S INTERESTING!

FL small talk
Nadiya's family

The big picture: Nadiya's family

1 Look at the picture of the family. In pairs, guess the answer to the questions.
   1 Where are they from?
   2 Are they saying hello or goodbye?
   3 Is it a special occasion? Why?

2 **2.1** Watch the video. Choose the correct words to complete the sentences.
   1 Nadiya is a British chef and lives in *the UK / Bangladesh*.
   2 Family meals *are / aren't* very important to Nadiya.
   3 She travels to Bangladesh to learn about her *family / culture*.
   4 Her family live in a *big city / small village* in Bangladesh.
   5 After one week with her family, she *goes home / continues travelling*.

3 **2.1** Put Nadiya's family in the correct columns. Watch again and check.

aunts	brothers	children	cousins
grandmother	husband	parents
sisters	uncles

Live in the UK	Live in Bangladesh

4 In pairs, discuss the questions.
   1 Do you have family who live in another country or another part of your country?
   2 Where do they live?
   3 When do you see them?
   4 How do you stay in touch with them?
   5 Is it normal to have family in other countries?

5 **2.2** Listen to Dev and Sophia talking about the video. Are the sentences true (T) or false (F)?
   1 They think that Nadiya's Bangladeshi family isn't important.   ....
   2 All of Dev's family live in the same town.   ....
   3 They think it's normal for people to have family in different countries.   ....
   4 Sophia has a Mexican friend called Sandra.   ....
   5 Sandra never visits Mexico.   ....

6 **2.2** Do Dev and Sophia sound interested when they talk? Watch the video again and tick (✓) the phrases you hear. How do you say these phrases in your language?
   1 Oh, right.   ☐
   2 That's cool!   ☐
   3 That's handy!   ☐
   4 Wow!   ☐
   5 That's great!   ☐
   6 Really?   ☐

Functional language

7 🔊 **2.14** Listen and match the conversations with the pictures.

1 .... 2 .... 3 ....

8 🔊 **2.14** In pairs, answer the questions for each picture. Listen again and check.

1 Where are the people in the conversations?
2 Do the people speaking know each other?
3 What do they talk about?
4 What happens at the end of the conversations?

9 🔊 **2.15** Match the questions with the answers. Listen and check.

1 How do you know Tracy? ....
2 What do you do? ....
3 Do you live near here? ....
4 Where are you from? ....
5 Do you know anyone in the building? ....
6 Do you work in finance, too? ....

a Yes, just around the corner.
b No, I'm in marketing.
c Yes, my brother lives in 5D.
d She's an old friend from school.
e I'm Italian.
f I work in the tax department.

10 How do the people show interest in the answers?

FL	small talk

Work/Study
What do you do?
Where do you work/study?
Do you work in …?

Home life
Where are you from?
Where do you live?
Do you live near here?

People in common
How do you know …?
Do you know …?
Do you live/work/study with …?

Showing interest
Oh, right. / Really? / Wow!
That's great/cool/interesting/handy!

11 🔊 **2.16** 🗨 showing interest 🗨 Listen to the phrases. Notice the intonation used to sound interested. Listen again and repeat.

1 Oh, right.   3 Wow!
2 Really?   4 That's great!

12 a Complete the sentences with information about your job, city and hobbies or interests.

1 I'm a/an ....
2 I live in ....
3 I like ....
4 I have ....

b In pairs, read the sentences to your partner. Respond showing interest.

Speaking

13 a In pairs, choose one of the situations from exercise 7. Use the functional language to make small talk. Remember to show interest.

b Swap partners and choose another situation from exercise 7. Invent details for the most interesting person you can imagine.

✎ Writing bank: page 145

REVIEW UNIT 2

Vocabulary
Verb collocations

1   a Match the halves to make sentences.
   1 My parents pay .... a a flat.
   2 I work .... b English.
   3 We study .... c alone.
   4 I want .... d as a waiter.
   5 I live .... e the bills.
   6 We share .... f to be a teacher.

   b In pairs, check your answers. Tell your partner three things about you.

Families

2   🔊 2.17 Look at the pictures. In pairs, complete the sentences with the words in the box. Listen and check.

   aunt   brother   cousin
   daughter   grandfather   wife

   1 Prince Harry is Prince William's ....
   2 Willow Smith is Will Smith's ....
   3 Bob Marley is Skip Marley's ....
   4 Brandy is Snoop Dogg's ....
   5 Julia Roberts is Emma Roberts's ....
   6 Amal Clooney is George Clooney's ....

3 Do you know of any other celebrity relations?

Grammar
Present simple (I, you, we, they)

4 a Write questions beginning Do you…? with the verbs in the box.

   | earn | like | live | want | work |

   1 .... to buy a house?   4 .... in an office?
   2 .... your job?   5 .... with your parents?
   3 .... a lot of money?

   b In pairs, ask and answer the questions.

Present simple (he, she, it)

5 a Complete the sentences with the correct present simple form of the verb in brackets.
   1 He _doesn't live_ alone. (live / -)
   2 Tom .... TV most evenings. (watch / +)
   3 She .... to help her parents. (try / +)
   4 Beth .... to go to university. (want / -)
   5 .... he .... children? (have / ?)
   6 He .... a flat with his friends. (share / +)

   b In pairs, ask each other the questions in exercise 4a and note down the answers. Write sentences for your partner using the present simple.
   He/She doesn't want to buy a house.

Question words

6 a In pairs, write eight questions using the words in the box. Use each word at least once.

   | How many | How old | What | When | Who | Why |

   b Ask and answer the questions.

Functional language
Small talk

7 Write the words in the correct order.
   1 do / you / what / do ?
   2 live / you / do / here / near ?
   3 from / you / where / are ?
   4 job / your / like / you / do ?

8 Ask the questions in exercise 7 to at least four students in your class. Remember to show interest in their answers. Answer their questions.
   I'm a reporter.
   Really? That's interesting.

⏱ Looking back

• What is your favourite part of this unit? Why?
• Do you want to look at something again? If yes, what?
• What five things can you say about you and your family?

24

Days of our lives

3

Grammar G
adverbs and expressions of frequency
modifiers

Vocabulary V
daily routine verbs
free-time activities
months and ordinals

Functional language FL
making suggestions

Skill
understand ideas in paragraphs

Video
a special day

Writing
a blog post

Exams
listening to a long conversation

The big picture: an empty city

1 Look at the picture. In pairs, guess the answers to the questions.

 1 Which city is it?
 2 What is unusual about the city?
 3 Which day of the year is it?
 4 What time of day is it?
 5 Where are all the people?

 The city is probably … or maybe …
 It's empty because …
 The people are at home/at work/on holiday, etc.

2 3.1 Listen to the information about the picture and check your answers.

3 In pairs, discuss the questions.

 1 What is your street like in the early morning?
 2 What is it like in the afternoon and at night?
 3 Do you get up early in the morning? At what time?
 4 Do you like early mornings? Why/Why not?
 5 What do you usually do in the morning?
 6 What do you do on a public holiday?

25

3.1 TIME ZONES

G adverbs and expressions of frequency
V daily routine verbs

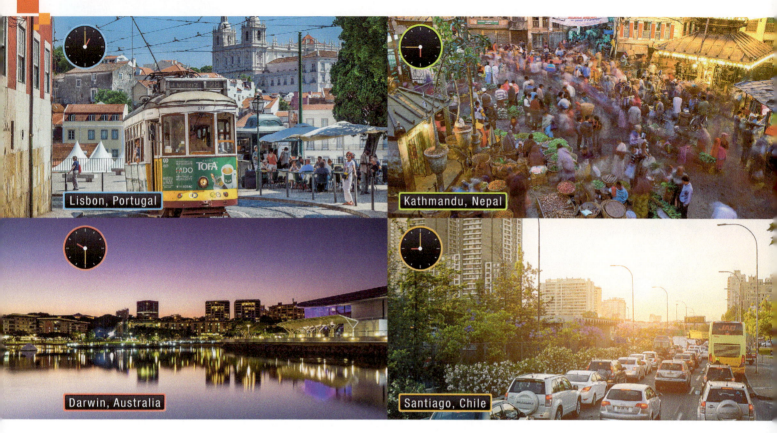

Listening

1 **a** Look at the pictures and the clocks. What time is it in each city?

   b Match the times of day in the box with the cities.

   | afternoon | evening | morning | night |

2 What's the time now? What time of day is it?

3 🔊 3.2 Listen to the people talking and match them with the cities.

   A .... C ....
   B .... D ....

4 🔊 3.2 Listen again and complete the sentences with speakers A, B, C and D.

   1 .... is happy to eat alone.
   2 .... is a student.
   3 .... has a long journey to work.
   4 .... does exercise.
   5 .... likes to be with his/her family.
   6 .... likes to prepare food.
   7 .... sleeps more at the weekend.
   8 .... lives with friends.

   🔍 **notice**

   We use *on*, *in* and *at* to talk about times and days.
   We use *on* with days: **on** Monday / **on** 15 December
   We use *in* with times of day: **in** the morning / **in** the afternoon
   We use *at* with times, *the weekend* and *night*: **at** 8 p.m. / **at** the weekend / **at** night

Vocabulary

5 Choose ten verbs from the box that you do every day. Write them in the order that you do them.

   V daily routine verbs

   🔊 3.3 Listen and repeat.

   call friends/family
   do housework/homework   finish work
   get dressed   get home   get ready for …
   get up   go to bed   have breakfast
   have … for lunch   have a shower/bath
   make dinner   start work   take a break
   take the metro/bus   wake up

   1 .... 6 ....
   2 .... 7 ....
   3 .... 8 ....
   4 .... 9 ....
   5 .... 10 ....

6 In pairs, ask and answer the question *When do you …?* with the verbs your partner wrote.

   When do you get up?
   I get up at half past seven, but on Sundays I get up at ten o'clock.

26

Grammar

7 🔊 **3.4** Match the halves to make sentences from the audio. Listen and check.

1 I **sometimes** go to the market ......
2 I **hardly ever** go to bed late ......
3 I **often** go to a local café ......
4 I **almost always** eat lunch ......
5 I'm **usually** on the bus ......
6 I **always** get up ......
7 I **occasionally** do housework ......
8 I **never** go to bed ......

a and have lunch.
b with my friends.
c during the week.
d later than 12.00.
e late once a week.
f on my own.
g on my way home.
h for two hours every day.

8 a Look at the adverbs of frequency in **bold** in exercise 7. Order them 1–8.

0%
1 ....
2 ....
3 ....
4 ....
5 ....
6 ....
7 ....
8 ....
100%

b Look at the sentences again and complete the rules.

1 Adverbs of frequency go *before* / *after* most verbs.
2 Adverbs of frequency go *before* / *after* the verb *to be*.
3 Expressions of frequency (*once* / *twice* / *three times a week*, *every day* / *week*, etc.) go at the *start* / *end* of the sentence.

> **G** adverbs and expressions of frequency
>
> *How often do you go to the gym?*
> *I usually go to the gym once or twice a week.*
> *How often is Carmen late for class?*
> *Carmen is always late for class. She's late every day.*
>
> → Grammar reference: page 134

9 🔊 **3.5** 🔊 **sentence stress** 🔊 Listen to the questions and answers. Notice how the adverbs of frequency are stressed.

1 How often do you go to bed late?
2 I never go to bed after 12.00.
3 How often do you sleep late?
4 I always sleep late at the weekend.

10 In pairs, read the sentences in exercise 7 again. Are they true for you? If not, change the adverbs of frequency to make them true.

I hardly ever go to the market on my way home.

Speaking

11 a In pairs, ask and answer the question *How often do you ...?* for the activities below. Remember to stress the adverbs of frequency. Make a note of the answers.

1 brush your teeth
2 do the housework
3 make dinner
4 do your English homework
5 go to the cinema
6 eat fast food
7 call your mother
8 check your phone

b Tell the class about your partner.

Sergio usually brushes his teeth three times a day.

3.2 TAKE IT EASY

G modifiers
V free-time activities

Reading

1 Look at the picture and answer the questions.
   1 Where are the people?
   2 How do they feel?
   3 Do you ever do this? If so, how often?

2 Look at the title of the text. What does 'take it easy' mean? In pairs, write a list of five ways to 'take it easy'.

3 Read the text. In pairs, discuss the questions.
   1 Are any of your ideas from exercise 2 in the text?
   2 Are the ideas in the text helpful?
   3 Do you have a busy life?
   4 Do you think it's difficult to take it easy?

Vocabulary

4 Look at the text again. Complete the free-time activities with the missing words.

   V free-time activities

1	.... an instrument
2	.... special meals
3	.... your bike
4	.... for a walk
5	.... a TV series
6	.... out for dinner
7	.... nature
8	.... up with friends
9	.... photos
10	.... video games
11	.... on social media
12	.... time with friends/family

   🔊 3.6 Listen, check and repeat.

5 a Write down five activities from the Vocabulary box that you do very often.

   b In pairs, compare your answers. Ask how often your partner does these activities.

   c Tell the class what you found out.

   Juan usually plays video games every weekend, but I never play video games.

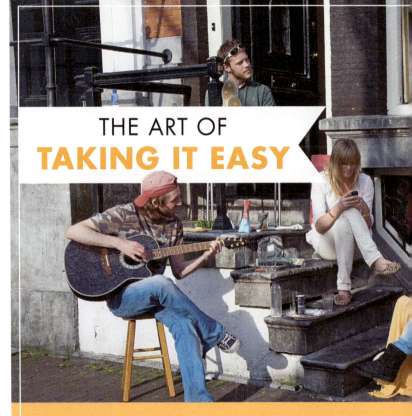

THE ART OF TAKING IT EASY

Our modern lives are very busy. We get up early, work all day, take the bus home, do the housework, make dinner, help the kids with their homework, watch a TV series or go on social media, go to bed … then the alarm clock goes off and we do it all again!

But some people's lives are too busy and they never relax properly. The problem of stress in many countries is quite serious and doctors say it's really important to know how to take it easy. So, here's a list of five quick tips. It isn't very difficult when you try.

1 DISCONNECT

Sometimes just stop. Turn off the TV, the radio and your laptop. Put your phone on silent. Close your eyes and think about nothing.

2 GO WITH THE MUSIC

Do you play an instrument? Or do you sing? They're great ways to relax. If not, you can listen to your favourite music. Put the volume up really high and dance around the house or sing out loud.

3 BE ACTIVE

Don't play video games, do some real sport! Ride your bike or simply go for a walk. The important thing is to move and do some exercise.

4 ENJOY NATURE

Go to a beautiful place – a park, a beach or a square, for example. Stop for a minute or two and look at the world around you. Maybe take photos, but don't share them online yet; you can do that later.

5 SPEND TIME WITH FRIENDS

Meet up with friends, go out for dinner or cook special meals for them. Have conversations late into the night and laugh out loud.

Do at least one of these things every day. Try to do all five at least once a week. Taking it easy isn't that difficult!

Grammar

6 a Look at the sentences from the text. What do the modifiers in **bold** do to the adjectives? Are they before or after the adjectives?

1 Our modern lives are **very** busy.
2 Some people's lives are **too** busy and they never relax.
3 The problem of stress in many countries is **quite** serious.
4 Doctors say it's **really** important to know how to take it easy.
5 It is**n't very** difficult when you try.

b Complete the rules with the modifiers.

! 1 .... makes the adjective negative (e.g. it's dangerous).
2 .... and .... make the adjective strong.
3 .... makes the adjective stronger than normal.
4 .... makes the adjective weak.

G modifiers

The coffee's **too** hot. Don't drink it!
The film is **very/really** good. I love it!
It's **quite** warm today. You don't need a jacket.
I'm **not very** tired. I want to go out tonight.

→ Grammar reference: page 134

---

7 🔊 3.7 ❝ emphasizing modifiers ❞ Listen to the sentences. Notice how the underlined modifiers are emphasized. Listen and repeat.

1 It's <u>quite</u> easy to do some exercise once a week.
2 It's <u>very</u> important to spend time with friends.
3 It's <u>too</u> difficult to switch off my phone!

8 a Make the sentences true for yourself using modifiers.

1 Going to the cinema is .... expensive.
2 It's .... fun to sing in the shower.
3 My neighbours are .... friendly.
4 Learning English is .... difficult.
5 The buses in the city are .... crowded.
6 It's .... dangerous to walk home alone at night.

b In pairs, say your sentences. Remember to emphasize the modifiers.

Speaking

9 a Move around the class and ask your classmates if they do the activities in the survey. If someone says yes, write down their name and ask the other questions.

b Tell the class what you found out.

Sam goes on social media. He uses Instagram every day. It's really easy to use!

| Home | About | Surveys | | Login | Sign up |

1 Do you go on social media? Name:
Which sites do you use? How easy are they to use?
How often do you use them?

2 Do you play an instrument? Name:
Which instrument do you play? How difficult is it to learn?
How often do you play it?

3 Do you ride a bike? Name:
Where do you ride it? How dangerous is it?
How far do you go?

4 Do you meet up with friends? Name:
Who do you meet up with? How friendly are they?
How often do you see them?

5 Do you cook special meals? Name:
What's your speciality? How good is it?
How often do you cook it?

✓ Exam practice: page 158

3.3 HAPPY BIRTHDAY

V months and ordinals
🔧 understand ideas in paragraphs

Reading

1. In pairs, look at the pictures and answer the questions.
   1. What can you see?
   2. Whose birthday is it?
   3. How old are the people?
   4. What are they thinking?

2. **a** In pairs, write down five things related to birthdays.
   1. ....
   2. ....
   3. ....
   4. ....
   5. ....

   b Read the text quickly. Tick (✓) the things on your list which are in the text.

   🔧 **understand ideas in paragraphs**

   It's useful to quickly understand the main idea of each paragraph.
   - Read the first sentence of each paragraph carefully. These are often topic sentences that summarize the main idea.
   - Read the rest of the paragraph quickly and check what it says.

3. Read the Skill box. Then read the highlighted topic sentences in the text carefully. Match headings a–d in with the correct paragraphs. Read the text again and check.
   a An enormous celebration
   b A popular song
   c Interesting traditions
   d Important ages

4. In pairs, answer the questions.
   1. Do you like birthdays?
   2. What do you usually do on your birthday?
   3. Which birthdays are important in your country?
   4. Does your country have any special birthday customs?

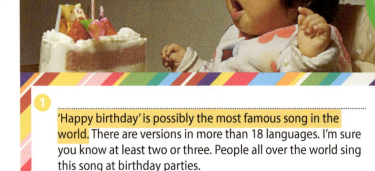

The truth about BIRTHDAYS

1 'Happy birthday' is possibly the most famous song in the world. There are versions in more than 18 languages. I'm sure you know at least two or three. People all over the world sing this song at birthday parties.

2 Of course, all birthdays are special, but some are *really* special. First birthdays are very important for parents, especially when it's their first child. Sixteenth birthdays are important in a lot of countries, such as the USA, for example. Eighteenth and twenty-first birthdays are important too as children become adults. And birthdays are not only for children. Adults enjoy birthdays, too. But whatever the birthday, the celebrations are usually the same: a cake, some candles, presents, family and friends.

3 But there are differences too – different countries have different customs. Everyone knows about piñatas in Mexico, but did you know that, in Spain, they pull people's ears on their birthday? One pull for each year. In some parts of Canada, they put butter on your nose. In China, you eat a bowl of very long noodles on your birthday. This brings good luck and a long life.

4 Everyone likes a good party, but which country has the biggest birthday party in the world? Most people say it's Vietnam. That's because everybody has their birthday on the same day! On New Year's Day (5 February this year) everybody celebrates their birthday together. They all have one big party – imagine all the cakes and candles they need! So, what about you? How do you celebrate your birthday? Do you have any special birthday traditions in your country?

Vocabulary

5 Match the dates in words with the numbers (day/month).

1 The first of January .... a 22/07
2 The eighteenth of March .... b 12/04
3 The twenty-second of July .... c 01/01
4 The fourth of October .... d 18/03
5 The twelfth of April .... e 04/10
6 The second of December .... f 02/12

> **notice**
> We write *5 February*, but we say *the fifth of February*.

6 Complete the tables with the correct months and ordinals.

V months and ordinals

Months

January, (1) ...., March, April, (2) ...., (3) ...., July, (4) ...., September, (5) ...., (6) ...., December

Ordinals

1	first	11	eleventh
2	(7)	12	twelfth
3	third	13	thirteenth
4	(8)	14	(11) ....
5	fifth	20	twentieth
6	(9)	21	twenty-first
7	seventh	22	(12) ....
8	eighth	23	twenty-third
9	ninth	30	thirtieth
10	(10)	31	(13) ....

🔊 **3.9** Listen, check and repeat.

7 Ask your classmates when their birthdays are. Whose birthday is closest to yours? Does anybody have the same birthday as you?

When's your birthday?
It's on 17 July.
Really? Me too!

8 Read the text. Are you surprised?

The birthday paradox

In a group of **23** people, there's a **50/50** possibility of two people having the same birthday. In a group of **75** people, there's a **99.5%** chance!

Writing

9 Read the text about a famous holiday and answer the questions.

1 When is the holiday?
2 What does it celebrate?
3 What do people do on this day?
4 What do they eat?

INTERESTING PUBLIC HOLIDAYS: PRESIDENTS' DAY

WHEN: the third Monday in February

WHERE: in the USA

WHO: George Washington's birthday, 22 February, and Abraham Lincoln's birthday, 12 February

WHAT: People celebrate the birthdays of George Washington and Abraham Lincoln on this day. Children don't go to school and a lot of people take a holiday from work. People have parades and street parties, and it's traditional to eat cherry pie.

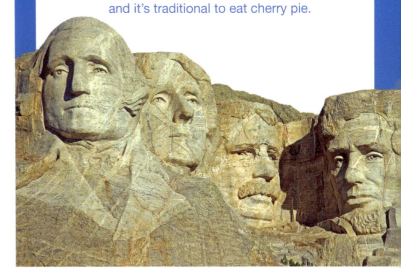

10 In pairs, choose an interesting public holiday in your country. Write a short encyclopedia entry. Remember to include answers to all the questions in exercise 9.

⇄ Mediation task: Student A page 126, Student B page 128

3.3

31

3.4 LET'S CELEBRATE!
FL making suggestions
🎥 a special day

The big picture: a special day

1. Look at the picture of a man from the Cocos Islands preparing for a wedding. In pairs, guess the answers to the questions.
   1. What does he have on his face?
   2. Why is he doing this?
   3. How does he feel?

2. 🎥 **3.1** Watch the video and check. Tick (✓) the things you see in the video.
   1. shopping for food
   2. cooking food
   3. building tents
   4. wearing special clothes
   5. eating a special meal
   6. dancing
   7. singing
   8. music

3. 🎥 **3.1** Watch the video again and complete the sentences with the correct words.
   1. The Cocos islands are in the .... Ocean, 2,750 km from Australia.
   2. People from Scotland and south-east Asia came to the islands .... years ago.
   3. In a Cocos Malay wedding, it is attractive to have .... skin.
   4. There is no food in the supermarket because the .... arrived late.
   5. A .... dance is a tradition at a Cocos Malay wedding.

4. In pairs, discuss the questions.
   1. How is a Cocos Malay wedding similar to a wedding in your country?
   2. How is it different to a wedding in your country?
   3. Do you like going to weddings? Why/Why not?
   4. How is life different on the Cocos Islands?
   5. Would you like to live there? Why/Why not?

5. 🎥 **3.2** Watch Dev and Sophia talking about the wedding. Are the sentences true (T) or false (F)?
   1. They think the Cocos Malay wedding is fun.
   2. Dev thinks it's easy to organize because everyone lives on a small island.
   3. He says the wedding was a success.
   4. Sophia says she likes to wear special clothes at parties.
   5. They decide to organize a party.

6. 🎥 **3.2** Watch again. Who makes the suggestions, Dev (D) or Sophia (S)?
   1. Why don't we have a party?
   2. How about this weekend?
   3. Let's do it in two weeks.
   4. Shall we have it at my flat?
   5. How about we speak to Agnes?

Functional language

7 Look at the picture and answer the questions in pairs.
1. What does it show?
2. Where is it?
3. Would you like to see it?

8 🔊 **3.10** Listen to Valerie and Jon talking about the parade. Complete the sentences with the correct words.
1. Valerie invites *Jon / Izzie* to see the parade.
2. They decide to go by *bus / car*.
3. *Jon / Valerie* agrees to call Izzie.
4. They agree to meet at *3.30 / 4.30*.

9 a 🔊 **3.10** Who says the sentences: Valerie (V) or Jon (J)? Listen again and check.
1. Do you want to go? ....
2. Yes, I'd love to. ....
3. How about we go together? ....
4. Why don't we ask Izzie, too? ....
5. That's a great idea. ....
6. Sorry, I can't. ....
7. Let's meet on the corner of my street. ....

b Which sentences are for making a suggestion and which are for responding?

FL making suggestions

Making suggestions	Responding
Do you want to ...?	Good idea!/That sounds great!
Let's ...	Yes, I'd love to!
Why don't we ...?	I'm not sure. / Maybe.
Shall I/we ...?	I don't think so. / Sorry, I can't.
How about we ...?	

10 🔊 **3.11** 💬 **sounding enthusiastic** 💬 Listen to the responses below. Notice the intonation used to sound enthusiastic. Listen again and repeat.
1. Good idea!
2. That sounds great!
3. Yes, I'd love to!

Speaking

11 Look at the pictures. In pairs, agree on the things below. Remember to sound enthusiastic.
1. where to go
2. who to go with
3. how to get there
4. where/when to meet

📝 **Writing bank: page 146** 33

REVIEW UNIT 3

Vocabulary
Daily routine verbs

1 a Complete the phrases with *get, have* or *do*.

1 .... dressed
2 .... home
3 .... homework
4 .... ready for work
5 .... lunch
6 .... up
7 .... a shower
8 .... the housework

b Choose the correct preposition to complete the sentences.

1 I usually wake up *in / on / at* 7 a.m.
2 I often have a sleep *in / on / at* the afternoon.
3 I always call my family *in / on / at* the weekend.
4 I take the bus *in / on / at* Mondays.

c In pairs, ask and answer the questions *When do you ...?* with the phrases in 1a.

Free-time activities

2 Complete the phrases with the verbs in the box.

| cook | go (x2) | enjoy |
| play (x2) | spend | take |

1 .... nature
2 .... video games
3 .... an instrument
4 .... out for dinner
5 .... on social media
6 .... photos
7 .... a meal
8 .... time with friends

3 Think of five free-time activities you do every weekend. In pairs, ask and answer questions about your interests.

Do you go for a walk every weekend?
Yes, if we have time.
And where do you usually go?
Sometimes we stay in the city and we go for a walk by the river, and sometimes we go for a walk in the countryside.

4 Find three free-time activities you and your partner **never** do.

Months and ordinals

5 a Look at the numbers and write the dates in words.

1 29/04   *The twenty-ninth of April*
2 14/02   ....
3 03/06   ....
4 22/11   ....
5 04/12   ....

b In pairs, think of three people you know, family or friends. When are their birthdays? Tell your partner.

My dad's birthday is on the 28th of September.

Grammar
Adverbs and expressions of frequency

6 Complete the list of adverbs of frequency.

100% (1) ....
usually
often
(2) ....
occasionally
hardly ever
0% (3) ....

7 a Look at the activities in exercise 1a. Write questions about three of them using *How often ...?*

b In pairs, ask and answer the questions. Use adverbs and expressions of frequency in your answers.

How often do you go on social media?
I hardly ever go on social media.

Modifiers

8 Choose four adjectives. Write a sentence for each.
Learning a language is easy.

9 Rewrite the sentences adding *too, quite, really* and *not very*.
Learning a language is not very easy.

Functional language
Making suggestions

10 Write the words in the correct order.
1 Anna / don't / we / too / ask / why ?
2 want / you / do / go / to?
3 meet / let's / at / station / the
4 I'd / to / yes / love

11 a 🔊 3.12 Complete the mini-dialogues. Use the expressions in exercise 10. Listen and check.

1 A Shall we go to the cinema?
  B ....
2 A ....
  B OK. That sounds great.
3 A ....
  B Good idea. I'm sure she'd like to come.
4 A ....
  B Sorry, I can't.

b In pairs, make and respond to suggestions about the weekend. Remember to sound enthusiastic.

🕐 Looking back

Think of five useful expressions or phrases from this unit.
- Where or when can you use them?
- How do you plan to remember them?
- Which section do you want to know more about?

Home life

4

Grammar G
there is/are
prepositions of place

Vocabulary V
houses and rooms
furniture
places in a town

Functional language FL
directions

Skill
listen for main ideas

Video
life on the road

Writing
asking for information

Exams
reading three short texts

The big picture: floating houses

1 Look at the picture. In pairs, choose the two best adjectives from the box to describe the houses.

| modern | expensive | big | beautiful |
| comfortable | unusual | light | |

2 Guess the answers to the questions.
　1　Where is it?
　2　Who lives in the houses?
　3　What are the good things about living here?

3 🔊 4.1 Listen to a reporter talking about the houses. Check your answers.

4 In pairs, discuss the questions.
　1　Would you like to live in Ijburg? Why/Why not?
　2　Do you live in a city or a village?
　3　What are the good things about living there?

4.1 A ROOF OVER YOUR HEAD

G there is/are
V houses and rooms

Vocabulary

1 **a** Look at the pictures of the bus and answer the questions.
   1 What is unusual about the bus?
   2 Who uses the bus?
   3 Where is it?

   b Read the text and check.

2 Match the words in the box with the numbers 1–12 on the pictures of the bus.

   V houses and rooms

bathroom	bedroom	ceiling	dining room/area
floor	ground floor	first floor	front door	kitchen
living room	roof	downstairs	upstairs	wall

   1 roof
   2 ....
   3 ....
   4 ....
   5 ....
   6 ....
   7 ....
   8 ....
   9 .... / ....
   10 .... / ....
   11 ....
   12 ....

   🔊 4.2 Listen, check and repeat.

Listening

3 🔊 4.3 Listen to a reporter talking about the bus. Which words from the Vocabulary box do you hear?

4 🔊 4.3 Listen again. Are the sentences true (T) or false (F)?
   1 Ipswich has a lot of homeless people. ....
   2 People use the bus all day. ....
   3 The bus has ten beds. ....
   4 This is the only bus for homeless people in the UK. ....

5 In pairs, discuss the questions.
   1 Do you think this project is a good idea?
   2 Does your city have a lot of homeless people?
   3 Do you know about any projects to help them?

Most people have a roof over their head, but some people aren't so lucky – they're homeless. Organizations like **The Bus Shelter** in the UK want to help. This bus is a temporary home for people living on the street in Ipswich.

Grammar

6 🔊 **4.4** Match the halves to make sentences from the audio. Listen and check.

1. There aren't any cheap homes
2. There isn't a bed
3. There's a small kitchen
4. There are some comfortable chairs
5. Is there a similar project
6. Are there any local organizations

a. here on the ground floor.
b. in your town?
c. here.
d. for them in the city.
e. for everyone.
f. for homeless people?

7 Answer the questions about the sentences in exercise 6.
1. Which sentences are singular? ....
2. Which sentences are plural? ....
3. When do we use *some*?
   A with positives   B with negatives   C with questions
4. When do we use *any*?
   A with positives   B with negatives   C with questions

G there is/are

	Singular	Plural
+	**There's** a living room.	**There are some** chairs.
–	**There isn't** a dining room.	**There aren't any** doors.
?	**Is there** a bathroom?	**Are there any** windows?
Y/N	Yes, **there is**. / No, **there isn't**.	Yes, **there are**. / No, **there aren't**.

→ Grammar reference: page 135

8 🔊 **4.5** 💬 **short answers** 💬 (Circle) the correct answers about the bus. Listen, check and repeat. Notice the underlined stressed words in the answers.

1. Is there a kitchen?   <u>Yes</u>, there <u>is</u>. / <u>No</u>, there <u>isn't</u>.
2. Is there a back door?   <u>Yes</u>, there <u>is</u>. / <u>No</u>, there <u>isn't</u>.
3. Are there any chairs?   <u>Yes</u>, there <u>are</u>. / <u>No</u>, there <u>aren't</u>.
4. Are there any TVs?   <u>Yes</u>, there <u>are</u>. / <u>No</u>, there <u>aren't</u>.

9 **a** Complete the questions using *is/are* and *a/any*.
1. .... there .... blackboard or .... whiteboard?
2. .... there .... posters on the wall?
3. .... there .... bags on the floor?
4. How many students .... there?
5. How many tables .... there?
6. .... there .... computer or .... TV?

b In pairs, ask and answer the questions about your classroom.

c Write three more sentences about your classroom using *there is/are*.

Speaking

10 **a** In pairs, think of another use for a double-decker bus. Choose an idea in the box or one of your own.

| a café | a family home | a language school |
| a library | an office | a restaurant |

b Draw a plan of your bus on the diagram. Then present it to the class.

On the first floor/upstairs there is/are …
On the ground floor/downstairs there is/are …
There isn't/aren't … because …

4.2 A HOME FROM HOME

G prepositions of place
V furniture

Vocabulary

1 Look at the pictures in the hotel review. Answer the questions in pairs.
   1 What rooms can you see?
   2 What is unusual about the hotel?
   3 Would you like to stay at this hotel? Why/Why not?

2 Tick (✓) the types of furniture you can see in the pictures.

   V furniture
   1 armchair   8 drawer
   2 blanket   9 fridge
   3 bookshelf   10 light
   4 carpet   11 mirror
   5 cupboard   12 pillow
   6 cooker   13 sink
   7 cushion   14 sofa

   🔊 4.6 Listen, check and repeat.

> **notice**
> We use **pillows** on beds. We use **cushions** on sofas and chairs.

3 In pairs, match the furniture in the Vocabulary box with the rooms. Some things can go in more than one room.

Kitchen	Bedroom	Living room	Bathroom

Reading

4 Read the review. In pairs, answer the questions.
   1 Does Maria like the hotel?
   2 Which positive words or phrases does she use?
   3 What does she like best about the hotel?
   4 Is there anything she doesn't like?

Maria Celdes
📍 Argentina
★★★★☆
REVIEWED 1 WEEK AGO

I really like this hotel! It's a great idea. It's all in the name, *Book and Bed*. I love the bedrooms, they're actually in the bookshelves. They're very small, but there's everything you need: a bed, a pillow, a blanket if you're cold … and a light, of course, so you can read your favourite book – that's very useful!

There are some cupboards for your bags, but there isn't a lot of space in them, and there are some drawers under the bedrooms where you can leave personal things. There's a big living room opposite the bookshelves. It has comfortable sofas and cushions – it's a great place to read or just relax.

Next to the bookshelves, there's a small kitchen area where you can make coffee and the bathroom has good, strong showers. My favourite thing is the big window behind the sofas in the living room. It has some fantastic views of Tokyo, especially at night when you can see all the city's lights. I certainly recommend this hotel if you are ever in Tokyo and you like books!

Book and Bed hotel
Tokyo, Japan

Grammar

5 a Match the furniture with the positions. Check your answers in the text.

1 drawers .... a **in** the bookshelves
2 sofas .... b **under** the bedrooms
3 window .... c **opposite** the bookshelves
4 bedrooms .... d **next to** the bookshelves
5 kitchen .... e **behind** the sofa

b Look at the prepositions of place in **bold**. How do you say them in your language?

6 Match the prepositions of place in the box with the pictures.

| above | behind | between | in | in front of |
| next to | on | opposite | under | |

1 .... 2 .... 3 ....

4 .... 5 .... 6 ....

7 .... 8 .... 9 ....

G prepositions of place

The window is **behind** the sofa.
The lights are **above** the sinks.
There's a pillow **on** the bed.
There aren't any tables **in** the living area.

→ Grammar reference: page 135

---

7 Look at the pictures. Write sentences to say where the things in the box are.

| orange cushion | blue blanket | kitchen sink |
| TV | armchair | drawers | pillows | cooker |

There's an orange cushion on the sofa in the living room.

8 🔊 **4.7** Listen to a description of the apartment in Lima. What are the five differences from the pictures?

Beautiful large apartment in Lima

Speaking

9 a In pairs, discuss the questions.
1 What is your favourite room in your house?
2 What do you do there?
3 How much time do you spend there every day?

b Draw a simple plan of the room including doors and windows, but not furniture. Give it to your partner.

c Describe the positions of all the furniture in the room. Draw what your partner says.

There's a big sofa next to the door.

4.3 THE UNDERGROUND CITY

V places in a town
🔧 listen for main ideas

Listening

1 Read about RÉSO in Montreal. In pairs, answer the questions.

1. What can people do in RÉSO?
2. What's surprising about it?
3. Would you like to go to there? Why/Why not?
4. Do you think people go there more in winter or summer? Why?

RÉSO is an underground city in Montreal, Canada and it is very, very big! There is so much to see and do **under** the streets of Montreal. Let's take a look at the city in numbers.

SHOPS: 2,000
BANKS: 40
HOMES: 1,600
CINEMAS: 40
OFFICES: 1,200
HOTELS: 7
RESTAURANTS: 200
UNIVERSITIES: 4
VISITORS PER DAY: 500,000
TOTAL SIZE: 32 km²

2 Read the Skill box.

🔧 **listen for main ideas**

When people speak, try to listen for the main ideas.
- Don't worry if you don't understand every word. Keep listening.
- Speakers often repeat or emphasize the main ideas.
- Listen for key words that help you understand the main ideas.

3 🔊 **4.8** Listen to three conversations with people at RÉSO. Complete the table with the topics in the box.

| free time | shopping | sports & fitness |
| studying | transport | work |

	Why is he/she at RÉSO?	What does he/she talk about?
1		
2		
3		

40

4 🔊 **4.8** Listen again. Choose the correct words to complete the sentences.

Conversation 1
1 Tomorrow I have a *gym / swimming* class.
2 In *summer / winter* I do a lot of outdoor sports.
3 It's really great to come here and forget about *work / the cold*.

Conversation 2
4 I live *in the underground city / on the other side of town*.
5 I *walk / run* to the campus.
6 *During the week / At the weekend* I come to the library to study.

Conversation 3
7 Do you know there are *30 / 40* banks here in RÉSO?
8 *Hundreds / Thousands* of people work here.
9 In winter, I prefer to be *in Montreal / underground*.

Vocabulary

5 Match the places in a town with the correct categories.

V places in a town

airport	bookshop	bus stop
department store	gym	library
museum	pharmacy	police station
post office	sports centre	stadium
swimming pool	train station	university

Transport	*airport*
Free time	
Study	
Services	
Shopping	

🔊 **4.9** Listen, check and repeat.

🔍 **notice**

You borrow books from a **library**. You buy books in a **bookshop**.

6 In pairs, ask and answer the question *How often do you go to a/an ...?* with the places in the Vocabulary box.

How often do you go to a train station?
I go to a train station once or twice a month.

Writing

7 a Read the description of a city and look at the picture. Which city is it?

b How many words from the Vocabulary box can you find in the text?

Intira Benjawan

I'm from ...., a very big Asian city. It has a population of over 14 million people! There are two airports and lots of train stations. Hua Lamphong is the main train station and it's next to the Sattru Phai district. This area is a great place to visit. The Golden Mount is a beautiful temple on a hill and it's next to the King Prajadhipok Museum. The Bobae Market is a great place to go shopping, but there are also some big department stores in the area. And if you want to watch sport, go to the Ratchadamnoen Boxing Stadium. There are lots of good restaurants, but my favourite is the White Flower restaurant – the pad Thai is delicious!

8 In pairs, write a similar description of your town/city.

... is a large/interesting/modern city.
It has a population of ... people.
There is/are ...
... is a great place to ...
If you want to ..., go to ...
You can visit the ...

⇄ Mediation task: All students, page 130   41

4.4 AN UNUSUAL HOME

FL directions
life on the road

The big picture: life on the road

1 **a** Look at the picture and guess the answers to the questions.
   1 Where does the girl live?
   2 What is strange about her home?
   3 Is she happy there?

   b 4.1 Watch the video and check your answers.

2 **a** Tick (✓) the things that are in the van.

   shelves ☐   fridge ☐
   cushion ☐   cupboard ☐
   drawers ☐   sink ☐
   bed ☐   sofa ☐
   cooker ☐   pillow ☐

   b Make sentences about the things in the van using *there is/are*.

   There's a bed, but there isn't a sofa.

3 4.1 Watch the video again and choose the correct words to complete the sentences.
   1 Hannah lives in her van *at the weekend / all week*.
   2 She lives in her van because *it's a cheap option / she can live where she likes*.
   3 It's important for her to be able to *cook / do yoga* in the van.
   4 Her favourite thing in the van is *the table / the plant shelf*.
   5 Hannah *has / doesn't have* a shower in the van.
   6 She *likes / doesn't like* living in a small space.

4 Would you like to live in a van like Hannah's? Why/Why not?

5 In pairs, say which items in the box are essential for you and which are luxuries you can live without.

television	shower	computer
plants	phone	cooker	fridge
sofa	bed	books

   A shower is essential for me, but I can live without a television, that's a luxury!

6 **a** 4.2 Watch Dev and Sophia talking about Hannah's van. Who is more positive about the idea?

   b 4.2 Complete the sentences with *Dev* or *Sophia*. Watch again and check.
   1 .... says the van has all the essential things.
   2 .... says the van is only OK for a short time.
   3 .... says the main problem is no bathroom.
   4 .... says there are bathrooms in other places.
   5 .... didn't know there's a van park in the town.

7 In pairs, answer the questions.
   1 Whose opinion is most similar to yours? Why?
   2 Is there a van park near your town?

4.4

Functional language

8 a 4.11 Listen to a conversation. Where does the person want to go?

b 4.11 Listen again and complete the conversation with the words in the box.

near	take	turn	get	straight	next to

A Excuse me, is there a van park (1) .... here?

B Yes, there is. It's (2) .... the stadium.

A Great, can you tell me how to (3) .... there please?

B Yes, of course. Go (4) .... on here, then (5) .... the second turning on the right. (6) .... left at the bus stop and the van park is on the corner, opposite the hospital.

9 a Look at the directions to the van park in exercise 8. Put the pictures in the correct order.

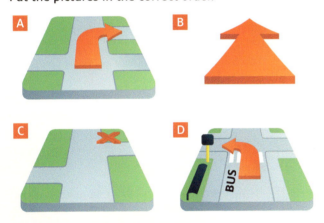

b Follow the directions and mark the van park on the map.

FL directions

Asking for directions
Is there a … near here?
Excuse me, where's the …. please?
Can you tell me how to get to …?

Giving directions
turn left/right at the …
go straight on
take the first/second/third turning on the left/right
it's on the right/left/corner
it's next to/opposite/between ….

10 4.12 Look at the map. Choose the correct words to complete the conversation. Listen and check.

A Excuse me, (1)*where / there* 's the police station, please?

B Oh, it's near here. (2)*Get / Go* straight on and turn (3)*right / left* at the post office. Take the (4)*first / second* turning on the right, and the police station is on the (5)*right / left*. It's (6)*next to / opposite* a pharmacy.

A Great, thanks a lot.

11 4.12 « **sentence stress** » Listen again. Notice how the speaker stresses the important direction words. In pairs, practise the conversation.

Speaking

12 In pairs, look at the map and take turns to ask for directions to the places in the box.

bus stop	hospital	park	pharmacy
post office	train station		

13 In pairs, think of places near your school. Practise asking for and giving directions to those places.

Writing bank: page 147

REVIEW UNIT 4

Vocabulary
Houses and rooms

1. In pairs, write the names of ten rooms or places in a home. How many do you have in your home?

2. In pairs, discuss the questions.
   1. Where do you usually eat?
   2. Where do you usually watch TV?
   3. Where do you usually study or read?
   4. Where do you spend most time? Why?

3. 🔊 4.13 Marco lives in a camper van. Listen to him answering the questions in exercise 2. Make a note of his answers.

Furniture

4. Write the names of two types of furniture for each description.
   1. something you sit on *an armchair, a sofa*
   2. something you use in the kitchen
   3. something you put things in
   4. something you put on a bed

5. Write definitions for three more types of furniture. Read the definitions to the class. Can they guess what the furniture is?

Places in a town

6. In pairs, look at the words in the box and answer the questions.

airport	bookshop	bus stop
department store	gym	library
museum	pharmacy	police station
post office	sports centre	stadium
swimming pool	train station	university

   1. Which places are five minutes from your English class?
   2. Which places do you visit most often? Why?
   3. Which places are more than half an hour from your home?

Grammar
there is/are

7. a Rewrite the sentences using *there is/are*.
   1. The street has two nice cafés.
   2. It doesn't have a bank.
   3. It doesn't have trees or plants.
   4. The nearest café has Wi-Fi.

   b Are the sentences true for the street you are in now?

8. Ask your partner about his/her neighbourhood. Use *Is/Are there …?* and the things in the box.

   | places to eat | places to do sports | public transport |
   | shops | things to do in your free time | |

Prepositions of place

9. Look at the picture of the hotel room. Write sentences describing where the things in the box are.

   | armchair | cushion | desk | lamp | mirror |
   | pillow | shower | sink | TV | |

   | above | behind | between | in front of |
   | next to | on | opposite | under |

10. Tell your partner three things about the room you are in. Use prepositions and *there is/are*.

    There's a desk next to the window.

Functional language
Directions

11. Work in pairs. Student A, tell your partner the best way to get to your home from the place you are in now. Student B, draw a map as you listen.

🕒 Looking back

- Think of five things you can say about your home and five about your neighbourhood.
- How can you practise this language at home or in class?

Shopping around

5

Grammar G
can/can't
present continuous
present simple and continuous

Vocabulary V
shopping
clothes and accessories

Functional language FL
shopping expressions

Skill
find information in a text

Video
our clothes

Writing
describing a photo

Exams
answering questions about a conversation

The big picture: a local shop

1 Look at the picture. In pairs, guess the answers to the questions.
   1 Where is the shop?
   2 What kinds of things does it sell?
   3 How old is the shop?
   4 How many customers come to the shop?
   5 What are the owner's plans for the future?

2 5.1 Listen to the information and check your answers.

3 In pairs, discuss the questions.
   1 Do you have local shops like this in your country?
   2 What do you buy there?
   3 Are they popular or do people prefer to shop in other places? Why?

45

5.1 THE END OF THE MALL

G can/can't
V shopping

Reading

1 In pairs, look at the pictures and answer the questions.
   1 Why are the shops closed and empty?
   2 Are there a lot of closed shops in your town?
   3 Why do these shops close?
   4 What other ways are there to shop?

   Some people don't have money to go shopping like before …

2 Read the introduction to the text and check your answers. Is the situation similar in your country?

3 Read the comments from some customers. Who are you most similar to?

4 Are the sentences true (T) or false (F)? Check your answers in the text.
   1 Patricia thinks things are very expensive online. ....
   2 Janine's grandmother takes the bus to the supermarket. ....
   3 Pierre goes shopping in his town. ....
   4 Francis finds good prices for clothes at the mall. ....

Is this the end of shopping as we know it?

In the UK, around sixteen shops in town centres close every day. Some customers want to spend their money in big shopping centres outside of town. But in the USA, shopping malls are closing because their customers prefer to shop online. So, is this the end of shopping as we know it? Let's find out what our readers have to say.

 Patricia: Things cost less online and there's so much choice! You can find anything you want, from electronics to clothes. And if you don't like it, then you can return it. There's one problem, though. You can spend a lot of money online! When you pay for everything by card, it's very easy to go crazy.

 Janine: My grandmother lives in the countryside and there aren't any local shops near her. And she can't drive, so she shops online. She thinks online supermarkets are great. She orders the food online and they bring her shopping to her house. It's really useful!

 Pierre: There are lots of good shops in my town. I like to talk to the shop assistants. I hardly ever shop online – you can't talk to a computer screen! I always shop locally for food. The market sells fresh fruit and vegetables. I usually pay in cash and the prices are good for the quality that you get.

 Francis: Can I say something about shopping centres? I love the mall near my town. I go there every weekend. I always buy my clothes in the sales. You can get really good discounts – 50% off the normal price. It's fantastic! And in a shop, I can try on clothes before I buy them so I know they're OK.

Vocabulary

5 Find the words in the box in the text. Put them in the correct columns. Which word appears as a noun <u>and</u> a verb in the text?

V shopping

buy	card	cash	cost	customer
discount	order	pay	the sales	sell
shop	shop assistant	spend	try on	

Nouns	Verbs

🔊 5.2 Listen, check and repeat.

6 a Complete the sentences with the correct forms of the words in the Vocabulary box.

1 When I .... locally, I usually .... in cash.
2 I don't like .... because the shops are too crowded.
3 Most supermarkets .... lots of international products.
4 I .... a lot of money in restaurants and cafés.
5 I only buy clothes if there's a good .... on them.
6 I .... something online about once a week.
7 I always .... shoes before I buy them.
8 My watch .... a lot of money.

b In pairs, say if the sentences are true for you. If not, change them so they are true for you.

Grammar

7 a Choose the correct words to complete the sentences from the text.

1 You *can / can't* spend a lot of money online!
2 She *can / can't* drive, so she shops online.
3 *Can / Can't* I say something about shopping centres?

b Which sentence is about:

a someone's ability? ....
b a general possibility? ....
c someone asking for permission? ....

G can/can't

+	You **can** get a big discount online.
–	The shop assistant **can't** speak French.
?	**Can** I pay by credit card?
Y/N	Yes, you **can**. / No, you **can't**.

→ Grammar reference: page 136

8 🔊 5.3 ❝ **sentence stress** ❞ Listen to the sentences. Notice how we stress *can't* in negative sentences and *can* and *can't* in short answers. Listen again and repeat.

1 Can you <u>buy</u> some <u>bread</u>?
2 <u>Yes</u>, I <u>can</u>. I can <u>go</u> to the <u>market</u>.
3 Can you <u>pay</u> by <u>card</u>?
4 <u>No</u>, I <u>can't</u>. I <u>can't find</u> my <u>credit card</u>!

9 In pairs, ask and answer the questions. Remember to stress *can* and *can't* correctly.

1 Can shops open on Sundays?
2 Can you pay by card everywhere?
3 Can you get a discount in any shops?
4 Can you buy food in the street?
5 Can you sell things you don't want online?

Speaking

10 In pairs, look at the things in the pictures and discuss the questions.

1 Where can you buy these things?
2 Can you buy them online?
3 Where can you get the best price?

fruit

phones

sports clothes

sunglasses

flowers

books

5.2 LOOKING GOOD

G present continuous
V clothes and accessories

Klaus Bernardo Marcella

Vocabulary

1 Match the clothes and accessories with the words in the box. Write down four more clothes or accessories you can see in the pictures.

V clothes and accessories

belt	boots	bracelet	earrings	
helmet	jacket	jeans	necklace	ring
sandals	scarf	shorts	suit	sweater
swimming costume		tie	tracksuit	trainers

1 .... 10 ....
2 .... 11 ....
3 .... 12 ....
4 .... 13 ....
5 .... 14 ....
6 .... 15 ....
7 .... 16 ....
8 .... 17 ....
9 .... 18 ....

🔊 5.4 Listen, check and repeat.

🔍 notice

The words *clothes*, *jeans*, *shorts* and *sunglasses* are always plural.

These are blue jeans. NOT *This is a blue jeans.*

2 In pairs, ask and answer the question *What do you usually wear ...?* with the phrases in the box.

| at the beach | at a party | at a wedding |
| at the weekend | at work | at home |

3 Look at the pictures again. Match the styles with the people.

1 surfer ....
2 biker   ....
3 hipster ....
4 exec   ....
5 street ....

4 In pairs, answer the questions.
1 Which of these styles do you see where you live?
2 Is your style similar to one of these? If so, which?
3 Are there any other styles in your country?
4 What clothes do these people wear?

Listening

5 🔊 5.5 What do you think the people in the pictures do at the weekend? Match them with the places. Then listen to the phone conversations and check.

1 the beach   ....
2 a concert hall   ....
3 a record shop   ....
4 a street market   ....
5 a department store ....

48

5.2

Lydia and Bruno   Ivan

Grammar

6 🔊 **5.6** Who says the sentences: Lydia (L), Bernardo (B), Ivan (I), Klaus (K) or Marcella (M)? Listen and check.
1 I'**m** just **buying** some earrings. ....
2 The shop assistant'**s coming**. ....
3 I'**m** not **shopping** ... I'**m** just **looking**. ....
4 We'**re** just **having** a look at the sandals. ....
5 What **are** you **wearing**? A green jacket? ....

7 Look at the sentences again. Answer the questions about the verbs in **bold**.
1 What do the verbs refer to? *an action in this moment / an action we do every day*
2 Which letters do we add to the main verb? ....
3 Which verb do we use with the main verb? ....

G	**present continuous**
+	She'**s buying** some sunglasses.
−	They **aren't wearing** helmets.
?	**Are** you **working** today?
Y/N	Yes, I **am**. / No, I'**m not**.

→ Grammar reference: page 136

🔍 notice

We often use *just* with the present continuous:
- to emphasize that the action is happening right now. I'm **just** buying some earrings.
- to mean 'only'. I'm **just** looking. (= I'm not shopping)

8 🔊 **5.7** 🎤 **-ing** /ɪŋ/ **sound** 🎤 Listen to the sentences. Notice the /ɪŋ/ sound in the main verbs. Listen and repeat.
1 What are you wear**ing**?
2 The shop assistant's com**ing**.
3 I'm not shopp**ing**.

9 **a** Complete the messages with the present continuous forms of the verbs in the box.

| come | do | have | look after |
| wait | not work | | |

b In pairs, act out the conversation. Remember to use the /ɪŋ/ sound.

14:10

Hi, what (1) .... you .... today? ✓✓

I (2) ....! 😊 I (3) .... just .... lunch at home. ✓✓

I (4) .... for the bus to the shopping centre. Do you want to come? ✓✓

Sorry, I can't. I (5) .... my nephew today. ✓✓

☹ OK. The bus (6) .... See you later! ✓✓

Bye!

Speaking

10 **a** In pairs, choose a place each. Think about the activities you can do there.

- on a bus
- in a café
- at the sports centre
- in the park
- at the train station
- in the shopping centre

b Imagine you are in these places right now. Have a phone conversation. Ask the questions.
1 How are you?
2 Where are you?
3 What are you doing?
4 Do you want to meet later?

✅ Exam practice: page 160

5.3 ON THE STREET

G present simple and continuous
🔧 find information in a text

a  b  c  d  e  f

Reading

1 In pairs, look at the pictures and discuss the questions.
  1 Do you know the names of these famous brands?
  2 What products are they?
  3 Are you wearing any famous brands of clothes today?
  4 Do you like brands? Do you have any favourites?

2 a Read the title and headings in the text. Guess the purpose of the text.
  1 to explain the legal problem
  2 to give information about the situation
  3 to give advice about what to buy

  b Read the text quickly and check your answer.

🔧 find information in a text

You often need to find information in a text quickly.
- Identify the information you need to find.
- Decide which paragraph has this information.
- Find the information you need in the paragraph.

3 a Read the questions and think about the information you need to find. Write the numbers of the paragraphs that have this information.
  1 Where can you buy fakes? ....
  2 Which brand products are popular? ....
  3 What problems can you have if you buy a fake? ....
  4 What problems can you have if you sell fakes? ....
  5 Who makes most money from fakes? ....
  6 Where do companies advertise their brands? ....

  b Read the paragraphs and <u>underline</u> the answers to the questions.

4 Choose the best answer for each question or write your own answer. In pairs, compare your answers.
  1 What do you think about fake goods?
    A They are good because the real thing is too expensive.
    B They are bad and create more crime.
    C Some fake goods are OK and they can be fun!
    D ....
  2 Do you ever buy fake goods?
    A No, never.
    B Yes, sometimes, because they're cheap.
    C Yes, I don't want to give money to big brand name companies.
    D ....

BRANDS:
the good, the bad and the ugly

1 The power of the brand
Brand names are all around us – on the TV, on our computer screens, in our magazines and even on the sides of buses! Brands are really important for companies because they want us all to know what products they sell. But they're also important for many customers. That's because the brands we choose tell the world about the type of people we are. Famous brands of clothes, shoes, watches and sunglasses are some of the most popular products that people want to buy. However, these products can be very expensive and not everybody can spend lots of money on them!

2 A cheap alternative
But there's another option. People who don't want to spend money on expensive brands can buy fakes instead! You can get copies of famous brand products for very good prices. People often sell these fakes in markets or on street corners. Some of them are quite good, almost as good as the original, but others are very poor quality. You need to be careful with what you buy. Remember, there's no guarantee for a fake watch and you can't return fake products to a shop if there's a problem!

3 The reality of fakes
And there's another thing we need to remember – fakes are illegal. The people who sell fake products can have problems with the police. It isn't an easy life. They often sell copies on the street because they can't find another job. It's the only way they can earn a little money. The people who make most money are the people who make the copies, but they aren't on the streets selling fakes!

Grammar

5 a Look at the pictures. In pairs, guess the answers to the questions.

1 Where is the market?
2 What kind of market is it?
3 What are the stalls selling?
4 Are the people buying or just looking?

b 🔊 5.9 Listen and check your answers. Are there any street markets like this in your town?

6 🔊 5.9 Listen again and complete the sentences.

1 The market opens at .... and closes at ....
2 The customer comes to the market every ....
3 Today, she's looking for a present for a ....
4 She wants to buy a .... or some ....

7 Look at the sentences in exercise 6. Which are present simple and which are present continuous? Complete the rules with the correct tenses.

1 We use the .... to talk about things that are always true or happen regularly.
2 We use the .... to talk about actions happening now. But we don't use state verbs (*like*, *love*, *want*, *need*, etc.) in the ....

G present simple and continuous

Present simple	Present continuous
Japanese people **buy** a lot of fish.	He**'s buying** a new suit at the moment.
I **go** to the market once a week.	We**'re going** to the café now.
I **need** a new laptop and smartphone.	I'm needing a new laptop.

→ Grammar reference: page 136

Writing

8 Look at the picture. Complete the text using the correct forms of the verbs.

This is Keiko. She (1) .... (live) in São Paulo. She (2) .... (make) paper decorations and she (3) .... (sell) them at the market. At the moment, she (4) .... (sell) special decorations to celebrate the new year. A lot of people (5) .... (want) to buy them! Keiko always (6) .... (wear) this hat, but today she (7) .... (wear) a coat, too. She (8) .... (not like) cold weather, but she (9) .... (love) new year!

9 Look at the picture. In pairs, use the information to write a similar description of Tony.

🔄 **Mediation task:** Student A page 127, Student B page 129

5.4 CAN I TRY IT ON?
shopping expressions
our clothes

The big picture: our clothes

1 Look at the picture. In pairs, guess the answers to the questions.
   1 Where are the people from?
   2 What are they doing?
   3 What clothes can you see?
   4 Where do the clothes come from?

2 a Which adjectives in the box describe the clothes the people are looking at?

> African   brand new   cheap
> expensive   second-hand   traditional

   b 5.1 Watch the video and check.

3 a Complete the sentences with adjectives from exercise 2a.
   1 People buy .... clothes in Ghana because they are cheap and ready to wear.
   2 There are small factories that make .... clothes using the material from second-hand clothes.
   3 .... clothes are important because they show the history and culture of Ghanaian people.
   4 People in the city think it's cooler to wear .... clothes.

   b 5.1 Watch again and check.

4 In pairs, discuss the questions.
   1 What do you do with your clothes when you don't want them any more?
   2 Were you surprised that second-hand clothes are popular in Africa?
   3 Do you ever buy second-hand clothes? Why/Why not?
   4 Do you ever wear traditional clothes? When?

5 5.2 Watch Dev and Sophia talking about the video. Are the sentences true (T) or false (F)?
   1 Dev was surprised that traditional clothes are more expensive. ....
   2 Sophia says that it's easy to make traditional clothes. ....
   3 Dev is wearing a second-hand jacket. ....
   4 The jacket cost £100. ....

6 5.2 Match the answers to the questions. Watch again and check.
   1 What do you think?   ....   a Just 30 pounds.
   2 How much was it?   ....   b It's great. I love it!
   3 Can I try it on?   ....   c I don't know.
   4 Do they have it in a small?   ....   d Yeah, of course.

Functional language

7 a Look at the pictures. In pairs, answer the questions.
1 Where are the people?
2 Are they buying something or just looking?
3 What are the people saying? Write two or three sentences for each picture.

b 🔊 5.10 Listen to the conversations and check. Did you guess what the people are saying?

8 🔊 5.10 Look at the sentences. Who says them: a customer (C) or a shop assistant (S)? Listen again and check.

1 Can I try this on? ....
2 Yes, of course. ....
3 Can I pay by card? ....
4 Type your PIN here. ....
5 Do you have another size? ....
6 And here's your change. ....

FL shopping expressions

Customer	Shop assistant
Excuse me.	How can I help you?
Can I try this/these on?	Of course, the changing rooms are over here.
Do you have a small/medium/large?	Yes, of course.
Does it/Do they come in blue/black?	I'm sorry. We don't have a ... one./have ... ones.
How much is that?	That's six euros.
Can I pay by card?	Yes, sure. Type your PIN here.
	No, sorry, we only take cash.
Here you are.	Thanks, and here's your change.

9 🔊 5.11 ❝ Yes/No questions ❞ Listen to the questions. Notice the intonation used. Listen again and repeat.
1 Can I try them on?
2 Do you have another size?
3 Can I pay by card?

Speaking

10 a In pairs, choose a situation. Have a conversation between a customer and a shop assistant. Remember to use the correct intonation in Yes/No questions.

b Swap partners and act out the other situation.

1
Student A: You work in the clothes department in a big department store. You are very friendly and always try to help your customers.
Student B: You're looking at some clothes in a department store. You want to try something on but you can't see the right size. You don't have any cash, you can only pay by card.

2
Student A: You're in a market. You want to buy a present for a friend. You see some earrings you like. You don't want to spend too much money.
Student B: You sell earrings in the market. You make the earrings yourself. You're very happy to help your customers. You can't accept cards, only cash.

✏️ Writing bank: page 148

REVIEW UNIT 5

Vocabulary
Shopping

1 In pairs, discuss the questions.
  1 Do you have a favourite shop?
  2 How often do you go there?
  3 What do you usually buy there?

2 a Complete the sentences with the words in the box.

card	cash	discount	order	shop	try on

  1 I always .... clothes before I buy them.
  2 I think online supermarkets are great. I .... food from them every week.
  3 If something costs a lot, I pay by ....
  4 I pay for smaller things, like cups of coffee, in ....
  5 I'm a student, so I get a .... in some shops.
  6 I prefer to .... online. It's quick and easy.

  b In pairs, discuss if the sentences in 2a are true for you.

Clothes and accessories

3 You are going to a friend's house for the weekend. Make a list of the clothes you want to take with you. Compare your list with a partner.

4 Write *This is* or *These are*.
  1 .... Caryn's scarf.
  2 .... his old trainers.
  3 .... an expensive necklace.
  4 .... my new suit.
  5 .... dirty boots.
  6 .... her earrings.
  7 .... a nice leather belt.
  8 .... the children's sandals.

Grammar
can/can't

5 Complete the sentences with *can* or *can't* and a verb from the box.

buy	find	give	hear	pay	speak

  1 The new supermarket is great. You .... everything you want in there.
  2 The music is too loud in this shop. I .... what you're saying.
  3 Where's my phone? I .... it anywhere.
  4 I don't have any cash. .... I .... by card?
  5 I'm very sorry, but we .... a discount on clothes in the sales.
  6 Why don't you ask the shop assistant? He .... English really well.

6 In pairs, ask and answer *Can you …?* for the activities in the box. Use *very well*, *quite well* or *not at all*.

| bake cakes | draw pictures | play tennis |
| play the guitar | ride a bike | speak Spanish |

  A *Can you play tennis?*
  B *Yes, I can, quite well./No, I can't, not at all.*

7 In pairs, write a list of five things you can't do (because it's not allowed or not possible):
  1 in your classroom. *You can't smoke.*
  2 in your town. *You can't ski – there's no snow.*

Present continuous

8 Write the *-ing* forms of the verbs.
  1 dance ....   5 study ....
  2 listen ....   6 talk ....
  3 put ....   7 use ....
  4 sing ....   8 write ....

9 In pairs, use the verbs in exercise 8 and your own ideas to say what people in the class are doing now.
  Carlos is sitting on a chair. He isn't standing.

Present simple and continuous

10 Choose the correct option to complete the questions. Then ask and answer the questions with a partner.
  1 *Do you study / Are you studying* for exams at the moment?
  2 What *do you usually do / are you usually doing* at the weekend?
  3 *Do you go / Are you going* to the shops every day?
  4 What sports *do you do / are you doing*?
  5 What *do you think / are you thinking* about now?

Functional language
Shopping expressions

11 🔊 5.12 Match the questions to the answers. Listen and check.
  1 Can I help you? ....   a What colour?
  2 Where are the   b Over there, next to
    changing rooms? ....   the shoes.
  3 Can I try these on? .... c Yes, of course!
  4 I'm looking for   d No, thanks, I'm just
    a shirt. ....   looking.

12 In pairs, continue two of the four conversations.

Looking back
- Which section of this unit was most useful for you?
- Write down five useful phrases from this unit.
- Tell a partner five things you can say to describe the people around you and what they're doing.

The great outdoors

Grammar G
like, love, hate + noun/*-ing* form
object pronouns

Vocabulary V
sports and leisure
the countryside
the weather

Functional language FL
telephone language

Skill
identify opinions

Video
storm chasers

Writing
messaging

Exams
discussing a topic

The big picture: an unusual football pitch

1. Look at the picture. In pairs, guess the answers to the questions.
   1. Which country are the children from?
   2. What are they doing?
   3. Where are they doing it?
   4. Why are they playing there?

2. 6.1 Listen to the information about the picture and check your answers.

3. In pairs, discuss the questions.
   1. Is football a popular sport where you live?
   2. Where do people usually play it?
   3. In what other places can you play it?
   4. What sports do you play?
   5. Where do you play them?

55

6.1 HOW DO YOU KEEP FIT?

G *like, love, hate* + noun/*-ing* form
V sports and leisure

Vocabulary

1 a 🔊 **6.2** Find the activities in the Vocabulary box and match them with the pictures. Listen and check.

b 🔊 **6.2** Which verbs do we use with these activities? Listen again and check.

2 Match the activities with the correct verbs.

V sports and leisure

athletics	baseball	bowling	cards
chess	cycling	fishing	golf	horse-riding
jogging	judo	Pilates	rock climbing
skiing	surfing	swimming	volleyball
weights	yoga

play	go	do
baseball		

🔊 **6.3** Listen, check and repeat.

3 Answer the questions about the activities in the Vocabulary box.
  1 Which activities do you usually do a) indoors? b) outdoors? c) both?
  2 Which do you usually do a) on your own? b) in a team?
  3 Which do you think are 'real' sports? Why?

4 In pairs, discuss the questions.
  1 Do you do any of the activities?
  2 How often do you do it?
  3 Where do you do it?
  4 Who do you do it with?

Reading

5 a What activities can people do to keep fit?

b Read the text. How do the people keep fit? Do they mention any of your ideas?

6 Read the text again. Match the people with the other good things about their activities.
  1 Jacques ....   a doesn't spend money.
  2 Maria   ....   b gets healthy food.
  3 Boris   ....   c meets other people.
  4 Alfred   ....   d gets to work early.

🔍 **notice**

We also use *go for a …* to talk about activities.
*I want to **go for a** swim / run / cycle / walk.*

Get fit by accident!

Not everybody is a sports star. And not everyone likes doing exercise. But that doesn't mean you can't get fit. Read about four people who keep fit by accident.

JACQUES: I hate doing sport of any kind. But I have a one-year-old dog and she's full of energy. She needs to run and play for at least an hour every day. I love going to the park and taking her for a walk. I throw a ball for her and play with her. It keeps me really fit and I often chat to other people with dogs. You don't need to go jogging or do weights to get fit … just get a dog!

MARIA: I can't stand the gym – it's so boring. And going for a run is the same. My favourite weekend activity is fishing. I know it isn't very 'sporty', but we walk miles to get to the right place and we carry all the heavy fishing gear. It's hard work, but I sometimes catch a fish for dinner! Doing that once a week keeps me fit.

6.1

Grammar

7 Look at the symbols and complete the sentences from the text with the verbs in the box. Do you agree with any of them?

| can't stand | don't like | don't mind |
| hate | like | love |

1. 😍 I .... going to the park.
2. 🙂 I .... going for a cycle.
3. 😐 I .... doing housework.
4. 😣 I .... sport at all.
5. 😖 I .... playing team sports.
6. 😠 I .... the gym.

8 Look at the sentences in exercise 7 again. Answer the questions.

1. Which sentences are about nouns? ......, ...
2. Which sentences are about activities? ......, ..., ..., ...
3. What form is the verb in when we talk about activities?
   ....

G *like, love, hate* + noun/*-ing* form

I love team sports/playing football.
Do you like your job/working as a doctor?
She doesn't mind the weather/being hot.

→ Grammar reference: page 137

9 Complete the text with the nouns and the correct form of the verbs.

| football | get up | life | play |
| run | train | win | |

USAIN BOLT NEEDS TO GET FIT?

This is Jamaican sprinter Usain Bolt. We all know he likes (1) .... very fast and loves (2) .... gold medals, but now he's retired from athletics, what's he doing? Well, he loves (3) ...., too and he wants to be a professional football player. Right now, he's playing for an Australian team – the Central Coast Mariners. His favourite team is Manchester United, but he doesn't mind (4) .... for another team. He likes (5) .... in Australia, but Usain says he needs to get fit – for football! He hates (6) .... early and doesn't like (7) ...., but right now he's working very hard and he's sure he can be a great football player.

10 🔊 6.4 🗨 **likes and dislikes** 🗨 Listen to the sentences. Notice how we emphasize the likes and dislikes phrases. Listen again and repeat.

1. I <u>hate</u> going for a walk!
2. I <u>don't like</u> playing chess.
3. I <u>like</u> doing Pilates.
4. I <u>don't mind</u> doing weights.

Speaking

11 In pairs, talk about your likes and dislikes with the activities below and explain your answers. Remember to use the correct intonation.

I can't stand going jogging because it's really boring!

watch / sport on TV	go / shopping
cook / food	take / bus
get up / early	go / jogging
play / cards	listen to / opera

 BORIS: My wife says I don't like sport at all, but that's not true. I love watching football on the TV! It's just that I hate playing team sports like football and basketball. I have a bike, though, and I like going for a cycle when I can. In fact, I'm going to work on my bike now. It's great – you don't spend ages in traffic and you get fit!

 ALFRED: I like doing yoga for fifteen minutes every morning. It's a good way to wake up, but it doesn't really get me fit. I don't like going jogging or swimming or anything like that. But I don't mind doing housework and that's how I keep fit. I listen to music and clean the house from top to bottom. It's free – not like an expensive gym, and I always have a clean house!

6.2 A VERY SPECIAL PLACE

G object pronouns
V the countryside

Vocabulary

1 Look at the pictures. In pairs, answer the questions.
 1 Which words from the Vocabulary box can you see in the pictures?
 2 Which words can't you see in the pictures?
 3 Which country do you think these places are from?

2 Put the words in the box in the correct columns.

V the countryside

beach	cloud	desert	field
forest	grass	hill	island	lake
mountain	river	sea	sky	trees

Water	Plants	Land	Air
lake			

🔊 6.5 Listen, check and repeat.

Listening

3 🔊 6.6 Listen to the descriptions and match pictures a–d with the places.
 1 Manuripi ……….   3 Lomas de Arena ……….
 2 Isla del Sol ……….   4 Uyuni ……….

4 🔊 6.6 Answer the questions. Listen again and check.
 1 Which country are they in?
 2 What is special about the countryside?
 3 Why can't you see beaches and the sea here?

🔍 notice

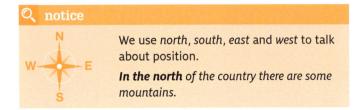

We use *north*, *south*, *east* and *west* to talk about position.

In the north of the country there are some mountains.

5 In pairs, discuss the questions.
 1 Do you like the countryside? Why/Why not?
 2 Which place in Bolivia would you like to visit most?
 3 What is the countryside in your country like?

In the south, there are some beautiful beaches. There are also lots of fields …

Grammar

6 a Look at the picture. Which place in Bolivia do you think it is?

b 🔊 **6.7** Listen to the tour guide and read the text. Check your answer to 6a.

Good morning, everyone. My name's Nacho and I'm your guide today. Can you hear **me** OK? There are twelve visitors on the tour to Uyuni today. We also have two other people travelling with **us**. Can I introduce **them** to **you**? Firstly, this is our driver, Carlos, and he's from right here in Uyuni. So if you have any questions about the area, you can ask **him**. And we also have Barbara. She speaks English, so you can ask **her** for help. Ah, this is interesting. There's an old train over there. Can you see **it**? It's almost 100 years old …

7 a Look at the highlighted words in the text. In pairs, find who or what they refer to.

'me' refers to Nacho.

b Match the object pronouns in the box with the subject pronouns.

her	him	it	me	them	us	you

1 I ....
2 you ....
3 he ....
4 she ....
5 it ....
6 we ....
7 they ....

8 Look at the sentences with object pronouns again. Complete the rules.

1 Object pronouns come *before / after* verbs.
2 Object pronouns come *before / after* prepositions.

G object pronouns

me	I'm lost. Can you help **me**?
you	You're Sally. I know **you**.
him	He's a teacher. I work with **him**.
her	She's nice. Everyone likes **her**.
it	It's broken. Can they fix **it**?
us	We're here. Call **us** when you want.
them	They're great books. I love **them**.

→ Grammar reference: page 137

---

9 a 🔊 **6.8** Put the object pronouns in brackets in the correct places in the sentences. Listen to the conversation and check.

A Hello, can I help? (**you**)
B Yes, please. We'd like some information about the trip to Uyuni. What can you tell about? (**us**, **it**)
A Well, it's a great trip. Are you taking children with? We have some great activities for. (**you**, **them**)
B Yes, we're taking our granddaughter. Do you have any special activities for? She's 8. (**her**)
A Yes, there's a special information centre for children at our first stop. She'll love. Look, here's a photo. (**it**)
B That's great!

b In pairs, act out the conversation.

Speaking

10 a Write three examples in each of the categories.

b In pairs, ask and answer the questions about the people and things.

What do you think of …? What about …? Do you like …?

Do you like mountains? No, I don't like them. I hate walking.
What about the beach? Yes, I love it. It's fun.

Exam practice: page 161   59

6.3 WHATEVER THE WEATHER

v the weather
⚡ identify opinions

Vocabulary

1 Look at the weather symbols. Complete the phrases with the words in the box.

v the weather

| cloudy | cold | foggy | hot | raining |
| snowing | stormy | sunny | warm | windy |

1 It's ....
2 It's ....
3 It's ....
4 It's ....
5 It's ....
6 It's ....
7 It's ....
8 It's ....
9 It's ....
10 It's ....

🔊 6.11 Listen, check and repeat.

🔍 notice

rain and *snow* are verbs. We can use them in the present simple and present continuous.
It **rains** a lot in the UK. It**'s raining** today.
It always **snows** here in January. It**'s snowing** now!

2 In pairs, discuss the questions.
   1 What's the weather like today?
   2 Is it usual for this time of year?
   3 Do you like this kind of weather? Why/Why not?

3 Which of the seasons in the box do you have where you live? Which months are they in?

| spring | summer | autumn | winter |
| dry season | rainy season | | |

4 Look at the pictures. Guess the answers to the questions.
   1 Which seasons do they show?
   2 What's the weather like?
   3 Where are they?

Listening

5 🔊 **6.12** Listen to a radio programme. Check your answers to the questions in exercise 4.

> 🔧 **identify opinions**
>
> When people talk about something they often give their opinions:
> - listen for verbs that express opinions, e.g. *love, hate, think, prefer.*
> - listen for positive and negative adjectives, e.g. *favourite, beautiful, dangerous.*

6 a 🔊 **6.12** Read the Skill box. Then listen again and say if the sentences are true (T) or false (F).
   1 Maria likes the colours of the trees in autumn. ……….
   2 She isn't happy when it rains. ……….
   3 Clause likes going skiing in winter. ……….
   4 His favourite season is spring. ……….
   5 Berta hates the beach in the summer. ……….
   6 Berta doesn't mind cold weather. ……….
   7 The rain isn't a problem for Hasan. ……….
   8 He doesn't like windy weather. ……….

   b Which words and phrases did the people use to give their opinions?

7 a In pairs, discuss the questions.
   1 What's your favourite season? Why?
   2 What's the weather like?
   3 What do you like doing at that time of year?
   4 Which season don't you like? Why?
   5 What's the weather like?

   b Tell the class your partner's opinions.

   Daniel loves the summer because it's hot and sunny. He likes finishing work early and going swimming. He thinks it's really fun.

Writing

8 Look at the picture and read the description. Then answer the questions.
   1 Where is the person?
   2 Why is she there?
   3 What's the weather like?
   4 Does she like the weather? Why/Why not?
   5 Is the weather normal for the time of year? Why/Why not?
   6 Does she like the place? Why/Why not?

I can't believe I'm here in Taksim Square in Istanbul. It's amazing! It's so big and empty – we're almost the only people here! It's really cold right now and it's snowing. My phone says it's –4°C, so I guess nobody wants to be outside on a cold day in winter, but I don't mind – I'm on holiday. I have a thick coat and I'm enjoying every minute! But it's strange, we usually see photos of Turkey in summer. We think it's a hot country, but it can get very cold here. I love it. Istanbul in the snow is very romantic!

♡ 27 likes

9 Find a picture of a place you like or are interested in. Write a description and include:
   1 what season the picture shows.
   2 what the weather is like in the picture.
   3 what the people are wearing and doing.
   4 what the weather is usually like.

➡ **Mediation task:** Student A page 126, Student B page 128

6.4 CAN I LEAVE A MESSAGE?

FL telephone language
storm chasers

The big picture: storm chasers

1 a Look at the pictures. In pairs, answer the questions.
   1 What weather can you see?
   2 Why is the van parked at the side of the road?
   3 What is in the man's hand?
   4 Where did it come from?

   b 6.1 Watch the video and check.

2 a In pairs, choose the correct options to answer the questions. Sometimes more than one option is correct.
   1 Why do Reed and his team chase the storm?
      a to take pictures of it
      b because they like danger
      c to see how big it is
   2 Why is it difficult to drive in the storm?
      a because the car has a problem
      b because there is lots of wind and rain
      c because the roads are bad
   3 Who does Reed call when they drive?
      a the police
      b a TV weather channel
      c his family
   4 Why do they stop chasing the storm?
      a because it is too dark
      b because the storm is finished
      c because the car is broken

   b 6.1 Watch the video again and check.

3 In pairs, answer the questions.
   1 Would you like to do the storm chasers' job? Why/Why not?
   2 Do you think that their job is necessary?
   3 Do you have bad storms in your country?
   4 Do you think storm chasers are necessary where you live?

4 6.2 Watch Dev and Sophia talk about the video. Are the sentences true (T) or false (F)?
   1 Sophia thinks the video is exciting. ....
   2 Dev thinks the video is very realistic. ....
   3 They have tornadoes in their country. ....
   4 They think storm chasers are necessary in their country. ....

5 6.2 In pairs, put the phrases in the correct order. Watch the video again and check.
   a ☐ Hello?
   b ☐ Thanks for your help.
   c ☐ Hi Sophia. Thanks for calling me back.
   d ☐ Hi Dev. It's me.
   e ☐ Hi, it's Dev here.
   f ☐ Can I speak to Sophia?

6.4

Functional language

6 Look at the picture. In pairs, guess the answers to the questions.

1 Which country is this?
2 What's the weather like?
3 What's the countryside like?
4 What activities can you do here?

7 🔊 **6.13** Listen to the telephone conversations and check your answers to exercise 6.

8 a 🔊 **6.13** Listen again and complete the table with the names in the box.

| Andy | Katia | Tom | Viviana |

	Person calling	Person answering
Conversation 1		
Conversation 2		
Conversation 3		

b What phrases did the people use to start and end the conversations?

FL telephone language

Person calling	Person answering
Hi …	Hello, (name of company), (your name) speaking. How can I help you?
This is … / It's … / My name's …	Thanks for calling back.
Can I speak to …?	Can you hold on, please?
Can I leave a message?	I'm afraid he/she can't come to the phone.
Can you ask (him/her) to call me back?	Can I take a message?
I'd like to …	Of course.
Thanks for your help.	Thanks for calling.

9 🔊 **6.14** Number the sentences in the correct order. Listen and check.

a ☐ Hi, Byron Surf School. Linda speaking.
b ☐ OK, that's great. Thanks for your help.
c ☐ Of course. They're every day at 10.00 and at 3.00.
d ☐ Hello, can I speak to Shane please?
e ☐ No problem. Thank you for calling.
f ☐ Yes, I'd like to ask about surf lessons.
g ☐ I'm afraid he's not here at the moment. Can I help you?

10 🔊 **6.15** 🗨 **sounding friendly** 🗨 Listen to people answering the phone. Notice how they use friendly intonation. Listen again and repeat.

1 Hi, Byron Surf School. Linda speaking.
2 This is Andy. How can I help you?

Speaking

11 a In groups of three, look at the diagram below. Decide who is the receptionist, the customer and Ashley. Use the Functional language box to have two conversations.

b Swap roles and repeat.

📝 **Writing bank: page 149**

REVIEW UNIT 6

Vocabulary
Sports and leisure

1 In pairs, can you think of:
   1 five sports you play with a ball?
   2 four sports you play in a team?
   3 three activities you can do indoors?
   4 three activities you can do on your own?
   5 one sport you're very good at?

2 Which activity doesn't go with the verb?
   1 **play:** cards, chess, judo, volleyball, golf
   2 **do:** athletics, weights, yoga, cards, Pilates
   3 **go:** swimming, cycling, volleyball, skiing, jogging

3 Look at the activities in exercise 2. Which do you do:
   1 almost every day?   3 on holiday?
   2 at the weekend?   4 never?

The countryside

4 Match the words with the pictures.
   1 beach ......   3 forest ......   5 mountain ......
   2 field ......   4 lake ......   6 river ......

5 Think of a place you know and use the words in exercise 4 to describe it to your partner.

   The Lake District is in the north of England. There are some beautiful mountains and lakes there ...

The weather

6 Complete the weather words with the correct vowels.
   1 s....nny   4 w....ndy   7 r........ning
   2 f....ggy   5 sn....wing   8 w....rm
   3 st....rmy   6 cl....dy   9 c....ld

7 In pairs, discuss the questions.
   1 What's the weather like now?
   2 What was it like yesterday?
   3 What's the weather usually like in your town in autumn, winter, spring and summer?
   4 What do you do in extreme weather – when it's really hot, cold, rainy, etc.?

Grammar
like, love, hate + noun/-ing form

8 **a** Order the phrases from most negative (1) to most positive (6).
   a ☐ I can't stand   d ☐ I don't like
   b ☐ I love   e ☐ I don't mind
   c ☐ I hate   f ☐ I like

   b Use the phrases in sentences that are true for you. In pairs, compare your answers.

   I can't stand doing the washing-up.

Object pronouns

9 Write the correct subject or object pronouns.

Subject	Object
I	1 ....
you	you
he	2 ....
3	her
it	4 ....
we	5 ....
6	them

10 Write the correct pronouns to replace the words in **bold**.
   1 She speaks Japanese so you can ask **Sheila** to help you.
   2 **Freya and I** have two dogs with us.
   3 There's a box on the table. Can you open **the box**?
   4 It's my dad's birthday so I'm cooking **my dad** a meal.
   5 They're wearing red hats. Can you see **Charlie and Ella**?

Functional language
Telephone language

11 In pairs, act out a phone call using the information below.

   Student A
   Call Student B and ask to speak to Joy. You want to talk to her about a game of tennis. You want to change the time to 6.30 p.m.

   Student B
   Student A calls you and asks to speak to Joy. Explain that Joy isn't in, she's at a music lesson. Take a message.

12 Swap roles and repeat the conversation.

Looking back

- Which section of this unit was most useful for you?
- Write down five useful phrases from this unit.
- Tell a partner three things you can do in English after doing this unit.

On the move

7

Grammar G
past simple of *be*, *there was/were*
past simple regular verbs

Vocabulary V
holiday phrases
past time expressions
transport

Functional language FL
using public transport

Skill
read in detail

Video
crazy rides

Writing
an informal email

Exams
reading a long article

The big picture: setting off on a trip

1 Look at the picture. In pairs, guess the answers to the questions.
   1 Where is the person?
   2 Where is she going? Why?
   3 How does she feel?

🔍 **notice**

trip is a noun to talk about going to a place and doing something: *I want to go on a camping trip next weekend.*
journey is a noun to talk about how you get from one place to another: *The train journey takes an hour and a half.*
travel is a verb: *I enjoy travelling by train.*

2 🔊 7.1 Listen to her talking and check your answers.

3 In pairs, discuss the questions.
   1 How often do you go on a trip away from your town?
   2 Where do you usually go?
   3 How do you travel there?
   4 How long is the journey?

65

7.1 BEFORE AND AFTER

G past simple of *be*, *there was/were*
V holiday phrases

a
b
c

Vocabulary

1 Look at the pictures. Which place do you prefer for a holiday? Why?

2 🔊 7.2 Listen to three people. Match them with the pictures.

1 .... 2 .... 3 ....

3 Match the verbs in the box with the words to make holiday phrases.

V holiday phrases

| book | go | have | rent | stay | visit |

1 .... in a hotel / in a hostel / in a tent / with friends/family
2 .... camping / sightseeing / hiking / abroad
3 .... a barbecue / a good time / a party
4 .... a museum / a castle / a park / the beach
5 .... a car / a bike / an apartment
6 .... a room / a ticket / a flight / a table at a restaurant

🔊 7.3 Listen, check and repeat.

4 In pairs, ask and answer the questions.
1 Where do you usually go on holiday?
2 Where do you stay?
3 What can you do there?
4 How do you get there?

Listening

5 🔊 7.4 Listen to the conversation about Same in Ecuador. Answer the questions.
1 How often does Sandra go to Same?
2 Where does she stay?
3 How does she get there?
4 Does she prefer Same now or in the past?

6 🔊 7.4 Are these things better in the past (P) or now (N)? Listen again and check.
1 transport   ....
2 jobs   ....
3 the beach   ....
4 prices for local people ....
5 activities for tourists ....

7 In pairs, discuss the questions.
1 Is tourism important for your country?
2 Where do tourists usually go?
3 What do they like to do?
4 Does it cause any problems for local people?

Grammar

8 Choose the correct words to complete the sentences about Same in the past.

1 Sandra's grandfather **was** a *fisherman / tour guide*.
2 It **wasn't** *a hard / an easy* job.
3 Her grandparents **were** *sad / happy*.
4 The *roads / boats* **weren't** very good.
5 **There were** *visitors from local towns / rich tourists*.
6 **There weren't** any *houses / apartments*.
7 **There was** a *local shop / big hotel*.
8 **There wasn't** *a bus station / an airport* nearby.

9 Look at the words in **bold** and answer the questions

1 What are the positive past simple forms of *be*?
.... and ....
2 What are the negative past simple forms of *be*?
.... and ....
3 What do *there was* and *there wasn't* describe?
plural / singular nouns
4 What do *there were* and *there weren't* describe?
plural / singular nouns

G past simple of *be, there was/were*

+	I **was** tired. They **were** quiet.	There **was** a restaurant. There **were** some houses.
−	She **wasn't** a teacher. We **weren't** on holiday.	There **wasn't** a big hotel. There **weren't** any tourists.
?	**Was** he a tour guide? **Were** you happy?	**Was there** a shopping centre? **Were there** any boats?
Y/N	Yes, he **was**. / No, he **wasn't**. Yes, we **were**. / No, we **weren't**.	Yes, **there was**. / No, **there wasn't**. Yes, **there were**. / No, **there weren't**.

→ Grammar reference: page 138

---

10 Complete the description of Shanghai with the correct form of *was* or *were*.

11 🔊 7.5 **short answers** Listen to the questions and answers. Notice how the underlined words in the short answers are stressed. Listen again and repeat the short answers.

Were there many tourists?
<u>No</u>, there <u>weren't</u>.
Was it a long journey?
<u>Yes</u>, it <u>was</u>.

12 In pairs, ask and answer the questions about Pudong 30 years ago. Remember to use the correct stress in the short answers.

1 Was Pudong very different 30 years ago?
2 Were there a lot of tourists?
3 Was it a busy town?
4 Were there a lot of tall buildings?
5 Were there any boats on the river?
6 Was there an airport?

Speaking

13 In pairs, think of a place you know well which was different in the past. Talk about the changes. Use the topics in the boxes and your own ideas.

Transport	Jobs
Entertainment	Food
Shopping	Population
Nature	Tourists

14 Tell the class about the changes. Are they generally good or bad? Explain your reasons.

The city is too crowded now. Twenty years ago there weren't lots of cars. It was easy to travel around the city.

today

30 years ago

SHANGHAI

Shanghai is a modern, high-tech city with a population of around 30 million. But it (1) .... always this way. Thirty years ago there (2) .... only seven million people in the city and it (3) .... very different. Look at this photo of the financial district of Pudong. It (4) .... a busy town, but it (5) .... anything like it is today. Thirty years ago there (6) .... any tall buildings. There (7) .... a lot of small boats on the river, but they (8) .... all working boats. There (9) .... only one airport and all the visitors (10) .... Chinese. Today, Pudong is full of restaurants, shops and parks and has all kinds of free-time activities for local people and visitors from all over the world.

7.2 MICROADVENTURES

G past simple regular verbs
V past time expressions

Reading

1 Look at the pictures and the title. What is a microadventure? Read the definition and check. Would you like to go on a microadventure? Why/Why not?

> **microadventure (n)** an adventure that is cheap, simple, short and close to home. You don't need to travel far or spend a lot of money to have a microadventure. You don't even need a lot of time. All you need is a spirit of adventure!

2 Read the interview and complete the plans for Nikki's microadventure.

Planning our microadventure!

Where do we want to go?
How can we get there?
What do we want to do there?
What can we eat and drink?
What time do we want to get back?

3 In pairs, plan a microadventure in your town. Tell the class about it.

We want to go the lakes outside the city. We can rent a car ...

Try a MICROADVENTURE

Microadventures are becoming very popular, but what exactly are they? We talked to Nikki Morgan, an account manager who works in the city centre, about her first ever microadventure.

Why did you want to try a microadventure?
Well, when I was a child we went camping, but I didn't like it. Then, a few weeks ago, I watched a video about Alastair Humphreys – he invented microadventures in 2012 – and it inspired me! It looked lots of fun and I wanted to try one.

Did you enjoy it?
Yes, I did. It was fantastic – I feel great! A friend and I planned it last week. We didn't want to go for a long time, just for one night. It was short, but we loved it.

Did you travel far?
No, we didn't. It was just us, a tent and public transport! There's a hill I can see from my office window. I look at it every day and it's very pretty, so we decided to visit it. We finished work yesterday afternoon, travelled by bus for about twenty minutes and walked up the hill. We stayed in the tent last night. A really simple little adventure.

Did you eat up there?
Yes, we did. We had some sandwiches and coffee. We tried to sleep, but it was difficult. We looked at the stars and talked a lot. This morning, we watched the sun come up. The city was so beautiful. I wanted to stay but I needed to get to work. So we walked back down and waited for the bus. I arrived at the office at 8.30.

You were back in time for work!
That's the great thing about microadventures. You don't need a lot of time. We did it all in just 12 hours. You don't need to travel very far. You can fit them easily into a working week. Everyone should try it!

68

Grammar

4 a Look at the text again. Find and write the past simple forms of the verbs.

1 watch ....
2 love ....
3 plan ....
4 try ....
5 stay ....
6 look ....

b Look at the past simple forms again. Match the descriptions to the spelling rules.

double consonant + ed	+ d
omit y + ied	+ ed

1 Most verbs
2 Verbs that end in *e*
3 Verbs that end in vowel + consonant
4 Verbs that end in consonant + *y*

5 Find a past simple question and a past simple negative in the text. Answer the questions.
1 How do we form a question in the past simple?
   .... + subject + infinitive
2 How do we form a negative?
   subject + ... + infinitive

G past simple regular verbs

+	I **loved** the trip.
–	My friend **didn't like** it.
?	**Did** you **stay** in a tent?
Y/N	Yes, I **did**. / No, I **didn't**.

→ Grammar reference: page 138

6 🔊 7.6 🔖 *-ed endings* 🔖 Listen to the sentences from the text. Pay attention to the past simple forms in **bold**. Which have one syllable? Which have two? Listen again and repeat.

1 We **tried** to sleep.
2 We **looked** at the stars.
3 I **wanted** to stay.
4 I **needed** to get to work.
5 We **walked** back down.
6 We **waited** for the bus.

🔍 notice

Some verbs are irregular and don't end in *-ed*.

go > went	We **went** on a camping trip.
do > did	We **did** it all in twelve hours.
have > had	We **had** some sandwiches.

Vocabulary

7 Look at the time expressions from the text. Put them in the correct order.

a few weeks ago   in 2012   last night   last week
this morning   when I was a child   yesterday afternoon

Past ▶
1 .... 2 ....
3 .... 4 .... 5 ....
6 .... 7 .... ▶ Now

8 Complete the phrases with the words in the box.

V past time expressions

ago   in   last   when   yesterday

1 .... + I was twelve / I was a child
2 .... + night / week / year
3 an hour / a few days / ten years + ...
4 .... + morning / afternoon / evening
5 .... + 2018 / March

🔊 **7.7** Listen, check and repeat.

9 a Write the past simple forms of the verbs in brackets.

1 .... dinner (cook)
2 .... the dentist (visit)
3 .... a sad film (watch)
4 .... for an exam (study)
5 .... in a tent (stay)
6 .... for a bus (wait)
7 .... (dance)
8 .... online (shop)

b Ask and answer the question *When was the last time you …?* with the phrases. Remember to pronounce the past simple endings with the correct number of syllables.

I cooked dinner last week when my parents visited me for the weekend.

Speaking

10 Think of a trip you went on recently. In pairs, ask and answer the questions.

When was it?
Where did you go?
Who did you go with?
How did you travel there?
Where did you stay?
What did you do?
What was the weather like?
Did you have a good time?

✅ Exam practice: page 162

7.3 COMMUTERS' TALES

v transport
read in detail

Vocabulary

1 Look at the pictures. In pairs, answer the questions.
  1 What types of transport can you see?
  2 What do they have in common?
  3 Where are the people going?

2 Match the different types of transport with the correct categories.

v transport

bike   boat   bus   car   ferry
motorbike   plane   scooter   taxi
train   tram   underground

Road   Rail

Sky   Water

🔊 **7.8** Listen, check and repeat.

🔍 notice

We use *by* + transport: *I travel **by car**, a lot of people get to work **by bus**.*

We say *on foot*: *The bus didn't come so we went **on foot**.*

Cities have different names for underground systems: **underground, metro, subway**

3 In pairs, answer the questions.
  1 Which types of transport does your town have?
  2 How often do you use these types of transport?
  3 Does it have an underground system? What's it called?
  4 How do you usually get to class?
  5 How long does it take?

  I usually travel to the centre by bus and then go on foot. It takes about thirty minutes.

Reading

4 a Read the text below quickly. Which three pictures show types of transport mentioned in the text?

b In pairs, answer the questions.
1 What is a commute?
2 Who is happy with her commute?
3 Who is unhappy with her commute?

read in detail

Sometimes you need to understand information in a text in detail.
- Find the information you need in the text and read it carefully.
- Think about how it relates to other details.
- Pay attention to the tense of the verbs – are they past or present?
- Check if the verbs are positive or negative.
- Pay attention to pronouns. Who or what do they refer to?

5 Read the Skill box, then read the text again. Are the sentences true (T) or false (F)?
1 Jennifer went to work on foot two years ago. ....
2 The ferry is busy early in the morning. ....
3 She has a good relationship with the people on the ferry. ....
4 Her office is near Grand Central Station. ....
5 Rosa's journey takes two and a half hours. ....
6 It takes her 20 minutes to walk to the bus stop. ....
7 The traffic in São Paulo is a problem. ....
8 She's happy to travel by metro. ....

6 In pairs, discuss the questions.
1 Do a lot of people commute to work or university in your town?
2 Does anybody you know commute as far as Jennifer?
3 Does anybody you know travel for two hours or more?
4 How long does your journey to work or university take?
5 What type of transport do you use?
6 Do you enjoy your commute? Why/Why not?

Writing

7 Read this short description of another commute. In what ways is it different from Jennifer and Rosa's stories?

247 posts

Last year I started going to work on my bike. It takes me about 40 minutes. Before I went by car, but it was really difficult to park near my office, so I decided to cycle. I really like it. I think it's a good way to start the day. It's true that in summer it can be very hot, but I can have a shower when I get to work. Sometimes in winter it rains a lot. I don't like cycling in the rain, so I travel by bus instead. Although the traffic is so bad in the rain, it actually takes more time on the bus!

👍 Like   💬 Comment

8 Write a short description of a journey you do regularly, or one that someone you know does. Explain what forms of transport you use, how long it takes and how you feel about it.

Our daily commutes

Every day, millions of people in cities all around the world travel for an hour or more to get to work. They use all types of transport: trains, buses, trams, ferries. Some people hate the commutes. Other people like them. Jennifer and Rosa talked to us about the two sides of the story.

Jennifer, Newburgh, USA
When I started working in New York, I lived in Manhattan and I walked to work. But two years ago, we had a baby and our apartment was too small, so we decided to move to Newburgh, about 60 miles away. Now it takes me two hours to get to work and two hours to get back again. I get up really early and travel by ferry across the Hudson river – that's my favourite part. There are only a few people on the ferry and we all know each other now. They're really friendly. On the other side, I take a train to Grand Central Station. Two hours later I'm walking through the door of my office, just a couple of blocks away. Some people think I'm crazy spending four hours on public transport every day, but I don't mind it – I read two or three books a week!

Rosa, São Paulo, Brazil
I take two buses and then go by metro to get to work. It usually takes two and a half hours. I start my journey at 5.30 a.m. every day. The bus stop is close to my house, but I sometimes wait 20 minutes for the bus to arrive. They're always crowded and I never get a seat. When I was a student I went to university by bus and the traffic wasn't so bad, but now there are lots of cars on the roads and it's a real problem. When I finally get to the metro station, it's about 7.30 a.m. The metro is busy, too, but it's also fast and it only takes 30 minutes to get to the city centre. I'm so happy when I get out of the station at the other end – it's so good to be out in the open air! I work all day and then it takes me another two and half hours to get home again. I don't have any free time. I want to find a job near my house!

⇄ Mediation task: Student A page 125, Student B page 130

7.4 GETTING AROUND

FL using public transport
▶ crazy rides

The big picture: crazy rides

1 Look at the pictures. What is unusual about the types of transport?

2 ▶ 7.1 Watch the video. In pairs, discuss the questions.
   1 Where can Mark and Theon use their vehicles?
   2 What do they use them for?
   3 How many people can travel in them?
   4 What are people's reactions to them?

3 ▶ 7.1 Watch the video again and complete the sentences with the correct words.
   1 Mark's car was originally a ....
   2 He worked on the vehicle for .... months.
   3 The work cost a little under $............................ .
   4 Theon likes .... things.
   5 He used the .... from a tractor on a houseboat.
   6 He worked on his crazy car in his ....

4 In pairs, discuss the questions.
   1 Do you think they're useful? Why/Why not?
   2 Do you think they're safe? Why/Why not?
   3 Which vehicle would you prefer to travel in? Why?

5 ▶ 7.2 Listen to Dev and Sophia talking about the vehicles. In pairs, answer the questions.
   1 Why does Dev think Mark's vehicle is dangerous?
   2 What are the two problems with Theon's vehicle?
   3 Why does Sophia want a floating car?
   4 How does Sophia usually travel to the city centre?
   5 What type of transport does Dev suggest?

6 ▶ 7.2 Listen again and complete the information about the train.
   1 Time to the city centre   ....
   2 Price of return ticket   ....
   3 Time of next train   ....

Functional language

7 🔊 **7.9** Listen to three conversations about transport. Match them to the pictures.

1 .... 2 .... 3 ....

8 🔊 **7.9** Listen again and answer the questions.

Conversation 1
1 What time is the next train to Oxford? ....
2 Which platform does it leave from? ....

Conversation 2
3 Where is the woman travelling to? ....
4 How long does the journey take? ....

Conversation 3
5 How often do buses leave for the centre? ....
6 Which bus stop do they leave from? ....

9 Look at the Functional language box. Which phrases did you hear in the conversations?

FL	using public transport

I'd like a single/return ticket to ...
I'd like a one-way/roundtrip flight to ...
Can you take me to ...?
How much is a ticket to ...?
How much is that?
What time is the next train/bus?
How long does it take to get to ...?
Where is the stop/platform/gate for ...?
Where does it leave from?

10 🔊 **7.10** 🗨 question intonation 🗨 Listen to the questions from conversation 3. Notice how the intonation goes down at the end. Listen again and repeat.

1 How can I help you?
2 When is the next bus to the centre?
3 Where does it leave from?

11 In pairs, change the details for conversation 3. Have a conversation. Remember to use the correct intonation in the questions.

Passenger	Excuse me.
Assistant	Yes, how can I help you?
Passenger	When is the next bus to ....?
Assistant	The buses leave every .... You can buy a ticket from the machine, over there.
Passenger	Thank you. And where does it leave from?
Assistant	From .... Out through these doors and on the left.
Passenger	Thank you.

Speaking

12 a Look at the information on the tickets. Choose a ticket and decide who is an assistant and who is a passenger. Have a conversation to buy the ticket.

b Swap roles and have another conversation to buy the other ticket.

Royal Air
One-way flight to Amsterdam, Netherlands
Date: 13 April
Flight: RA376-B
Departure: London (Heathrow) 10.45
Arrival: Amsterdam (Schiphol) 12.15
Price: €157.00
Gate: C35

```
Day Return to Manchester
Date:   28 Nov
From:   London Euston Station
        (platform 4) 15.40
To:     Manchester Piccadilly
        (platform 11) 17.20
Price:  £68.50
```

Writing bank: page 150

REVIEW UNIT 7

Vocabulary
Holiday phrases

1 Choose the correct verbs to complete the sentences.
   1 Jack likes to *go / stay* camping, but I prefer to *rent / stay* in a hotel.
   2 Shall we *book / visit* a museum or *be / go* sightseeing?
   3 You can *rent / stay* an apartment by the sea and *make / have* a good time on the beach.
   4 We usually *go / visit* abroad. Karl *books / rents* the flights.
   5 I often *visit / stay* with friends and *do / go* hiking.

Past time expressions

2 a Complete the sentences with the words in the box.

   | ago | in | last | when | yesterday |

   1 She went to the cinema a few days _____.
   2 Max cooked a meal _____ night.
   3 He visited the doctor _____ afternoon.
   4 We had exams _____ June.
   5 I started to play the guitar _____ I was twelve.

   b Write five sentences that are true for you using the past time expressions in the box.

   | an hour ago | in 2017 | last week |
   | yesterday evening | when I was a child |

   I had some lunch an hour ago.

Transport

3 a Rank the forms of transport in order of preference (1–6) for use in your town.

   | bike | bus | car | taxi | tram | underground |

   b In pairs, discuss the questions.
   1 Which form of transport do you usually use? Why?
   2 Which did you use today?
   3 How was your journey? How long did it take?

4 🔊 7.11 Listen to Paul and Jo discussing transport in Lyon. Are the sentences true (T) or false (F)?
   1 Paul says the new bike service is really cheap. ____
   2 Jo thinks bikes and scooters are equally popular. ____
   3 Paul says that people drive cars a lot because of the weather. ____

5 In pairs, talk about transport in your town/city.
   Public transport is cheap but slow because the traffic is bad.

Grammar
Past simple of *be*, there *was/were*

6 Complete the sentences with *was/were* or *wasn't/weren't*.
   1 There _____ a really nice restaurant in the hotel but it _____ very expensive.
   2 You _____ in class yesterday. Where _____ you?
   3 I _____ at work last week because I _____ ill.
   4 A _____ there any boats on the sea?
     B No, there _____.

Past simple regular verbs

7 Write the past simple form of the verbs. Some are common irregular verbs.
   1 decide _____   5 try _____
   2 do _____   6 have _____
   3 go _____   7 wait _____
   4 travel _____   8 stay _____

8 a In pairs, talk about the first time you did something. Use your own ideas or the ideas in the box.

   | go to another country | move house |
   | have a party | stay in a hotel |

   b Write a short paragraph about it. Try to use verbs in the past simple. Compare answers with your partner.

   The first time I went to another country: It was four years ago – I went to Greece with my family. It was our summer holiday. I had a great time!

Functional language
Using public transport

9 Write the words in the correct order.
   1 next / what / bus / is / to / city / centre / the / the / time ?
   2 you / me / take / the / to / can / please / train station ?
   3 long / how / take / get / to / to / does / the / cathedral / it ?
   4 train / this / does / go / the / park / to ?
   5 to / ticket / much / is / how / a / Edinburgh ?

10 Read the questions again. In pairs, continue the conversations.

⏲ Looking back

- Which section of this unit was most useful for you?
- Tell a partner what you did last weekend.
- Tell a partner what you did on holiday last year.

In the news

8

Grammar
past simple irregular verbs
verb + *to* + infinitive
sequencers

Vocabulary
life stages
entertainment

Functional language
responding to news

Skill
listen for facts and figures

Video
Sophie's goals

Writing
a biography

Exams
completing a factual text

The big picture: watching the news

1 Look at the picture. In pairs, guess the answers to the questions.
   1 Where are the people?
   2 What are they doing?
   3 Is it a good place to watch the news? Why/Why not?
   4 What other things can you do there?

2 🔊 **8.1** Listen to the information and check your answers.

3 Look at the different ways to find out about the news. In pairs, discuss the questions.

   magazines   newspapers   online news sites
   radio   social media   TV

   1 How often do you use these to find out about the news?
   2 Do you use different ways for different types of news?
   3 Is it important to know the news every day? Why?

   I listen to the news on the radio every morning. I buy a newspaper once a week to read about the sports news.

75

8.1 I MADE THE NEWS

G past simple irregular verbs
V life stages

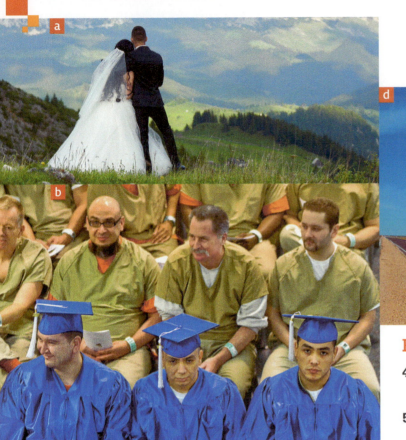

Vocabulary

1 Look at the pictures. Which life stages from the Vocabulary box can you see? What is unusual about the situations?

2 Match the pictures with the titles.
1 Success behind bars ....
2 On top of the world ....
3 Florida, here we come! ....
4 Never too late ....

3 Put the life stages in the typical order that they happen.

V life stages

be born	become famous	die
fall in love	get married	get a job
go to school	graduate	have children
learn to drive	leave home	make friends
move house	retire	

1 .... 8 ....
2 .... 9 ....
3 .... 10 ....
4 .... 11 ....
5 .... 12 ....
6 .... 13 ....
7 .... 14 ....

 8.2 Listen and check.

Reading

4 Look at the picture and the title of the article. What is it about? Read the text quickly and check.

5 Read the text again. Are the sentences true (T) or false (F)?
1 Dagny is only famous in Sweden.
2 She was married to Harry for a long time.
3 She joined a computer class because she wanted to write a blog.
4 She often writes about important life events.
5 She thinks it's important to try new things.
6 Her blog isn't useful for young people.

LIFE BEGINS AT 100

Dagny Carlsson is the world's oldest blogger. She started her blog, *BLOGGA MED MIG!* (Blog with me) when she was 100. She soon became famous not just in her home country of Sweden, but all over the world.

She was born in 1912. As a child, she wanted to be a teacher or a writer, but her family was very poor and she got a job in a factory. She went to college when she was older and later she met her husband, Harry. They were very happy together and loved dancing, but sadly he died when she was in her 90s.

When Dagny was 99, her younger sister gave her an old computer. She didn't know how to use it and so she went to computer classes. Her teacher saw her learn quickly and said she should write a blog. She used the name Bojan because she thought it was a modern name. But why did her blog become so popular?

She writes posts that compare how things are now with how they were years ago.

Grammar

6 Match the halves to make sentences from the text. Check your answers in the text.

1 When Dagny was 99, her younger sister **gave** her ....
2 She used the name Bojan because she **thought** it was ....
3 She **wrote** that there were ....
4 In 2014, she **wore** ....
5 In 2018, she **won** ....
6 She **said** that curiosity helped her to become ....

a a blogger.
b two ingredients for a long life.
c a VR headset for the first time.
d an old computer.
e a modern name.
f an award for all her hard work.

7 a Look at the past simple forms of the irregular verbs in **bold**. Write the infinitive forms.

1 ....   4 ....
2 ....   5 ....
3 ....   6 ....

b Find an example of the past simple negative and question form with irregular verbs in the text. Answer the questions.

1 Is the structure different from regular verbs?
2 Which word do we use with the infinitive in negatives?
   ....
3 Which word do we use with the infinitive in questions?
   ....

c In pairs, find six more irregular past simple verbs in the text. What are the infinitives?

In her posts about the past, she speaks about the moments that were important to her during her life. The day she moved house, left home, or got married.
In one of her most famous posts, she wrote that there were two ingredients for a long life: good genes and curiosity. In fact, she said that curiosity helped her to become a blogger. And that curiosity continues. In 2014, she wore a VR headset for the first time, and she opened an Instagram account. In 2018, she won an award for all her hard work.
Her life is not very unusual, but her optimism and curiosity are wonderful. Dagny helps a lot of people. She is an inspiration for young and old people all over the world.

G past simple irregular verbs

+ She **wrote** a blog.
− She **didn't know** how to use a computer.
? **Did** she **win** an award?
Y/N Yes, she **did**. / No, she **didn't**.

See page 168 for a list of common irregular verbs
→ Go to Grammar reference: page 139

8 a 🔊 8.3 ❝ **past simple irregular verbs** ❞ Listen and repeat the past simple irregular verbs. Notice the vowel sounds.

1 gave   /eɪ/   3 went   /e/
2 thought   /ɔː/   4 wrote   /əʊ/

b 🔊 8.4 Say the past simple irregular verbs in the box. Put them in the correct columns. Listen, check and repeat.

| ate | broke | bought | caught | felt | made |
| paid | read | rode | said | saw | spoke |

gave /eɪ/	thought /ɔː/	went /e/	wrote /əʊ/

9 a Write the correct past simple form of the verbs in brackets.

1 The last time I .... shopping, I .... (go, buy)
2 The last time I .... to my parents, I .... (speak, say)
3 The last time I .... someone a card, I .... (give, write)
4 The last time I .... a film, I .... it was ... (see, think)
5 The last time I .... my friends, we .... (meet, go)
6 The last time I .... something, I .... (break, feel)

b In pairs, complete the sentences so they are true for you. Remember to pronounce the verbs with the correct vowel sounds.

Speaking

10 Think of a celebrity who is not alive. In pairs, ask and answer questions to guess who the celebrity is.

Where was he/she born?

Why did he/she become famous?

Did he/she get married?

Did he/she have any children?

When did he/she die?

8.2 CULTURE NEWS

G verb + *to* + infinitive
V entertainment

Vocabulary

1 Look at the news website. In pairs, answer the questions.
1 What type of news does the website show?
2 Which story is about music?
3 Which is about art?
4 Which is about TV?
5 Which words from the Vocabulary box are related to the stories?
6 What do you think the stories are about?

2 Put the words in the box in the correct columns.

V entertainment

actor	album	artist	band
concert	DJ	exhibition	festival
film	gallery	painter	painting
screen	series	singer	stage

Music	Art	Cinema/TV
		actor

🔊 **8.5** Listen, check and repeat.

3 🔊 **8.6** 〝 schwa sound 〞 Listen and repeat the words. Notice how the parts in **bold** have the same /ə/ sound. Listen again and repeat.

1 act**or**
2 festiv**al**
3 sing**er**
4 conc**e**rt
5 exhibit**io**n
6 alb**u**m

4 🔊 **8.7** Match the halves to make sentences. Say them with the correct pronunciation of the schwa sound. Listen, check and repeat.

1 The actors were in ......
2 The lead singer made ......
3 The painters had ......
4 The festival had ......

a an exhibition in the local gallery.
b some great concerts this year.
c a new album last year.
d a funny series before.

Watching the *Night Watch*

📅 March 23   💬 Comments (23)

Listening

5 🔊 **8.8** Listen to an entertainment report. Match the three stories with the news stories in the website.
1 ......   2 ......   3 ......

6 🔊 **8.8** Are the sentences true (T) or false (F)? Listen again and check.
1 You can only listen to DJs at the Coachella festival. ......
2 It's difficult to book tickets for the festival. ......
3 You can watch the restoration of *The Night Watch* online or at the Rijksmuseum. ......
4 There is a special exhibition about the painting at the gallery. ......
5 Al Pacino and Robert De Niro are working on a new TV series. ......
6 More people watch films at the cinema nowadays. ......

7 In pairs, discuss the questions.
1 Which story from exercise 5 do you think is the most interesting? Why?
2 Do you read entertainment news online?
3 Which entertainment stories are in the news in your country?

🔍 **notice**

the news is uncountable and takes a singular verb:
What's **the news**?   **The news** is that ...

Grammar

8 ◆)) 8.9 Complete the sentences from the report with the correct form of the verbs in the box. Listen and check.

| be | change | go | show | visit | watch |

1 The organizers **decided** .... the format.
2 If you **'d like** ...., book your tickets now.
3 You **need** .... fast!
4 The museum **is planning** .... the restoration work online.
5 If you **want** .... the gallery, there is a special exhibition.
6 People today **prefer** .... the small screen.

9 Look at the verbs in **bold** in exercise 8. Which word comes after them and before the infinitive?

G verb + *to* + infinitive

decide	I **decided to go** to an exhibition.
would like	Would you **like to come** to the festival?
want	I **don't want to watch** that series.
prefer	The band **prefers to play** at small concerts.
hope	They're **hoping to make** a new album.
plan	She **isn't planning to visit** the gallery.
need	I **didn't need to book** tickets for the film.
learn	I **learned to play** the guitar at school.

→ Grammar reference: page 139

10 a Complete the sentences with the correct form of the verbs in the box.

| get | go away | live | study | watch |

1 I'm planning .... this weekend.
2 I decided .... English really seriously.
3 I hope .... abroad in the future.
4 I don't want .... the news every day.
5 I'd like .... a new job soon.

b In pairs, say which sentences are true for you. Change the others so they are true.

I'm planning to stay at home this weekend.

Speaking

11 In groups of four, ask and answer the questions. Who is most similar to you?

What job did you want to do when you were young?

Why did you decide to study English?

What do you want to do this weekend?

What are you planning to do after class?

Where would you like to travel to next summer?

Carlos is similar to me. We both wanted to be astronauts when we were young.

✓ Exam practice: page 163

8.3 EYEWITNESS ACCOUNTS
G sequencers
🔧 listen for facts and figures

Listening

1 a Look at the pictures. In pairs, say what is happening and put them in the correct order.

b Read the newspaper story and check.

'SPIDERMAN' ARRESTED AFTER CLIMBING LONDON TOWER

Alain Robert, also known as 'the Human Spider', climbed Heron Tower today – the tallest building in the City of London. This was a 'free climb' and he didn't use any ropes or safety equipment, just his hands. Hundreds of people stopped work to watch as he climbed the tower. When he reached the top of the tower, police officers entered and arrested him. Robert has climbed more than a hundred skyscrapers around the world, including the Burj Khalifa in Dubai.

2 🔊 **8.10** Listen to a news report about the climb. Answer the questions.
1 How is the report different from the newspaper story?
2 Which do you prefer? Why?
3 How would you describe Alain Robert?
4 What would you do if you saw someone climbing a building?

🔧 listen for facts and figures

Sometimes you need to listen for specific information.
- Identify the type of information you need, e.g. a number, a time, a place.
- Think about the words you might hear, e.g. for a time you might hear *minutes* or *hours*.
- Listen carefully and write down the information you need.

3 🔊 **8.10** Read the Skill box. Listen again and answer the questions.
1 What nationality is Alain?
2 How tall is the Heron Tower?
3 How long did it take him to climb the tower?
4 How many floors are there?
5 When did Alain start climbing buildings?

80

Grammar

4 Put the sentences from the story in the correct order.

a ☐ **40 minutes later**, he reached the top of the tower.
b ☐ **Then**, he started climbing up the building.
c ☐ **After a few minutes**, the police arrived.
d ☐ **In the end**, they freed him and he went home.
e ☐ **After that**, he waved to everyone on the ground.
f ☐ **Finally**, the police went in and arrested him.
g ☐ **First**, I saw a man arrive.

5 Look at the words in **bold**. Answer the questions.
1 How do they make the story easier to follow?
2 Which give information about time?
3 What punctuation mark comes after them?

G	sequencers
first	*First*, I bought some shoes.
then	*Then*, we had a coffee.
after that	*After that*, we watched a film.
finally	*Finally*, we had lunch.
in the end	*In the end*, I decided to go home.
after + time	*After a while*, she left.
time + later	*An hour later*, she came back.

→ Grammar reference: page 139

6 a Read about another climb. How is it different from the one in London?

b In pairs, add the sequencers in the box to make the text easier to follow. There are different possible answers.

after six hours	after that	finally
half an hour later	~~first~~	then	in the end

Writing

7 Complete the text using the correct words.

Yesterday was a long day. (1)_____, I had an interview in the morning. (2)_____, I went to work. In the evening, I met some friends for dinner and (3)_____ that, we decided to go dancing. (4)_____ a few hours I left, but I missed the last train, so in the (5)_____ I went home by taxi. (6)_____ I went to sleep at about 3 a.m. Four hours (7)_____, my alarm clock went off – it was time to get up again!

🔍 notice

We use *in the end*, to talk about the result of a problem or to give unexpected news.
*My computer broke, but **in the end**, I fixed it.*
*I wanted to go to the concert, but **in the end**, I didn't.*

8 Write about what you did yesterday. Use as many sequencers as possible.

Spiderman climbs world's tallest building

Alain Robert was on top of the world yesterday after a record-breaking climb of the 800-metre-tall Burj Khalifa in Dubai. *first* He arrived at the tower at around 5.30 p.m. and he prepared for the climb. As it was an official climb, he had ropes and a harness for safety. He started to climb up the building. Lots of people waited in the streets below to watch him. It started to get dark, so they shone lights onto Alain. He was almost at the top, when he started to get a pain in his legs, but he continued the climb. He reached the top just after midnight. He waved at everybody on the ground below. He came down using the lift and celebrated his achievement.

Mediation task: Student A page 127, Student B page 129

8.4 I DON'T BELIEVE IT!

FL responding to news
🎬 Sophie's goals

The big picture: Sophie's goals

1 Look at the pictures that represent three goals Sophie wants to achieve. In pairs, guess what they are.

2 🎬 8.1 Watch the video and check. Which goals does she achieve after three weeks?

3 🎬 8.1 Watch the video again. Are the sentences true (T) or false (F)?
   1 Sophie made the goals because she is on holiday. ....
   2 She thinks the video can help her achieve the goals. ....
   3 She is German, but she is living in the Netherlands. ....
   4 She didn't study any Japanese in three weeks. ....
   5 She can go horse riding in Germany at the weekend. ....
   6 She started driving lessons in English. ....

4 In pairs, discuss the questions.
   1 Was Sophie happy with what she achieved in October?
   2 Are Sophie's goals easy to achieve?
   3 Is making a list of goals each month a good idea?
   4 What are your goals for next month?
   5 Do you think you can achieve them?

5 🎬 8.2 Watch Dev and Sophia talking about the video. Choose the correct words to complete the sentences.
   1 Dev thinks he's *similar to / different from* Sophie.
   2 Sophia says that Japanese is a *difficult / strange* subject to study.
   3 Dev *makes / doesn't make* a list of goals each month.
   4 Dev is *good / bad* at dancing.
   5 Dev is *happy / unhappy* with the dance lessons.

6 🎬 8.2 Watch the video again. Match Dev's news to Sophia's reactions.
   1 Dev writes a list of goals. ....   a Sophia is surprised.
   2 Dev's brother's wedding.   ....   b Sophia is very surprised.
   3 Dev can't dance.   ....   c Sophia is worried.
   4 Dev started salsa classes. ....   d Sophia is pleased.

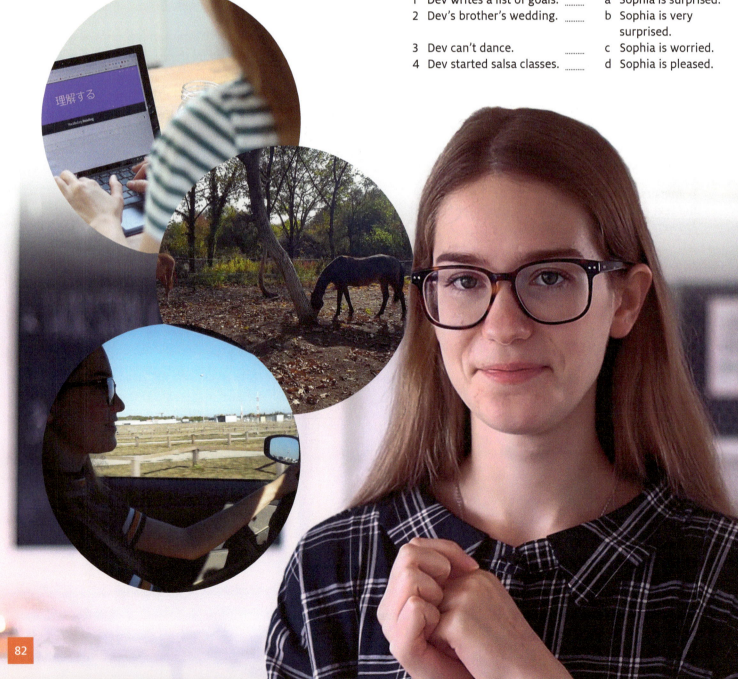

82

Functional language

7 🔊 **8.11** Look at the pictures. Listen and match them to the conversations.

1 ___ 2 ___ 3 ___ 4 ___ 5 ___

8 🔊 **8.11** Listen again. Complete the sentences with the correct time expressions.

1 José and Beth moved to a new house _____.
2 Erika and Kristoff had a baby girl _____.
3 Adam lost his job _____.
4 I passed my driving test _____.
5 I can't come to your party _____.

9 Match the reactions with conversations 1–5.

a Did they? Wow, that's great! ___
b That's great news! Congratulations! ___
c A hundred people? That's awful! ___
d Can't you? What a shame! ___
e Is she? Fantastic! ___

FL	**responding to news**
Good news	Wow! / That's great (news)! / Fantastic! / Congratulations!
Bad news	Oh no! / What a shame! / That's awful! / I'm so sorry.
Surprise	Really? / You're joking! / I don't believe it!

🔍 notice

We often use echo questions (auxiliary + subject pronoun + ?) to show surprise:

I went to the exhibition.	**Did you?**
Sandra's learning to drive.	**Is she?**
I can't swim.	**Can't you?**

10 🔊 **8.12** 💬 **echo questions** 💬 Write echo questions for the news. Listen and check. Notice the intonation goes up. Listen again and repeat the responses.

1 I failed my exam – again.
   _____? Oh no! What a shame!
2 David was at the theatre last night.
   _____? I don't believe it!
3 Carla's working at the local radio station now.
   _____? That's great news!

11 In pairs, say the news and respond using echo questions and phrases from the Functional language box.

1 My football team won the Champions League!
2 I didn't get tickets for the concert.
3 I was really ill all weekend.
4 I finished the marathon in my best time!
5 We're going to the beach for a party.
6 I lost my wallet on the bus.

Speaking

12 Think of some good or bad news about the topics. In pairs, give your news and respond appropriately.

1 travel   4 health
2 work   5 education
3 money   6 entertainment

✏️ Writing bank: page 151   **83**

REVIEW UNIT 8

Vocabulary
Life stages

1 **a** In pairs, look at the life stages below. Choose four that happened to you.

be born	fall in love	get married	get a job
go to school	graduate	have children	
learn to drive	leave home	make friends	
move house	retire		

b When did these things happen? Ask and answer questions with your partner.

A When did you move house?
B I moved house three years ago.

Entertainment

2 Look at the nouns in the box. Are they people, things or events? Put them in the correct category.

actor	album	artist	concert	DJ
exhibition	festival	painter	painting	
screen	singer	stage		

1 People: ....
2 Things: ....
3 Events: ....

3 Choose the correct option to complete the sentences.
1 My brother is in a *band / series*. He plays the drums and his best friend sings.
2 She's a well-known *DJ / actor* in films and on stage.
3 Some great bands are playing at the *gallery / festival*.
4 I love this song. It's the best one on the *album / screen*.
5 Some of the artist's most famous *painters / paintings* are now at the *gallery / concert*.

4 In pairs, discuss the questions.
1 Who is your favourite singer or band?
2 What's the name of their album?
3 Do you ever go to festivals or concerts? Where?

Grammar
Past simple irregular verbs

5 **a** Complete the sentences with the past simple form of the verb in brackets.
1 I .... about 20 text messages yesterday. (write)
2 I .... the news headlines this morning. (read)
3 I .... my friend an email today. (send)
4 I .... my friends for a coffee. (meet)
5 I .... a mistake in my homework. (make)

b Are the sentences true for you? If not, write sentences with the same verbs that are true for you. Compare your answers with a partner.

Verb + *to* + infinitive

6 Complete the sentences so they are true for you.
1 I decided to go ....
2 I wanted to see ....
3 I'm learning to play ....
4 I'm planning to visit ....
5 I prefer to watch ....

7 In pairs, ask and answer the questions.
1 What do you need to do this evening?
2 What would you like to eat right now?
3 When do you want to go to bed?
4 Where are you planning to go tomorrow?

Sequencers

8 **a** Look at the actions and tick (✓) the ones you did this morning.

read the news ☐	have a coffee ☐	get a bus ☐
listen to the radio ☐	have a shower ☐	call a friend ☐
go shopping ☐	go to work ☐	go to class ☐

b Tell a partner about your morning with the sequencers in the box.

after that	after + *time*	finally	first	then

First, I had a shower. After that, …

Functional language
Responding to news

9 🔊 **8.13** Listen to some people announcing some news. Choose the best response in the box to each piece of news.

Did they?	When?	Did she?	I didn't know that!
Wow, that's great news!		Oh no!	What a shame!

10 In pairs, read the information below and take it in turns to respond to your partner's news.

Student A
I passed the exam. I got an A.
Dad bought a new car last week.
I left my bag on the train!

Student B
I failed my driving test – again! That's the fifth time!
I'm planning to get a dog.
Sorry, I can't play tennis with you tomorrow.

⏱ Looking back

- What's the most interesting news story in this unit?
- What good news and bad news did you have recently?
- How many irregular past simple verbs can you now use?

84

Food matters

9

Grammar G
countable and uncountable nouns
quantifiers
should

Vocabulary V
food
describing food

Functional language FL
eating out

Video
soul food

Skill
guess the meaning of words

Writing
a review

Exams
understanding details in short dialogues

The big picture: street food

1 Look at the picture. In pairs, guess the answers to the questions.
   1 Where do you think the people are?
   2 What type of food are they cooking?
   3 What are the good things about this type of food?
   4 Would you like to eat here? Why/Why not?

2 🔊 9.1 Listen and check your answers.

3 In pairs, discuss the questions.
   1 Is street food popular where you live?
   2 What kind of food can you eat?
   3 Do you like street food? Why/Why not?
   4 What's your favourite street food?

You can always buy street food in the park near my house. We often go there on Sunday for a walk and we get a snack. I usually have a kebab or some Greek salad.

85

9.1 BREAKFAST TIME

G countable and uncountable nouns
V food

Vocabulary

1 Put the food in the correct columns.

V food

> ~~apples~~   bananas   ~~beans~~   ~~carrots~~   chicken
> eggs   fish   grapes   meat   melons
> mushrooms   olives   peas   potatoes
> tomatoes

Fruit	Vegetables	Protein
apples	carrots	beans

> ~~biscuits~~   ~~bread~~   ~~butter~~   cereal   cheese
> chocolate   crisps   milk   nuts   pasta
> rice   toast   yoghurt

Dairy	Carbohydrates	Snacks
butter	bread	biscuits

 9.2 Listen, check and repeat.

2 9.3 ❝consonant clusters❞ Listen to the words. Notice the groups of letters in **bold** and how they are pronounced. Listen again and repeat.
  1 bi**scu**i**ts**
  2 cho**co**late
  3 cri**sps**
  4 ve**get**ables
  5 mu**shr**ooms

Listening

3 Look at the pictures. Answer the questions.
  1 What food can you see in each picture?
  2 Which breakfast would you most enjoy? Why?

4 9.4 Listen to a radio programme. Match the pictures with the types of breakfast.
  1 Turkish breakfast   ....
  2 Mexican breakfast   ....
  3 Full English breakfast   ....
  4 American breakfast   ....

5 In pairs, discuss the questions.
  1 Which breakfast in pictures a–d is best for your health?
  2 Which is most similar to a traditional breakfast in your country?
  3 What do you usually have for breakfast during the week?
  4 What do you usually have for breakfast at the weekend?
  5 Do you think breakfast is an important meal? Why/Why not?
  6 Do you ever have cereal or other breakfast food in the evening? Why?

Grammar

6 a Read the sentences from the programme. Which of the words in **bold** is uncountable?

> I had some **coffee** and a **biscuit**.

> Then I had an **apple** and some **nuts**.

b Look at the words in **bold** again. Answer the questions.
1. Which words do we use before singular countable nouns? .... and ....
2. Which word do we use before plural countable nouns instead of a number? ....
3. Which word do we use before uncountable nouns? ....

7 Read the conversation from the programme and answer the questions.

> Do you eat any meat?

> No, I don't. And I don't eat any fish, but cheese is OK.

1. Which word do we use before uncountable nouns in negatives and questions? ....
2. What form of *be* do we use with uncountable nouns? *is / are*

G countable and uncountable nouns

	Uncountable	Countable (singular)	Countable (plural)
+	I'd like **some bread**.	I'd like **an apple**.	I'd like **some tomatoes**.
–	I don't want **any coffee**.	I don't want **a biscuit**.	I don't want **any peas**.
?	Do you have **any meat**?	Do you have **a melon**?	Do you have **any eggs**?

→ Grammar reference: page 140

🔍 notice

Some nouns can be countable and uncountable.

I'd like **some ice cream**.   I'd like **an ice cream**.

8 a Look at the words in the box. Are they countable or uncountable in your language? And in English?

| cheese | coffee | fruit | meat |
| rice | soup | tea | toast | pasta |

b 🔊 9.5 Match the words with the expressions to make them countable. Listen and check.
1. a bowl of .... / .... / ....
2. a piece of .... / .... / .... / ....
3. a cup of .... / ....

Speaking

9 a In pairs, ask and answer the questions. Make a note of your partner's answers.
1. What did you have for breakfast today?
2. What do you usually have for lunch?
3. What's your favourite dinner?
4. How often do you cook lunch or dinner?
5. Do you eat with friends, family or alone?

b Swap partners and make sentences about your last partner.

Maria had a cup of coffee and a piece of toast for breakfast.

9.2 A HEALTHY DIET?

G quantifiers
V describing food

Vocabulary

1 Put the adjectives in the box in the correct columns.

V describing food

~~baked~~   boiled   delicious   disgusting
fresh   fried   frozen   grilled
homemade   raw   roast   spicy
sweet   takeaway   vegetarian

Opinion/Flavour	Type of food	Type of cooking
		baked

🔊 9.6 Listen, check and repeat.

2 In pairs, ask the question *How would you describe …?* for the words in the box.

chocolate cake   chicken   curry   eggs
fruit juice   hamburger   pizza   sushi

Well, most people say pizza is takeaway food, but it can be homemade or you can buy it frozen. I think it's delicious!

Reading

3 Look at the pictures. In pairs, discuss the questions.
   1 What food can you see?
   2 How would you describe the food?
   3 Which is the healthiest? Why?

4 Read the text quickly and match the diets to the photos.

5 Read the text again and answer the questions.
   1 Which diet does the writer choose? Why?
   2 What are the problems with the other diets?
   3 Which diet would you choose?
   4 Do you know any other diets?
   5 What can/can't you eat on those diets?

a

b

c

DO YOU NEED A NEW DIET?

How many magazines do you read with celebrities talking about what you need to eat to be healthy, happy and beautiful? There are too many diets around at the moment! How do they work, and what can you eat? I looked at three to see which was best for me.

THE UNCOOKED DIET
You can only eat raw food. This means you eat a lot of fresh fruit, some vegetables and nuts. You can also have a little milk or a raw egg. And some people also eat raw fish or meat! I don't know if it's healthy, but it sounds disgusting!

THE PALEO DIET
The paleo diet consists of food that people ate over 10,000 years ago. That means no bread, no pasta and no rice. It contains a lot of grilled or roast meat and fish and some fruit and nuts. You can have a few eggs, too, but you can't eat any cheese, yoghurt or other dairy foods. Most importantly, you can't eat any sugar, so no sweet snacks or chocolate. This diet is not for me!

THE FLEXITARIAN DIET
Basically, this is a vegetarian diet with a little meat or fish. Flexitarians believe that we eat too much meat, and this is bad for our health and the environment. How much meat can you eat? That depends on you, but flexitarians generally try to eat a lot of beans, peas and nuts instead. It's an easy diet to follow and it's very healthy. I want to be a flexitarian!

Grammar

6 Match the halves to make sentences from the text. Check your answers in the text.

1 **How many** ....
2 There are **too many** ....
3 This means you eat **a lot of** ....
4 You can also have **a little** ....
5 It contains **a lot of** ....
6 You can have **a few** ....
7 We eat **too much** ....
8 **How much** ....

a diets around at the moment!
b milk or a raw egg.
c fresh fruit.
d magazines do you read?
e grilled or roast meat and fish.
f eggs, too.
g meat, and this is bad for our health.
h meat can you eat?

7 Look at the words in **bold** in the sentences in exercise 6 again. Answer the questions.

1 Which words do we use to talk about a big quantity?
....
2 Which words do we use to talk about a small quantity?
.... and ....
3 Which words do we use to talk about more than you need? .... and ....
4 Which words do we use to ask about a quantity?
.... and ....

G quantifiers

Uncountable	Countable
How much coffee do you drink?	**How many** eggs do you eat?
I drink **a lot of** tea.	I eat **a lot of** vegetables.
She only wants **a little** milk.	We have **a few** apples.
We eat **too much** meat.	Don't eat **too many** biscuits!

→ Grammar reference: page 140

8 a 🔊 9.7 **/uː/ and /ʌ/ sounds** Listen to the words. Notice the pronunciation of the vowels in **bold**. Listen again and repeat.

1 /uː/ t**oo**   2 /ʌ/ m**u**ch

b 🔊 9.8 Say the words in the box and put them in the correct columns. Listen, check and repeat.

| butter | cup | few | food | fruit | some |

/uː/ too	/ʌ/ much

9 🔊 9.9 Choose the correct words to complete the conversation with an Olympic swimmer. Listen and check.

A So, William, I heard that you eat (1)*how much / a lot of* food every day. Two breakfasts! Is that true?
B It's true, I have two breakfasts. First, I eat (2)*a little / a lot of* fruit before I train in the morning – just a banana or a pear. But when I finish, I have a big breakfast: some cereal, (3)*a few / a little* pieces of toast, some cheese and tomatoes, (4)*too many / a few* eggs …
A (5)*How much / How many* eggs?
B Four or five.
A That's (6)*a lot of / too much* eggs!
B Maybe, but I need (7)*a lot of / too much* energy because I swim ten kilometres every day!
A OK, what next?
B I go to the gym, but I don't like it. There are (8)*too much / too many* people. Then I have lunch. I usually have a big bowl of pasta, some meat or chicken and (9)*a few / a little* vegetables. Two hours later, I'm back in the swimming pool.
A And what do you have for dinner?
B Pasta again!
A Really? That's (10)*too much / a little* pasta for me!

Speaking

10 a In pairs, complete the questions with *much* or *many*. Ask three or four people in the class the questions. Make a note of their answers.

1 How .... cups of coffee do you drink?
2 How .... meat do you eat?
3 How .... junk food do you eat?
4 How .... pieces of fruit do you eat?
5 How .... water do you drink?
6 How .... chocolate do you eat?
7 How .... snacks do you eat?
8 How .... fish do you eat?

b In pairs, discuss your answers.

Most people drink a little coffee every day – one or two cups, but Carlos drinks too much coffee. He has five cups a day!

Most people eat a lot of meat but I only eat a little meat at the weekend, and Ana is vegetarian.

Exam practice: page 164

9.3 LOVE FOOD, HATE WASTE

G *should*
🔧 guess the meaning of words

Reading

1 Look at the title and the pictures. In pairs, answer the questions.
  1 How much food do we waste every year?
  2 Which type of food do we waste most?
  3 In what ways do people waste food?
  4 What can we do to help the situation?

2 Read the text and check your ideas from exercise 1.

3 In pairs, discuss the questions.
  1 Did the text surprise you? Why?
  2 How much food do you waste?
  3 Which piece of advice is most useful?
  4 Do you do any of these things already?

🔧 **guess the meaning of words**

You can often guess the meaning of new words from the context.
- Look at the sentence the word is in. Is it a verb, noun or adjective?
- Read the sentences before and after the new word to understand the context.
- Think of a word that makes sense in the context.

4 a Read the Skill box. Find the words in the text. Are they nouns, adjectives or verbs?
  1 rotten   ....
  2 defrost   ....
  3 leftovers   ....
  4 packed lunch   ....
  5 peel   ....
  6 picky   ....

b Read the sentences before and after. In pairs, guess the meaning of the words.

5 Match the words from exercise 4 to the definitions to check.
  1 to take off the skin of a fruit or vegetable
  2 to let frozen food reach room temperature
  3 food which remains after the rest is used
  4 cold food you can carry in a bag or box
  5 describing something you can't eat because it is old and bad
  6 describing someone who finds a lot of problems with things

Food WASTE makes us cry

We throw away one third of the food we buy. That's **1.3 billion** tonnes of food every year around the world. The worst problem is with fruit and vegetables, where **45%** ends up in the bin – that's almost half of all the fruit and veg we buy! But why do we waste all this food? There are three main reasons:

Firstly, we buy too much food. Many people shop once a week in supermarkets to save time and money, but the food often becomes ⁽¹⁾**rotten** before we can use it and we throw it away. It isn't easy to go shopping every day, so what should we do? Well, we should plan our meals more and only buy the food we need. Another good idea is to cook large quantities of food when the food is fresh. You can eat what you want and freeze the rest. A few days later, you can take out the frozen food and ⁽²⁾**defrost** it. You have another meal ready. It's a great way to save food, time and energy!

Secondly, we put too much food on our plates. We often can't eat it all, so we throw it away. We should try to cook the exact amount we need. When there are ⁽³⁾**leftovers**, we shouldn't throw them away. You can keep them for another meal. Put them in the fridge and use them for a ⁽⁴⁾**packed lunch** to take to work or school the next day – or have them for breakfast. And be careful when you prepare vegetables. For example, you don't need to ⁽⁵⁾**peel** your potatoes. You can clean them and cook them with their skins.

9.3

Finally, farmers throw away a lot of food because big supermarkets don't want 'ugly' fruit and vegetables. We shouldn't be so (6)**picky** about the food we buy. Fruit and vegetables don't need to look perfect. They taste great whatever shape they are. We should all tell the supermarkets that we're happy to buy 'ugly' food. They need to know that we love food and hate waste!

Grammar

6 a Look at the sentences from the text. Match them to the definitions.
   1 What should we do?
   2 We should try to cook the exact amount we need.
   3 We shouldn't throw them away.
   a It's a good idea to do this.
   b It's a bad idea to do this.
   c What advice is there?

b What other examples with *should* or *shouldn't* can you find in the text?

G should

+	We should learn more about our food.
–	We shouldn't throw food away.
?	Should we be careful with food?
Y/N	Yes, we should. / No, we shouldn't.

→ Grammar reference: page 140

7 9.11 **should and shouldn't** Listen and repeat the sentences from exercise 6a. Notice how we pronounce *should* and *shouldn't*.

8 Complete the conversation with *should* or *shouldn't*. In pairs, practise the conversation.
   A I invited my boss to dinner, but she told me she's a vegetarian. What (1) .... I do?
   B You (2) .... go to a vegetarian restaurant.
   A I can't. It's too late to book a table.
   B Well, you (3) .... cook a complicated dish. Do something simple.
   A (4) .... I cook pasta? That's easy.
   B Yes, you (5) .... Everyone likes pasta!

Writing

9 Read the list of tips. Complete the title.

> **Five top tips to** ....
> • You shouldn't drink any coffee in the afternoon.
> • You should listen to some relaxing music.
> • You should have a warm bath or shower.
> • You shouldn't eat a big meal late in the evening.
> • You shouldn't watch TV before you go to bed.

10 In pairs, choose another topic and write at least five tips.

   Top tips to save money.   Top tips to be happy.
   Top tips to get fit.   Top tips to speak English.

⇆ Mediation task: All students, page 131

9.4 WHAT'S ON THE MENU?

FL eating out
🎥 soul food

The big picture: soul food

1 a Look at the pictures. In pairs, answer the questions.
   1 How would you describe the dishes?
   2 What ingredients can you see?
   3 Which countries do they come from?
   4 Where can you buy them?

   b 🎥 9.1 Watch the video and check your answers.

2 🎥 9.1 Choose the correct words to complete the sentences. Watch again and check.
   1 Peckham is a *traditional London / multicultural* neighbourhood.
   2 Jennifer is more interested in making *money / good food*.
   3 Her restaurant is popular with *West Indians / different nationalities*.
   4 *Sally / Sally's husband* is from Iran.
   5 Sally thinks food is important to *bring people together / be healthy*.
   6 She cooks a *traditional Iranian / multicultural* meal.

3 In pairs, discuss the questions.
   1 Are there any neighbourhoods like this in your city?
   2 What types of food can you buy in your neighbourhood?
   3 Do you like to try food from different countries?
   4 Is eating a meal with people important to you?

4 🎥 9.2 Watch Dev and Sophia talking about the video and answer the questions.
   1 How often does Sophia think you should eat with friends or family?
   2 Why can't Dev eat with his flatmates?
   3 When did Sophia live in the old part of town?
   4 What type of food does Sophia want to eat?

5 🎥 9.2 Put the parts of the meal in order. Watch again and check.
   a ☐ coffee   c ☐ dessert
   b ☐ main course   d ☐ starter

92

Functional language

6 In pairs, read the menu and answer the questions.
1 What kind of restaurant is it?
2 Are there any restaurants like this in your town?
3 Do you like this type of food?

7 🔊 9.12 Listen to the conversation. Complete the table with the correct food and drinks.

	Man	Woman
Drink		
Starter		
Main course		
Dessert		

8 🔊 9.12 Listen again and tick (✓) the phrases you hear in the Functional language box.

FL eating out

Customer
Do you have a table for ... please?
We have a reservation for ...

Can I have ...?
I'll have ...
I'd like ...
... for me, please.
Nothing for me, thanks.

Can you bring us the bill, please?

Waiter
Do you have a reservation?
Come with me, please.

Here's the menu.
Can I get you anything to drink?
Still or sparkling?
Are you ready to order?
Anything else?

Here's the bill.

9 🔊 9.13 ❝ sentence stress ❞ Listen to the questions. Notice how the important words are stressed. Listen again and repeat.
1 Do you <u>have</u> a <u>table</u> for <u>two</u>, <u>please</u>?
2 Can I <u>get</u> you <u>anything</u> to <u>drink</u>?
3 I'd <u>like</u> the <u>mozzarella</u> and <u>tomato</u> <u>salad</u>.
4 Can you <u>bring</u> us the <u>bill</u>, <u>please</u>?

Speaking

10 a In groups of three, decide who is the waiter and who are the customers. Act out ordering a meal at a restaurant.

b Swap roles and act out another conversation.

THE GOURMET BURGER BAR

STARTERS

Mozzarella and tomato salad
The finest mozzarella and beef tomatoes with fresh basil, pesto and extra virgin olive oil.

Chicken wings
Barbecued chicken wings served with homemade mayonnaise and green jalapeño peppers.

MAIN COURSES

Habanero cheeseburger
100% organic beef, mozzarella cheese, hot and spicy sauce, salad and mayonnaise.

Veggie burger
Vegetarian burger, aubergine, goat's cheese and mixed-leaf salad.

Italian chicken burger
Organic chicken burger, avocado, pesto sauce and salad.

DESSERTS

Chocolate brownie and ice cream
Freshly baked brownie served with vanilla ice cream.

Fruit of the day
Fresh strawberries topped with a blend of honey and fresh yoghurt.

 Writing bank: page 152

REVIEW UNIT 9

Vocabulary
Food

1 In pairs, discuss the questions.
1 Which are your favourite foods?
2 Are there any foods you don't like or can't eat?
3 Which foods do you eat every day?

Describing food

2 In pairs, talk about how you would describe these foods.
1 fruit salad and ice cream
2 a cup of tea with four spoons of sugar
3 chicken curry and rice
4 a hamburger with cheese and fries

Grammar
Countable and uncountable nouns

3 Choose the correct words to complete the sentences.
Breakfast
I had (1)*a coffees / some coffee* and (2)*a piece / some piece* of toast with (3)*a butter / butter* and (4)*honey / honeys*.
Lunch
I had some (5)*salad / salads*, (6)*a / a bowl of* pasta and some (7)*bread / breads*.
Dinner
I had (8)*rice / rices* with (9)*a / some* meat and (10)*a glass of water / some waters*.

4 What did you have to eat yesterday?

5 In pairs, ask and answer questions using *Do you have a/an/any ...?* and the words in the box (✓ = answer yes, ✗ = answer no).

| banana ✓ | bread ✗ | carrots ✓ | cheese ✓ |
| crisps ✗ | egg ✓ | grapes ✓ | rice ✗ |

A *Do you have any grapes?*   B *Yes, I have some grapes.*

Quantifiers

6 Complete the questions with *much* or *many*.
1 How .... fruit do you eat?
2 How .... meat do you eat in a week?
3 How .... cups of coffee do you have each day?
4 How .... water did you drink yesterday?
5 How .... different vegetables did you eat yesterday?

7 In pairs, ask and answer the questions in exercise 6. Who has the healthiest diet, you or your partner?
I eat a lot of fruit.   *I eat too much meat.*

should

8 Complete the sentences with *should/shouldn't* and the verbs in the box.

| buy | drink | eat | plan | tell |

1 If you want to stay healthy, you .... more fruit and vegetables.
2 We're wasting too much food. We .... our meals each week.
3 He .... more food than he needs. He's always throwing it away.
4 You .... too much coffee. Have a glass of water instead.
5 We .... Anna that we're vegetarian so that she doesn't cook any meat.

Functional language
Eating out

9 Read these dishes from a menu. Are they starters (S), main courses (M) or desserts (D)?
1 bread and olives ....
2 chicken burger with fries and side salad ....
3 southern-fried chicken wings ....
4 chocolate fudge cake and ice cream ....
5 fresh fruit salad ....
6 three fish curry with rice and green beans ....

10 a 🔊 9.14 Order the phrases to form short dialogues. Listen and check.
1 a ☐ Certainly. Come with me.
  b ☐ Yes, do you have a table for two, please?
  c ☐ Are you waiting for a table?
2 a ☐ Yes, the chicken for me, please.
  b ☐ Sparkling water, please.
  c ☐ And can I get you anything to drink?
  d ☐ Are you ready to order?
3 a ☐ Yes, thanks. Can you bring us the bill, please?
  b ☐ Is everything OK?
  c ☐ Certainly. Just a moment.
  d ☐ I'm sorry, we only accept cash.
  e ☐ Can I pay by card?

b In groups of three, practise a conversation at a restaurant. Use language from the dialogues in 10a.

🕒 Looking back

- Think of five questions you can ask about food and eating.
- What other foods would you like to know the name of in English?
- Can you describe your favourite meal?

Technology

10

Grammar G
comparatives
going to

Vocabulary V
electronic devices
communication verbs
parts of the body

Functional language FL
invitations

Skill
identify reasons

Video
bionic boots

Writing
an online post

Exams
understanding short texts

The big picture: vinyl collector

1 Look at the picture. In pairs, guess the answers to the questions.
   1 Where is the person?
   2 What is he looking at?
   3 How does he feel?
   4 Why does he want to buy it?

2 🔊 **10.1** Listen and check your answers.

3 In pairs, discuss the questions.
   1 Do you know anyone who has vinyl records?
   2 How often do they listen to them?
   3 How do you listen to music?
   4 Why do some people like using old technology?

4 Do you have any of the devices in the box? How often do you use them?

analogue camera	CD player	MP3 player
DVD player	FM radio	VHS player

95

10.1 TECHNOLOGY TIMELINE
G comparatives
V electronic devices

Vocabulary

1 Look at the photos. In pairs, answer the questions.
   1 Where are the people?
   2 What are the people doing?
   3 Who is having more fun? Why?

2 Which devices from the Vocabulary box can you see?

3 Put the devices in the box in the correct columns.

V electronic devices

> ~~blender~~   dishwasher   drone   freezer
> game console   headphones   keyboard
> mouse   PC   printer   tablet
> speakers   vacuum cleaner   virtual assistant
> VR headset   washing machine

Housework/ Cooking	Entertainment	Work/Study
blender		

🔊 **10.2** Listen, check and repeat.

4 In pairs, discuss the questions.
   1 Which devices do you have at home?
   2 Which do you use every day?
   3 Which are most important for you? Why?

Listening

5 a Look at the pictures of some devices from the past. What are they?

   b Where do they go on the technology timeline?

Technology timeline

1876	first telephone
1889	first ....
1901	first ....
1932	first colour television
1937	first washing machine
1940	first freezer
1964	first ....
1972	first computer keyboard
1977	first ....
1976	first PC
1983	first 3D printer
2014	first virtual assistant

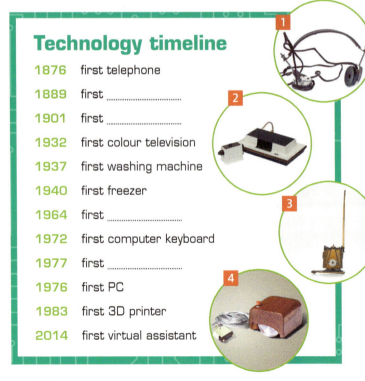

6 🔊 **10.3** Listen to a radio programme. Check your answers to exercise 5 and write the devices in the correct place.

96

Grammar

7 Look at the sentences from the programme. They all compare two things. What are they comparing? Which preposition connects the two things?

1 The sound quality is **worse** than headphones today.
2 Modern headphones are **more comfortable** than these.
3 The games are **easier** than the games on the PlayStation.
4 It's **smaller** than the original vacuum cleaner.
5 Vacuum cleaners from the 1940s are **bigger** than the cleaners we use today.
6 It's **better** than the original mouse.

8 a Look at the comparatives in **bold** in exercise 7. Match them to the adjectives.

1 small ....
2 big ....
3 bad ....
4 easy ....
5 good ....
6 comfortable ....

b Match the comparatives with the spelling rules.

1 adjectives with one syllable: add *er* ....
2 adjective with one syllable ending in vowel + consonant: double consonant and add *er* ....
3 adjective ending in *y*: omit *y* and add *ier* ....
4 adjectives with two syllables or more: use *more* + adjective ....
5 Some adjectives are irregular: .... and ....

G comparatives

+ er	This computer is **faster** than my laptop.
double consonant + er	Modern TVs are **bigger** than old TVs.
omit y + ier	A washing machine is **heavier** than a dishwasher.
more + adjective	The headphones are **more expensive** than the speakers.
irregular	Your phone is **better** than Alex's phone. I think CDs are **worse** than records.

→ Grammar reference: page 141

9 🔊 10.4 ❝ **pronouncing -er** ❞ Listen to the sentences. Notice how we don't stress the *er* ending, but we stress *more*. Listen again and repeat.

1 The new TV is bigger and better.
2 Yes, but it's more expensive!

10 a Look at the pictures. Write five sentences comparing them, using the adjectives in the box.

big	bad	cheap	difficult to use
easy to use		expensive	heavy
good	light	small	

b In pairs, compare your sentences.

1940s washing machine

modern washing machine

Speaking

11 In pairs, ask and answer the questions. Explain your answers using comparative forms.

1 What do you prefer to eat for lunch, a salad or takeaway food? Why?
2 Where do you prefer to watch a film, at home or at the cinema? Why?
3 Which season do you prefer: summer or winter? Why?

I prefer to eat a salad for lunch. It's healthier than takeaway food and I think it's more delicious!

12 Write three more questions like the ones in exercise 11. In pairs, ask and answer the questions.

10.2 CONNECTING PEOPLE

G going to
V communication verbs

Vocabulary

1 Look at the picture. Guess what the boy is doing on his phone.

2 Match the verbs in the box with the icons.

V communication verbs

| call | chat with | download | receive | share |
| search for | send | transfer | upload | |

1 .... 2 .... 3 ....
4 .... 5 .... 6 ....
7 .... 8 .... 9 ....

🔊 **10.5** Listen, check and repeat.

3 In pairs, make sentences with the communication verbs and the nouns in the box.

| emails | family | files | friends | information |
| messages | money | music | photos | |

I chat with my friends every day.

Reading

4 Read an article about mobile phones. Tick (✓) the topics it mentions.

1 health ☐   4 holidays ☐
2 shopping ☐ 5 education ☐
3 banking ☐   6 agriculture ☐

5 Read the text again. Match the countries with the services.

1 Malawi ....   5 Tanzania ....
2 Mexico ....   6 Rural areas
3 Nepal ....   everywhere ....
4 Dominican Republic ....

a receive information about weather and prices
b pay bills and transfer money
c get quick medical attention
d give health care to new mothers
e contact patients
f connect hospitals and health centres

Small things can make a
big difference

We send messages every day. We can chat with friends, arrange a meeting, or tell someone we're going to be late. But did you know that text messages make a big difference to the lives of millions of people around the world?

In Malawi, hospitals send messages to medical centres in villages hundreds of miles away. It's cheaper, quicker and easier than sending doctors out to visit. In Mexico, doctors send messages to their patients to remind them to take their medicine. In Nepal, health workers use mobile phones to organize visits to mothers in rural areas before and after their babies are born and share information with health centres in the towns.

In the Dominican Republic, emergency services use text messages to help people who need medical attention. When an accident happens, the emergency services send a message to all their medical staff. Any paramedics who are near the accident know where to go and they can arrive quickly, much more quickly than an ambulance. This service helps save lives every day!

Medicine is not the only area using text messages to help people. In Tanzania, farmers receive information about the weather and the prices in the market. This helps them plan what they're going to grow and also to know when to get the best prices. All over the world, people contact their banks, pay bills and transfer money on their phones using PIN numbers which arrive by text message. This is very important for people who don't have a bank account and live a long way from the nearest town.

6 🔊 **10.6** Listen to three people talking about how they use mobile phones. Which services from exercise 5 are they talking about?

1 .... 2 .... 3 ....

Grammar

7 🔊 **10.6** Complete the sentences with the words in the box. Listen again and check.

market	money	medicine	patients
prices	school		

1 I'**m going to send** .... to my mother.
2 My little brother **is going to start** at a new .... next week.
3 We'**re going to send** messages to all our .... who are over 70.
4 They **aren't going to forget** to take their ....
5 I'**m not going to take** my mangoes to the .... tomorrow.
6 I'**m going to wait** to see what the .... are like next week.

8 a Look at the sentences in exercise 7 again. Are they about the past, the present or the future?

b Look at the words in **bold.** Which verb do we use before *going to*?

G *going to*

+	I'**m going to send** the files tonight.
–	They **aren't going to share** the photos.
?	**Are** you **going to call** your family?
Y/N	Yes, I **am**. / No, I'**m not**.

→ Grammar reference: page 141

9 🔊 **10.7** Complete the conversation with *going to* and the verbs in brackets. Listen and check.

A So, there are no classes tomorrow. What ⁽¹⁾ .... you .... (do)? ⁽²⁾ .... you .... (study) for the exam?
B No, I'm not! I ⁽³⁾ .... (not work) at all! I ⁽⁴⁾ .... (meet) with Sue for coffee. She has a new job! She ⁽⁵⁾ .... (tell) me all about it.
A When ⁽⁶⁾ .... she .... (start)?
B Next week.

10 🔊 **10.8** 🗨 *going to* /gənə/ 🗨 Listen to the sentences. Notice how *going to* is pronounced. Listen again and repeat.

1 What are you **going to** do?
2 I'm not **going to** work at all!
3 She's **going to** tell me all about it.

11 a Write questions using the prompts and *going to*.

1 you / go out / tonight?
2 you / have a coffee / after class?
3 what / you / do / next weekend?
4 what / you / do / next summer?

b In pairs, ask and answer the questions. Try to pronounce *going to* like /gənə/.

Speaking

12 a Imagine you are in these situations. In pairs, decide what you are going to do.

1 Your car breaks when you are in a different country.
2 You invited some friends for dinner, but you burned it.
3 You broke your mother's favourite vase.

b Tell the class about your solutions to each problem.

Well first, we're going to try to fix the car ...

✓ Exam practice: page 165

10.3 ROBOT SUITS

V parts of the body
🔧 identify reasons

Vocabulary

1 Look at the pictures. Match the words in the box with the parts of the body.

V parts of the body

ankle	arm	back	elbow	fingers
foot	hand	head	knee	leg
neck	shoulder			

1 .... 5 .... 9 ....
2 .... 6 .... 10 ....
3 .... 7 .... 11 ....
4 .... 8 .... 12 ....

🔊 10.9 Listen, check and repeat.

2 Look at the pictures again. In pairs, answer the questions.
  1 What are the people doing?
  2 What parts of their body are they using?
  3 Do you think it's hard work? Why/Why not?
  4 How is technology helping them with their work?

Listening

3 🔊 10.10 Listen to a news report about robotics in the workplace. Check your answers to the questions in exercise 2.

🔧 **identify reasons**

It's important to understand the reasons for something.

- Listen to questions with *why* that ask about reasons, e.g. *Why did you call Richard?*
- Listen to answers with *because* or *to* that give reasons, e.g. *Because I needed to talk to him. / To talk to him.*
- Listen to explanations with *so*, e.g. *I needed to talk to Richard, so I called him.*

4 🔊 **10.10** Listen again. Choose the correct reasons to answer the questions.

1. Why is building cars hard work?
   a because the factories are dangerous
   b because the workers repeat the same job
   c because they build hundreds of cars
2. Why do car companies want to use robotic suits?
   a to give people's jobs to robots
   b to help workers with the hard work
   c to make the workers work harder
3. Why was the car industry the first industry to use these suits?
   a because there were a lot of accidents
   b because the car industry had more money
   c because other industries are going to use them too

5 In pairs, discuss the questions.

1. Do you think robotic suits are a good idea? Why/Why not?
2. Do you know someone with a dangerous job?
3. What does he/she do?
4. Can you think of other jobs where robotic suits can be useful?

Writing

6 Read about another use for robot suits. Who does it help? How does it help them? What parts of their body does it support?

7 Look at the picture and read the notes. In pairs, write a short text about how the new robot suit is going to help firefighters.

FIREFIGHTER
OF THE FUTURE

SPECIAL FEATURES

STRONGER LEGS
– climb a lot of stairs in tall buildings

STRONGER ARMS
– carry people/heavy objects; break doors

TOOLS ATTACH TO ARM
– don't need to carry them

AUTOMATIC TORCH ON SHOULDER
– see in the dark

OXYGEN ON BACK
– not breathe in smoke

Learning to walk with a
robotic suit

Doctors are using robot suits to help patients learn to walk after an accident. The suit supports their legs, especially the ankles and knees, so it's easier for patients to walk. Their legs get stronger quickly and soon they can walk without the robot suit.

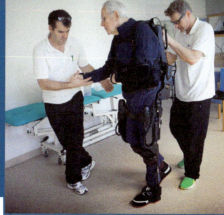

⇄ Mediation task: All students, page 131

10.4 DO YOU FANCY GOING FOR A RUN?

FL invitations
🎥 bionic boots

The big picture: bionic boots

1 Look at the picture. In pairs, think of three adjectives to describe the boots.

2 🎥 **10.1** Watch the video and answer the questions.
   1 Which city are they in?
   2 Why did Keahi invent the boots?
   3 Where does he use them?
   4 Which is faster, the boots or the bike?
   5 Are the boots easy to use?

3 🎥 **10.1** Complete the sentences using the comparative form of the adjectives in the box. Watch again and check.

   | easy | fast | good | hard | light | smart |

   1 Thanks to technology we can be ...., faster, and even have superpowers.
   2 Keahi is working on reducing the weight of the boots because the .... the boot, the faster you can go.
   3 He thinks his bionic boots are .... than bicycles because they're faster and .... to carry around.
   4 In the race through San Francisco, Keahi's boots were a lot .... than the bicycle.
   5 Justin found out that using the boots is a lot .... than it looks.

4 In pairs, discuss the questions.
   1 Would you like to try the boots? Why/Why not?
   2 Do you think that the boots are going to be popular in the future? Why/Why not?
   3 Which 'superpower' would you like to have: run faster, jump higher, be stronger or be smarter? Why?

5 🎥 **10.2** Watch Dev and Sophia talking about the video. Who prefers boots and who prefers bikes?

6 🎥 **10.2** Answer the questions. Watch the video again and check.
   1 What does Dev invite Sophia to do?
   2 Why can't Sophia go tomorrow?
   3 When do they agree to go?

102

Functional language

7 Look at the poster. In pairs, answer the questions.
1 What kind of film is it?
2 Would you like to see this film? Why/Why not?

8 🔊 **10.11** Listen to three friends talking about the film. Do they all want to see it?

9 🔊 **10.11** Listen again and answer the questions.
1 What day are they going to see the film?
2 Why isn't Tim going to watch the film?
3 What time is it on?
4 Where are Jack and Kate going to meet?
5 At what time?

10 🔊 **10.12** Complete the phrases from the conversation with the words in the box. Listen and check.

can't	come	coming	good	love	next

1 Do you fancy .... to see it on Saturday?
2 Yeah, I'd .... to.
3 Would you like to .... ?
4 Thanks, but I ....
5 Maybe .... time.
6 When's .... for you?

11 🔊 **10.13** ❝ **positive and negative intonation** ❞
Listen to the phrases. Notice the difference in the intonation between the positive answer and the negative answer. Listen again and repeat.
1 Yes, thanks, I'd love to!
2 Thanks, but I can't.

FL invitations

Making an invitation
Would you like to go ...?
Do you fancy going ...?
I'm going to ..., would you like to come, too?

Accepting
Yes, that'd be great.
Yes, I'd like that.
Yes, I'd love to.

Refusing
Thanks, but I can't.
I'm sorry, I'm going to ...
Maybe next time.

Arranging to meet
When's good for you?
Are you free on Saturday?
When are you free?

Speaking

12 Invite your classmates to the events below. Accept and arrange to meet, or refuse and make an excuse.
Would you like to watch the match at my place tonight?
Sorry, I'm going to meet some friends in town.

- do some sport
- go to a restaurant for a meal
- see a film
- watch some sport at home
- go shopping
- visit a friend

✏ Writing bank: page 153

REVIEW UNIT 10

Vocabulary
Electronic devices

1 In pairs, write ten electronic devices. Answer the questions.
 1 Which do you have at home?
 2 Which can't you live without? Why?
 3 Which do you never use?
 4 Which do you really hate? Why?

Communication verbs

2 a Choose the correct verb from the box to complete the sentences. There are two verbs you don't need.

| chat with | download | receive |
| search for | share | send |

 1 I usually .... text messages because it's quicker than calling and it's cheaper.
 2 I .... a lot more emails than I send to other people.
 3 I never .... videos to my phone. It's difficult to watch them on a small screen.
 4 I prefer to .... friends online. It's easier than meeting up with them.

b Do you agree with these sentences? Discuss your answers with a partner.

3 a Match the halves to make sentences.

 1 I usually call ...... a photos of my holiday.
 2 I like to upload ...... b for information online.
 3 I send ...... c with people on social media.
 4 I always search ...... d my parents every week.
 5 I chat ...... e about fifty text messages a day.

b In pairs, check your answers. Are the sentences true for you? If not, change them to make them true for you.

Parts of the body

4 a 🔊 10.14 Listen and point to the parts of the body you hear.

 b 🔊 10.14 Listen again and write them down.

 c Can you remember all the parts of the body from 4b, without looking at your list?

Grammar
Comparatives

5 Write the comparative form of the adjectives in brackets.

My new headphones were (1).................... (expensive) than others you can buy, but the sound quality is much (2).................... (good). My old headphones were (3).................... (small) and (4).................... (easy) to carry around, but these new ones are far (5).................... (comfortable) to wear, and although they're a lot (6).................... (big), I still wear them when I travel to work.

6 In pairs, write sentences comparing you and your partner.
I am older than Julia.

going to

7 a Look at the activities. Tick (✓) the ones that you are going to do today or tomorrow.

watch TV ☐	have a coffee ☐	get a train ☐
listen to music ☐	have a shower ☐	call a friend ☐
send a message ☐	go to work ☐	go shopping ☐

b In pairs, ask and answer questions.
 A *Are you going to call a friend?*
 B *No, I'm not. I'm going to send a message.*

c What else are you going to do? Tell your partner.
I want to book a holiday, so I'm going to search for flights online.

Functional language
Invitations

8 In pairs, act out a conversation using the information.

Student A
Ask student B if he/she is free on Saturday afternoon. Say that there is a new exhibition at the art gallery that you are going to go to. Ask student B if he/she would like to come with you.

Student B
You are free on Saturday morning, but not in the afternoon. Thank student A for the invitation. Explain that you can't come because you are going to visit your parents. Say that you would like to visit the gallery another time.

9 Swap roles and repeat the conversation.

🕘 Looking back

- What did you discover in this unit about technology?
- Think of six different forms of communication and six different situations in which they would be appropriate.
- Think of three things you can say about your plans for the next few days.

A working life

11

Grammar G
(don't) have to
superlatives
will for predictions

Vocabulary V
school subjects
jobs

Functional language FL
offers and requests

Skill
scan a text

Video
comic book writer

Writing
a formal email

Exams
listening and completing notes
understanding the general idea of conversations

The big picture: learning

1 Look at the picture. In pairs, guess the answers to the questions.
   1 Who is the teacher and who is the student?
   2 How do you know?
   3 What is the subject?
   4 How would you describe the class?

2 🔊 11.1 Listen and check your answers.

3 In pairs, discuss the questions.
   1 What are you learning at the moment?
   2 Do you have a good teacher? Why/Why not?
   3 What makes a good teacher?

   I'm learning to drive. It's really difficult but my teacher is great, she's very patient with me.

105

11.1 MY SPACE

G (don't) have to
V school subjects

Vocabulary

1 a In pairs, answer the questions.

1 When was the Berlin wall destroyed?
2 What is the capital of Morocco?
3 Is gravity stronger on Earth or Mars?
4 How do you say 'hello' in Japanese?
5 Who is the president of Canada?
6 What does 'www' mean on the internet?
7 How many legs does a spider have?
8 Who painted *Guernica*?
9 What is H_2O?
10 What is $\sqrt{49}$?

/10

b 🔊 **11.2** Listen and check. Write your mark on the test.

2 Match the subjects in the box with questions 1–10. Add two more subjects.

V school subjects

Art   Biology   Chemistry
Computer science   Geography   History
Languages   Maths   Physics   Politics

1 ....   6 ....
2 ....   7 ....
3 ....   8 ....
4 ....   9 ....
5 ....   10 ....

🔊 **11.3** Listen, check and repeat.

3 a 🔊 **11.4** ❝ **word stress** ❞ Listen and repeat the words. Notice the underlined syllables that are stressed.

1 <u>Che</u>mistry   3 <u>Phy</u>sics
2 Com<u>pu</u>ter   4 Ge<u>o</u>graphy

b 🔊 **11.5** Say the words and underline the stress. Listen, check and repeat.

1 History   3 Biology
2 Languages   4 Politics

4 In pairs, discuss the questions.

1 Which subjects did you like at school?
2 Which subjects didn't you like?
3 Did you get good marks at school?
4 Do you have a degree from a university?
5 Do you think exams and tests are fair?

a

b

Listening

5 Look at the pictures and answer the questions.

1 Where are the people studying?
2 Do you study or work in places like this?
3 Which do you think is better? Why?
4 Do you prefer to work alone or with other people?

6 🔊 **11.6** Listen and match the people with the pictures.

Bruno ....   Janice ....   Karl ....

7 🔊 **11.6** Listen again and complete the table. How is Bruno different to the others?

	Which subject do they study?	Where do they study?	Why do they study there?
Bruno			
Janice			
Karl			

Grammar

8 Who said the sentences, Bruno (B), Janice (J), Karl (K) or the presenter (P)?

1 I **don't have to** walk far. ....
2 I **have to** spend a lot of time in front of the computer. ....
3 **Do** you **have to** work together? ....
4 My friend Katrina **has to** get a 9 or 10 in the exam. ....

9 Look at the words in **bold** in exercise 8. Answer the questions.

1 Which sentences say something is necessary? .... and ....
2 Which sentence says something isn't necessary? ....
3 Which sentence asks if something is necessary? ....

G (don't) have to

+ We **have to do** exams at university.
  Alice **has to start** work at 8.00.
− You **don't have to pay** – it's free!
  Salem **doesn't have to get up** early today.
? **Do** you **have to speak** English for the job?
  Does your brother **have to come** with us?
Y/N Yes, you **do**. / No, you **don't**.
  Yes, he **does**. / No, he **doesn't**.

→ Grammar reference: page 142

10 a Complete the text with the correct form of *have to* and the verbs in the box.

| be | go | teach | wait | worry |

Like all children in Italy, Sofia Viola (1) .... to school, but she (2) .... about problems with her classmates. That's because she is the only pupil at the school! Her teacher (3) .... all the subjects in a normal classroom. 'Everything is exactly the same – except it's a little calmer than a normal school,' she says. Luckily, Sofia (4) .... alone every day. She goes to a bigger school twice a week to play with other children. How long (5) .... they .... before more children join the school? Not long, next year four new pupils are going to start.

b In pairs, say what Sofia and her teacher *have to* or *don't have to* do.

Sofia has to answer all the teacher's questions.

Speaking

11 a In pairs, ask and answer the questions about work or studies. Make a note of the answers.

1 What time do you have to start work/class?
2 Do you have to wear a uniform or formal clothes?
3 Do you have to work/study at the weekend?
4 Do you have to take public transport?
5 Who do you have to work with?

b Tell the class about your partner.

Paula doesn't have to wear formal clothes to work, but she has to start early.

11.2 THE HAPPIEST PROFESSION

G superlatives
V jobs

Vocabulary

1 Look at the pictures and write the correct jobs from the box.

V jobs

chef   dentist   engineer   farmer
hairdresser   mechanic   nurse   pilot
police officer   receptionist

1 .... 6 ....
2 .... 7 ....
3 .... 8 ....
4 .... 9 ....
5 .... 10 ....

🔊 **11.7** Listen, check and repeat.

2 In pairs, ask and answer the question *In which job do you have to ...?* with the phrases in the box.

work long hours   travel   help people
use special tools

3 In pairs, discuss the questions.
1 Do you work?
2 If so, what's your job?
3 What did you want to do when you were a child?
4 What's your 'dream job'?

Reading

4 a Read the job satisfaction survey. Tick (✓) the three most important things for you. In pairs, compare your answers and explain why they are important.

b Which job do you think is number one in a job satisfaction survey?

The Job Satisfaction Survey

What's most important for you?

☐ Friendly colleagues   ☐ A good boss
☐ Good money   ☐ Being creative
☐ A relaxed working   ☐ Helping people
   atmosphere   ☐ Good holidays
☐ Flexible working hours

108

5 Read the article and check your answer to exercise 4b. What do Tony, Sandra and Phil say are the most important reasons why they are happy?

6 Are the sentences true (T) or false (F)?
1 Hairdressers don't work at the weekend. ....
2 Hairdressers generally earn a lot of money. ....
3 Hairdressing is a creative job. ....
4 Being friendly and happy is part of the job. ....
5 Hairdressers usually wear formal clothes. ....
6 Salons are often relaxed and friendly places. ....

🔍 notice

job is countable: *It's a great job!*
work is uncountable: *It's hard work.*

The happiest profession

A recent survey showed that hairdressing is the happiest profession in a list of over eighty different jobs. But why? Is it the money? No. Hairdressers aren't the richest people in the world. They earn less money than many other professions, but they are a lot happier than doctors, engineers or pilots who have high salaries, but also a lot of stress. It isn't the working hours either. Hairdressers often have to work long hours, and weekends are the busiest time for them.

So, what's the answer? We talked to some happy hairdressers to find out.

'It's hard work, but we make people happy,' said Tony, who took part in the survey. 'I love the creative side of the job, too – that's the most important thing for me.'

Sandra, a manager at a large salon, said 'A good hairdresser has to smile, chat with the customers and make jokes. I think it's the best part of the job!'

'It's a great job! I don't have to get up early in the morning, wear a suit and tie, or sit in front of a computer all day – those are the biggest advantages for me,' said Phil, who became a hairdresser last year. 'A lot of the customers are my friends now. I feel like I'm at home, not at work! And you ask me why I'm happy?'

So, if you think you have the worst job in the world, or you're looking for a change of career, you know what to do … become a hairdresser!

Grammar

7 a Look at the superlative in **bold** in this line from the text. Are there any professions on the list that are happier than hairdressing?

Hairdressing is **the happiest** profession in a list of over eighty different jobs.

G superlatives

Nurses work **the longest** hours.
Saturday is **the busiest** day of the week.
The biggest problem is my boss.
It's **the most expensive** place to live.
It's **the best** job in the world!
He's **the worst** chef in the restaurant.

→ Grammar reference: page 142

b Find the superlatives in the text for the adjectives.
1 rich   the ....
2 important   the ....
3 busy   the ....
4 good   the ....
5 big   the ....
6 bad   the ....

8 🔊 11.8 *the* /ðə/ and /ðiː/ Listen to the sentences. Notice how *the* is pronounced /ðə/ before a consonant and /ðiː/ before a vowel. Listen again and repeat.
1 /ðə/   Pilots have the best job.
2 /ðiː/ Receptionists have the easiest job.

9 a Complete the questions with the superlative form of the adjectives in brackets.
1 Who is the .... person in your family? (old)
2 What is the .... restaurant near your home? (good)
3 Which unit in this book is the ....? (interesting)
4 Which subject is the .... to study? (easy)
5 What is the .... place in your country? (hot)

b In pairs, ask and answer the questions. Remember to pronounce *the* correctly.

Speaking

10 Discuss the question *Who has the … job in the world?* with the superlatives in the box. Give reasons for your answers.

best	most boring	dirtiest	easiest
coolest	most interesting	most dangerous
most difficult	most respected	worst

Pilots have the coolest job because they can travel all over the world.

✅ Exam practice: page 166   109

11.3 THE CHANGING WORKPLACE

 will for predictions
scan a text

a   b

Reading

1   Look at the pictures. In pairs, match them with the descriptions.

1   machines on a biscuit production line ....
2   a drone delivering a package ....
3   early robots in a car factory ....
4   a robot at work in the service industry ....

2   In pairs, discuss the questions.

1   Do the photos show the past, present or future?
2   Who did these jobs before robots?
3   Are you worried about robots doing our jobs? Why/Why not?

scan a text

You sometimes need to find information in a text quickly.
- Identify the key word(s).
- Move your eyes quickly over the text looking for the key word.
- When you find it, stop and read the sentence in detail.
- Make a note of the information you need.

3   Read the questions below. Notice the key words in **bold**. Scan the text to find the key words and answer the questions.

1   Which company used the **first robot**?
2   Which new job did robots do in the **1970s**?
3   How do robots help **doctors**?
4   What job do **drones** do?
5   Which robot has a **friendly face**?
6   Which robot helps **teachers**?
7   What's the name of the **robot dog**?
8   What do we need to do in **difficult situations**?

4   Read the article properly and answer the questions.

1   Why were robots popular in the past?
2   In which industries do robots work today?
3   Why shouldn't we worry about robots taking our jobs?
4   Is the author generally positive or negative about robots?

ROBOTS THEN AND NOW

Robots are all around us now, but when did we first start to use them … and what will happen in the future?

YESTERDAY
The first robots, or machines controlled by computers, worked in car factories. The American car company General Motors used the first robot in its factories in 1961. The robot, called *Unimate*, lifted large pieces of hot metal and made work safer for the people in the factory. In the 1970s, robots started to do simple, repetitive jobs for factory workers in the food industry, too. And by the end of the 20th century, robots were common on most production lines. They were quicker and cheaper than humans, and most people were happy because they did the most boring jobs.

TODAY
Today, robots don't only work in factories, they also help people in all kinds of different jobs. For example, doctors use robots during difficult operations. Online shops use drones to deliver packages. We use robots to control cars and other vehicles in dangerous situations where it's impossible for people to work. For example, we sent the 'rover' robot to Mars to see if there is life there.
We're also starting to see robots in the service industry, too, in hotels, restaurants, museums, and even at home. *Pepper*, a robot with a friendly face, can speak a number of different languages and can give information to guests and customers in hotels, airports and conference centres. Another robot called *Nao* is smaller than Pepper, but has hands and legs and helps teachers in class. *Nao* can follow the students' instructions and can talk to them. There's also *Miró*, a robot dog. It helps old people in their homes. These robots are not taking the place of people. They're working with them to make their jobs easier.

TOMORROW
What about the future? Will robots take our jobs? Well, a lot of jobs that people do today will disappear. Robots will probably take the place of shop assistants, receptionists and farmers, for example. But don't worry, because in the future, humans will need to do different jobs that don't exist today. And there are some jobs that robots definitely won't take, like nurses and police officers. That's because in the most difficult situations, we won't want to speak with robots, we'll want a real person. So, welcome to a wonderful future of humans and robots working side-by-side!

110

Grammar

5 Look at the predictions from the text. Do you agree with them?

1 Robots **will probably take** the place of shop assistants, receptionists and farmers.
2 In the future, humans **will need** to do different jobs that don't exist today.
3 There are some jobs that robots **definitely won't take**, like nurses and police officers.
4 In the most difficult situations, we **won't want** to speak with robots.

6 a Look at the words in **bold**. Answer the questions about the predictions in exercise 5.

1 Which word do we use for a positive prediction? will / won't
2 Which word do we use for a negative prediction? will / won't
3 Which word do we use if we aren't sure about a prediction? ....
4 Which word do we use if we are very sure about a prediction? ....

b Look at the last paragraph of the text. Can you find the contracted form for *we will*? ....

G will for predictions

+ *I'll (probably/definitely) become a police officer in the future.*
− *Hannah (probably/definitely) won't work in a factory.*
? *Will robots replace us?*
Y/N *Yes, they will. No, they won't.*

→ Grammar reference: page 142

7 Complete the predictions using *will/won't* so they are true for you. In pairs, compare your answers.

1 It .... rain tomorrow.
2 I .... go to bed early tonight.
3 The teacher .... give us homework.
4 I .... pass the next English test.
5 I .... have a new job next year.

8 In groups, write three more predictions about the future. Use *probably* and *definitely* to say if you are sure about them or not.

Atlético Madrid probably won't win the Champions League.

Writing

9 Complete the text about the future of food with *will/won't* and the verbs in the box. Do you agree with the predictions?

| be | eat | have | prepare | sell | work |

The future of food
What (1) .... we .... in the future? We (2) .... definitely .... a lot of choice with fruit and vegetables from different countries around the world, but shops (3) .... meat because we (4) .... probably all .... vegetarians! Robots (5) .... food in factories, but people (6) .... as chefs in restaurants because it's a creative job.

10 In pairs, choose a topic from the boxes. Write a short text about how things will be different in the future.

transport   entertainment   sports and hobbies
education   shopping

Mediation task: Student A page 125, Student B page 130

11.4 DREAM JOB
FL offers and requests
🎬 comic book writer

The big picture: comic book writer

1 Look at the picture. In pairs, answer the questions.
   1 What can you see?
   2 Do you know the character in the comic book?
   3 Who does the character look like?
   4 Do/Did you like comic books?

2 🎬 **11.1** Watch the video. Match the jobs in the box with the people.

   actor   artist   writer   shop owner

Chris

Thor

Chris's dad

the Protector

3 🎬 **11.1** Are these sentences true (T) or false (F)? Watch again and check.
   1 Chris wants the shop to sell his comic book. ....
   2 Chris's dad helps his son a lot. ....
   3 Chris wears the Protector costume and is in the film. ....
   4 Thor isn't impressed by Chris's ideas. ....
   5 People like the Protector comic book. ....

4 In pairs, discuss the questions.
   1 How does Chris achieve his dream? *he's lucky / he works hard / both*
   2 What is your 'dream job'?
   3 What do you need to do to get this job?
   4 Do you think you'll work in this profession in the future?

5 🎬 **11.2** Watch Dev and Sophia talking about the video. Answer the questions.
   1 How do Dev and Sophia think Chris achieved his dream?
   2 What is Dev's dream job?
   3 Why does he think he won't do this job?
   4 What is Sophia's dream job?

6 🎬 **11.2** Watch again and answer the questions.
   1 What does Sophia offer to do to help Dev?
   2 How does Dev respond?
   3 What does Dev ask Sophia to do to help him?
   4 How does Sophia respond?

112

Functional language

7 🔊 **11.11** Listen to four conversations. Match them with the pictures.

1 .... 2 .... 3 .... 4 ....

8 a 🔊 **11.11** Listen again. Complete the phrases with the words in the box.

Can you	I'll	Let me	Shall I

1 .... help you with that.
2 .... read it, please?
3 .... look at it for you?
4 .... wash these and you can clean the tables.

b Which of the sentences are offers? Which are requests? How did the other people respond?

FL offers and requests

Making an offer	Accepting and refusing an offer
Let me …	Thanks, that's great!
I'll …	No, really. It's OK.
Shall I …?	I'm fine, thanks.
Making a request	**Accepting and refusing a request**
Can you … please?	Sure, no problem.
	Of course.
	Sorry, I can't help you there.

9 🔊 **11.12** Look at the Functional language box. Complete the conversation with the correct words. Listen and check.

A I have to cook dinner for eight people tonight.
B Really? (1) .... me help you.
A I'm (2) ...., thanks.
B I (3) .... wash the vegetables, if you want.
A No, really. It's OK.
B (4) .... I make some dessert?
A Honestly, I'm fine! But (5) .... you make me a coffee, please?
B (6) ...., no problem.
A Thanks!

10 🔊 **11.13** 🔊 **sounding helpful** 🔊 Listen to the offers. Notice the intonation to sound helpful. Listen again and repeat.

1 Let me help you.
2 I'll wash the vegetables.
3 Shall I make some dessert?

Speaking

11 Look at this 'to-do' list of jobs that you have to do. In pairs, say the jobs and make offers or requests. Try to sound helpful when you make an offer.

I have to wash the car today.
Shall I help you?
No, really, it's fine. But can you clean the kitchen, please?
Sure, no problem.

To-do list
- wash the car
- clean the kitchen
- cook lunch
- call the dentist
- go to the bank
- buy some milk
- do homework
- pay the phone bill

✎ Writing bank: page 154

REVIEW UNIT 11

Vocabulary
School subjects

1 Match the subjects to the topics.

1 Biology	....	a	light, sound, gravity
2 Geography	....	b	politicians and laws
3 Maths	....	c	plants and animals
4 Politics	....	d	numbers
5 History	....	e	the earth and countries
6 Physics	....	f	people and things in the past

2 🔊 **11.14** Underline the stressed syllable in the subjects in exercise 1. Listen and check your answers.

Jobs

3 a In which jobs do you have to do these things? Add your ideas to the table.

Travel	Wear a uniform	Work at the weekend	Work in an office
pilot		chef	

b In pairs, think of a job that matches both of the phrases in 1–3.
1 use special tools / work outside
2 be creative / earn a lot of money
3 help people / work long hours

c Which job(s) would you never do? Why?

4 Think of five friends or family members who work. Write the jobs they do and explain them to a partner.

My uncle's a doctor. He works at the hospital. He loves his job.

Grammar
(don't) have to

5 Complete the sentences with the correct form of (don't) have to and a verb from the box.

ask	pay	start	travel	wear

1 She .... a lot for her new job. She's going to Singapore next week.
2 We .... work at 8 a.m.
3 Do you .... a uniform for your job?
4 I .... my boss if I want to work from home.
5 You .... for coffee in the office – it's free.

6 What do you have to do today? What don't you have to do? Write sentences that are true for you.

I have to walk home, but I don't have to cook a meal ...

Superlatives

7 In pairs, make sentences to compare the jobs in the photos. Use the correct superlative forms.

bad	boring	creative	difficult
easy	exciting	good	stressful

I think the DJ has the best job!
I think the mechanic has the most boring job.

will for predictions

8 Where will Eva be at these times? Complete the predictions using the words in brackets and will/won't.
1 At 10 a.m. today, she *'ll be at work*. (at work / ✓)
2 It's Saturday tomorrow, so she .... (in the office / ✗)
3 On Saturday afternoon, she .... (definitely / at the gym / ✓)
4 In the evening, she .... (probably / out with friends / ✓)
5 She .... before midnight. (in bed / ✗)

9 In pairs, write three predictions about your life next year. Use *probably* and *definitely*.

In June, I'll definitely finish my course.

Functional language
Offers and requests

10 a Complete the requests and offers using one word.
1 .... me help you with that. It looks heavy.
2 .... you give me another one of those? They're really delicious.
3 .... you hold this for me, please? My hands are full.
4 Don't worry. I .... get some when I go out.
5 Will you do me a favour, ...? Can you get the keys from my pocket? Thanks.

b 🔊 **11.15** Listen and check. What is happening in situations 1–5?

🕒 Looking back

- What's the most useful thing you've learned in this unit?
- Which exercise was the most interesting? Why?
- Which three jobs would you like to do? Why?

Live life to the full 12

Grammar G
present perfect
present perfect and past simple
tense review

Vocabulary V
feelings and emotions
measurements

Functional language FL
recommendations

Skill
listen in detail

Video
sleeping in the sky

Writing
an information leaflet

Exams
writing a short story

The big picture: an amazing experience

1 Look at the picture. In pairs, guess the answers to the questions.
   1 Where is the person?
   2 What is she doing?
   3 Does she like the experience?
   4 How does she feel?
   5 Why did she do it?

2 12.1 Listen to the conversation and check your answers.

3 In pairs, discuss the questions.
   1 Would you like to try this activity? Why/Why not?
   2 Why do people like doing scary things like this?
   3 Do you like doing scary things?
   4 What kind of scary things do you like?

115

12.1 TRY SOMETHING NEW

G present perfect
V feelings and emotions

Vocabulary

1 a Look at the pictures. What are the people doing?

b In pairs, use the feelings in the Vocabulary box to describe how the people feel.

He feels nervous.

2 Put the feelings in the correct columns.

V feelings and emotions

afraid	angry	bored	happy
interested	nervous	relaxed	sad
stressed	surprised	tired	worried

Positive	Negative	Neutral
	afraid	

🔊 **12.2** Listen, check and repeat.

3 In pairs, ask and answer the question *How do you feel when …?* with the situations.
1 a friend remembers your birthday
2 you have a difficult exam
3 your teacher asks you an easy question
4 it's the weekend and the sun is shining
5 you watch a video about Hollywood actors
6 you're alone and you hear a strange sound

Reading

4 Read a blog post about feelings. Match the pictures to the paragraphs.

Paragraph 1 ....   Paragraph 3 ....
Paragraph 2 ....   Paragraph 4 ....

5 In pairs, say what you do when you're bored, angry or stressed. How does it make you feel?

6 🔊 **12.3** Listen to the conversation between Ollie and Martha. Tick (✓) the activities Martha has done.
1 eat Japanese food ☐
2 eat Korean food ☐
3 dance salsa ☐
4 dance samba ☐
5 see *Singing in the Rain* ☐

✓ The daily routine

Have you ever felt stressed at work or worried by exams? Do you feel bored and tired of your daily routine? Of course! It happens to all of us. But what can you do to make things better? Here are three simple ways to feel happier.

Try something new
Think of something you've never done, something you really want to do – and just do it! Maybe you haven't tried Japanese food because you're too nervous. Or you haven't danced salsa because you're too afraid. Or you haven't seen that classic film everyone talks about. Now is your chance to do it. You'll feel so happy you did!

Make a small change to your routine
Think of something you do every day and do it differently. Have you ever changed your route to work in the morning? Walk through the park, or cycle to work, or stop for a coffee on the way. A little change can make a big difference. Break your routine. You won't be bored, I promise you!

Do something for someone else
The best way to feel better is to do something nice for someone. Have you ever bought coffee for your colleagues at work? Have you ever helped someone on the bus with their heavy bags? Have you ever made a cake for a neighbour? If you haven't – try it tomorrow. They'll be surprised and very happy, and the smile you get in return will make you feel fantastic all day long!

116

Grammar

7 🔊 **12.3** Order the present perfect sentences from the conversation. Listen again and check.

a ☐ I've never **seen** *Singing in the Rain*.
b ☐ Yes, I **have**. I've **had** Japanese, Chinese, Thai – I love them!
c ☐ **Have** you ever **eaten** Japanese food?
d ☐ I **haven't danced** salsa, but I **have danced** samba.
e ☐ **Have** you ever **danced** salsa?

8 Look at the words in **bold** in the sentences in exercise 7. Answer the questions.
1 Are they about actions at a specific time in the past, or about experiences in their lives?
2 What are the two parts of the verb? .... + past participle
3 Which past participles are different from the past simple? .... and ....
4 Which word do we use with questions to mean 'in your life'? ....
5 Which word do we use to emphasize 'not in my life'? ....

G	present perfect
+	I've **tried** Moroccan food. Irene's **danced** tango.
–	I **haven't seen** that film. Sam **hasn't driven** a car.
?	**Have** you (ever) **made** a cake? **Has** your boss (ever) **bought** you a coffee?
Y/N	Yes, I **have**. / No, I **haven't**. Yes, she **has**. / No, she **hasn't**.

→ Grammar reference: page 143

9 How many examples of the present perfect can you find in the text?

10 🔊 **12.4** 🎤 **weak form of *have*** 🎤 Listen to the question and short answer. Notice the difference in the pronunciation of *have*. Listen again and repeat.

Have you ever eaten Japanese food?
Yes, I have.

11 a Write questions with *Have you ever …?* and the present perfect.
1 eat / Japanese food
2 dance / tango
3 see / a black and white film
4 drive / a fast car
5 organize / a surprise party
6 help / someone to move house

b In pairs, ask and answer the questions. Remember to use the correct pronunciation of *have*.

c Say what you discovered about your partner.
Julio has never eaten Japanese food.

Speaking

12 a Write a list of five things you think everyone should do at least once. Think about the topics in the boxes and your own ideas.

books	places
music	people
films	food
activities	drink

b Move around the class and ask *Have you ever …?* for the five things on your list. Make a note of people's answers. Who has done the most activities?

117

12.2 EXTREME ADVENTURES

G present perfect and past simple
V measurements

Vocabulary

1 a 🔊 **12.5** In pairs, answer the questions. Listen and check your answers.

THE BIG GEOGRAPHY QUIZ

1 Where's the coldest place on Earth?
   A) the Arctic   B) the Antarctic
2 Which country has the longest coastline?
   A) Canada   B) Indonesia
3 Who is the fastest swimmer in the world?
   A) César Cielo   B) Michael Phelps
4 What is the biggest land animal?
   A) the Asian elephant   B) the African elephant

b 🔊 **12.5** Listen again. Add the missing number to the measurements.

1 −89.........°C   3 ....91 seconds
2 ....,000 km   4 ....,000 kg

2 Put the units in the correct columns.

V measurements

centimetres   degrees   grams   ~~hours~~
kilograms   kilometres   kilometres per hour
metres   miles   miles per hour   minutes
seconds

Time	Temperature	Distance/Height
hours		

Weight		Speed

🔊 **12.6** Listen, check and repeat.

🔍 **notice**

We use *how* + adjective to ask about measurements.
How cold is the Antarctic?
How fast does César Cielo swim?
How heavy is an African elephant?

3 a In pairs, look at the measurements. Guess which questions they answer.

1 9.58 seconds   3 8,848 metres
2 173,000 kg   4 57.6°C

b 🔊 **12.7** Listen and check your answers.

4 Write questions to find the answers. In pairs, ask and answer the questions.

How tall are you?
I'm 1.72 metres.
1 your partner's height
2 the time he/she takes to travel to class
3 the speed he/she can drive
4 his/her weight when he/she was born
5 the temperature last night

Listening

5 Look at the pictures of two adventurers. In pairs, answer the questions.
1 Where are the people?
2 What are they doing?
3 What is the adventure?

6 🔊 **12.8** Who do you think has done the things: Felicity (F) or Ross (R)? Listen and check. What do they have in common?

1 has run a marathon in the Sahara desert   ....
2 has climbed Mount Everest   ....
3 has given a TED talk   ....
4 has run a marathon pulling a car   ....
5 has written a book   ....
6 has crossed the Antarctic alone   ....

118

7 🔊 **12.8** Listen again and complete the statistics for the two record-breaking adventures.

Antarctic crossing
Time: ....
Distance: ....
Weight carried: ....
Temperature: ....

The Great British Swim
Total distance: ....
Total time: ....
Time swimming per day: ....
Distance per day: ....

8 In pairs, discuss the questions.
1 Which adventure was more difficult? Why?
2 Why do people try these types of adventures?
3 Would you like to try an adventure like these?

Grammar

9 🔊 **12.9** Match the questions about Felicity with the answers. Listen and check.
1 What incredible things has she done? ....
2 Was she alone? ....
3 How long did the journey take? ....
4 How far did she ski? ....

a Yes, she was.
b The journey lasted 59 days.
c She's crossed the Antarctic on skis.
d She covered 1,744 kilometres.

10 Look at the questions and answers in exercise 9. Answer the questions.
1 What tenses are they in?
2 Which question is about an experience in Felicity's life? ....
3 Which questions are specific details about the experience? ....

G present perfect and past simple

Present perfect
What's the most amazing thing Ross Edgley has done?
He's swum around the coast of Great Britain.

Past simple
How far did he swim every day?
He swam 30 to 50 kilometres a day.

→ Grammar reference: page 143

11 a 🔊 **12.10** 🗣 **irregular past participles** 🗣 Listen to the sentences. Pay attention to the pronunciation of the past participles in **bold**. Listen again and repeat.
1 He has **swum** all the way around the coast of Great Britain.
2 She's even **given** a TED talk about her experience.

b What are the infinitive forms of the verbs? What are the past simple forms?

12 🔊 **12.11** Complete the table of verbs. How are the past participles pronounced? Listen, check and repeat.

Infinitive	Past simple	Past participle
begin		
	took	
		spoken
do		
	sang	
		eaten

13 a Look at the questions in the present perfect. In pairs, think of two questions about specific details in the past simple.
1 Have you ever swum in a river?
   How far did you swim? Was it cold?
2 Have you ever done yoga?
3 Have you ever taken part in a competition?
4 Have you ever sung karaoke?

b In pairs, ask and answer the questions. Ask follow-up questions in the past simple if your partner has done the activity.

Speaking

14 Match the halves to make questions.
1 What's the longest journey ....
2 What's the hardest exam ....
3 What's the scariest film ....
4 What's the most beautiful place ....
5 What's the best present ....
6 What's the most delicious dish ....

a you've ever eaten?
b you've ever visited?
c you've ever been on?
d anyone has ever given you?
e you've ever done?
f you've ever watched?

15 a Ask at least three of your classmates the questions from exercise 14. Ask follow-up questions to find out more.

b Tell the class about any amazing experiences you learned about.

✓ Exam practice: page 167

12.3 FACE YOUR FEARS

G tense review
🔧 listen in detail

Listening

1 Look at the pictures. In pairs, answer the questions.
1. How does each situation make you feel?
2. Do any of them make you feel afraid or nervous?
3. Why do you think some people are afraid of these things?
4. Which two do you think are the most common fears? Why?

2 🔊 **12.12** Listen to a radio interview. Answer the questions.
1. Which phobia does Glen talk about?
2. How did he face his fear?

🔧 listen in detail

You sometimes need to understand detailed information.
- Listen once to understand the general ideas.
- Listen again and pay attention when they discuss the information you need.
- Think about the tenses of the verbs: if they're positive or negative, what they refer to, etc.
- Think about all the information you hear and how it fits together.

3 🔊 **12.12** Read the Skill box. Listen again and choose the correct option to complete the sentences.
1. Glen *had / has / has never had* a phobia of lifts.
2. He still feels *nervous / afraid / relaxed* when he's in a lift.
3. His mother *wasn't afraid of / hated / has been stuck in* lifts.
4. He *is / was / isn't* afraid of flying.
5. He *used / didn't use / was stuck in* the lift today.
6. To control his fear, he started by going into a lift *with the doors closed / on his own / with his therapist*.
7. Now he's trying to take the lift *with a friend / on his own / to the top floor*.
8. He says it's *easy / difficult / impossible* to control your fears.

120

Grammar

4 a Look at the sentences from the radio programme. What tenses are the verbs in **bold**?

a I sometimes **feel** nervous when I take a lift.
b **Did** you **have** a bad experience as a child?
c I**'ve** never **been** afraid of flying.
d I**'m** still **working** on that.
e That**'s going to be** the next step!
f I know it**'ll take** time.

b Match the sentences with the functions.

1 an action or situation that happens regularly ....
2 an action in progress now ....
3 a plan for the future ....
4 a prediction about the future ....
5 a finished action in the past ....
6 an experience in someone's life ....

G tense review

Present simple	Kim usually takes the lift when he gets to work.
Present continuous	I'm waiting for the lift at the moment.
Past simple	I didn't take the lift this morning.
Present perfect	Have you ever been stuck in a lift?
will	The lift will be quicker than the stairs.
going to	Alex is going to take the lift to reception.

→ Grammar reference: page 143

5 🔊 **12.13** Choose the correct tenses to complete the questions. Listen and check.

1 *Did you have / Do you have* a phobia when you were a child?
2 What *were / are* you afraid of?
3 *Do you have / Did you have* the same fear now?
4 *Have you done / Are you doing* anything at the moment to control it?
5 *Are you going to do / Do you do* anything about it in the future?
6 How long do you think *it has taken / it will take*?

6 In pairs, ask your partner if he/she is afraid of anything or knows anyone who has an extreme fear or phobia. Use the questions in exercise 5 to help you.

Writing

7 a Read the text about a personal experience. In pairs, choose another title for it.

a The worst food in the world!
b The food I hated as a kid
c Try a new type of food
d It's healthy, but disgusting

b Choose the correct words to complete the text.

Learning to love *cabbage*

⁽¹⁾*Did / Have* you ever eaten cabbage? Did you ⁽²⁾*like / liked* it? When I was a child, I really hated cabbage! I ⁽³⁾*don't / didn't* like the taste or the smell. When my mother cooked cabbage for dinner, I said that I was ill so I didn't have to eat it! But now I ⁽⁴⁾*love / loving* it! When I was a student, I lived with some Asian students, and they ⁽⁵⁾*cooked / cooking* cabbage in a very different way from my mother. I tried it and I really liked it. Now I cook cabbage, too. I still ⁽⁶⁾*don't / isn't* like the way my mother cooks it, but I'm ⁽⁷⁾*tried / trying* to teach her some new ways. Every week, we try a new recipe together. This week I ⁽⁸⁾*'m / 'll* going to make a Chinese soup. She ⁽⁹⁾*didn't / hasn't* tried it before, but I think she ⁽¹⁰⁾*'ll / 's* like it.

8 Choose a title about a personal experience and write a short text about it. Remember to talk about the past, present and future.

> The food I hated as a kid
> A fear I had as a child
> An important event that changed me
> A person who had a big influence on me
> An amazing experience I want to repeat

9 In pairs, read each other's stories and ask any follow-up questions to find out more.

⇆ **Mediation task:** All students, page 131

12.4 COULD YOU RECOMMEND A HOTEL?

FL recommendations
▢ sleeping in the sky

The big picture: sleeping in the sky

1 Look at the picture of an unusual hotel. In pairs, guess the answers to the questions.
  1 What is unusual about it?
  2 Which country is it in?
  3 What type of people stay there?
  4 How is it different from a normal hotel?

2 ▢ 12.1 Watch the video and answer the questions.
  1 Where is the hotel?
  2 What's its name?
  3 How do you go up the mountain?
  4 How do you come down it?

3 ▢ 12.1 Answer the questions. Watch the video again and check.
  1 How high up is the Sky Lodge?
  2 How many rooms does it have?
  3 What are the walls of the hotel made of?
  4 What do they have for breakfast?
  5 How many ziplines do they have to take to go down?
  6 How did Thomas describe the Sky Lodge?

4 In pairs, discuss the questions.
  1 Would you like to stay in the Sky Lodge?
  2 What would be the best part?
  3 What would be the worst part?
  4 What's the most unusual place you've ever stayed in?
  5 Where was it and what was unusual about it?

5 In pairs, order the things from 1 (most important) to 6 (not important) for a hotel.

| beautiful views | big rooms | central location |
| comfortable beds | good price | quiet street |

6 ▢ 12.2 Watch Will and Laura talking about the video. Answer the questions.
  1 Would they like to stay at the Sky Lodge hotel?
  2 What reasons do they give?
  3 Where is Will going at the weekend?

7 ▢ 12.2 Tick (✓) the recommendation that Will chooses. Watch again and write why. What are the problems with the others?
  a Portishead campsite ▢
  b Royal Plaza ▢
  c Bristol Backpackers ▢

122

Functional language

8 How do you get recommendations about places to go on holiday? In pairs, say how often you do the things.
   A look on websites like TripAdvisor
   B read guidebooks about places
   C ask friends and family
   D speak to a travel agent

9 🔊 **12.14** Look at the pictures. What is the person's job? Listen and check.

10 🔊 **12.14** Match the speakers with the type of holiday, the place and the activities. Listen again and check.

1	romantic holiday	Oaxaca	go shopping
2	cultural holiday	Puerto Vallarta	go hiking
3	beach holiday	San Cristóbal	visit archaeological sites

11 🔊 **12.15** Complete the phrases with the words in the box. Which are for asking for recommendations and which are for making recommendations? Listen and check.

| best | have | love | makes |
| recommend | say | should | why |

1 Could you _____ a place to go here?
2 _____ not try San Cristóbal de las Casas?
3 People _____ it's beautiful.
4 What _____ it so special?
5 You'll _____ it!
6 You _____ to visit the market in the old town.
7 What's the _____ place to go to?
8 You _____ go to Oaxaca.

FL recommendations

Asking for a recommendation	Making a recommendation
Could you recommend a …?	Why not try …?
Can you suggest a …?	People say it's …
What's the best …?	You'll love it!
What makes it so special?	You should …
What else can you …?	You have to …

12 🔊 **12.16** 🎤 **emphasis in recommendations** 🎤
Listen to the recommendations again. Notice how the underlined words are emphasized. Listen again and repeat.
1 People say it's <u>beautiful</u>.
2 You'll <u>love</u> it!
3 You <u>have</u> to visit the market in the old town.

13 In pairs, ask for and make recommendations for places in your country for the types of holidays in the box. Remember to emphasize the recommendations.

| adventure holiday | beach holiday | cultural holiday |
| nature holiday | romantic holiday | |

Speaking

14 In pairs, look at the situations. Take turns asking for and making recommendations.

FOOD:
Student A: You want to cook a meal for your boss, but don't know what to make.
Student B: Recommend a delicious recipe.

FILMS:
Student B: You feel sad and want to watch something funny.
Student A: Recommend a film to make B feel happier.

SPORT:
Student A: You need to get fit and want to do an activity.
Student B: Recommend a hobby that is easy and will get A fit.

HOBBY:
Student B: You have just arrived in a new town and want to meet new people.
Student A: Recommend a hobby that will help B socialize.

✏️ Writing bank: page 155   123

REVIEW UNIT 12

Vocabulary
Feelings and emotions

1 🔊 **12.17** Listen to the speakers and tick (✓) the correct emotion.

1 surprised ☐	relaxed ☐	stressed ☐
2 stressed ☐	tired ☐	afraid ☐
3 tired ☐	happy ☐	interested ☐
4 stressed ☐	bored ☐	nervous ☐
5 afraid ☐	angry ☐	worried ☐
6 worried ☐	interested ☐	bored ☐

2 Complete the sentences so they are true for you. Compare your answers with a partner.
1 Sometimes I feel worried about ....
2 I'm always happy when ....
3 I get very angry when ....
4 One thing I'm interested in is ....
5 I was really surprised when ....

Measurements

3 a Match the questions to the answers.
1 How long is your little finger?
2 How much do you weigh?
3 How tall are you?
4 How long do you sleep at night?
5 How far do you travel to class?
6 How long can you hold your breath?

a Seven hours.
b Four miles.
c 20 seconds.
d 6 centimetres.
e 65 kilograms.
f 1.6 metres.

b In pairs, ask and answer the questions in 3a so that they are true for you.

Grammar
Present perfect

4 a In pairs, write questions with *Have you ever ...?* and the present perfect form of the verbs. Which past participles are irregular?
1 write / a book or poem
2 work / in a shop
3 win / a prize
4 live / in another country
5 fly / in a helicopter
6 fail / an exam

b Ask and answer the questions in 4a.

c Think of one more *Have you ever ... ?* question and ask your partner.

A *Have you ever eaten sashimi?*
B *No, I haven't, but I've eaten sushi.*

Present perfect and past simple

5 a Put the words in the correct order to make questions.
1 ever / have / Peru / been / you / to ?
2 what's / ever / had / the / holiday / best / you / have ?
3 have / done / really / ever / exciting / you / something ?
4 thing / eaten / you / have / worst / what's / the / ever ?

b In pairs, ask and answer the questions. If the answer is yes, ask and answer more questions in the past simple to get or give more information.

A *Have you ever been to Peru?* B *Yes, I have.*
A *Where did you go?* B *I went to Lima.*

Tense review

6 a Choose the correct tenses.
1 How old were you when you *begin / began* to study English?
2 How often *are you having / do you have* English classes?
3 Who *was / is* your first English teacher?
4 What *have you found / will you find* difficult?
5 Where *are you going to study / have you studied* English next year?

b In pairs, ask your partner the questions in 6a.

Functional language
Recommendations

7 🔊 **12.18** In pairs, put the conversation in the correct order. Write 1–8. Listen and check.
a ☐ You can also do water sports on the lakes. You'll love it there.
b ☐ You should try the Lake District.
c ☐ Really? What makes it so special?
d ☐ Could you recommend a place to go hiking?
e ☐ What else can you do there?
f ☐ Can you suggest a hotel?
g ☐ There are some high mountains. It's very beautiful.
h ☐ People say The Derwent is a good place to stay.

8 In pairs, ask for and make recommendations for:
1 a good place to eat out
2 an interesting thing to do in your home town
3 a city to visit

A *What's the best restaurant near here?*
B *Why not try Pablo's on the high street?*

Looking back

- Which section of this unit is the most memorable?
- Think of five phrases from this unit you can use tomorrow.
- Think of five things you can say to describe your experiences and achievements.

MEDIATION

1.3 Work in a group: All students

1. In groups of three, look at the pictures. Choose a restaurant to go to together. Student A will lead the discussion. Student B will take notes about your opinions. Student C will be the spokesperson for the group.

   Student A
   What do you think about this restaurant, Maria?
   Student B
   I think it looks great! / I think it looks expensive.

2. Tell the class which restaurant you chose and why.

   Student C
   We chose … because …

7.3 Simplify a text: Student A

1. You are planning a journey from London to Paris. Look at comments about two ways to travel and highlight the important information.

2. Tell your partner the important information about these two ways to travel. Listen to your partner tell you about two more ways to travel.

   The train costs …
   The journey takes …

3. In pairs, decide how you would like to travel.

Train

We took the train from London to Paris – the Eurostar. It was really quick. It only took two and a half hours, but we had to be at the station 30 minutes before the train left. It was quite cheap. It cost about £200. It was also really easy. We got on the train in the centre of London and got off in the centre of Paris. You can have lunch on the train and you can see some beautiful views of the countryside … when the train isn't underground!

Bus and ferry

I love boats, so I wanted to take the ferry to France. The journey was quite long, but it wasn't very expensive. The bus from London to Dover took two and a half hours – and only cost £10! The ferry from Dover to Calais took an hour and a half. It cost £50 and it was fantastic! At Calais, I got on another bus to take me to Paris. This was also very cheap – only £15, but it took about six hours. So it was a very long journey. But I loved travelling by ferry, so I was happy!

11.3 Explain in your own words: Student A

1. Read the text. Write notes on the good things and bad things about robots.

Good things about robots	Bad things about robots

2. Close your book. Tell your partner everything you can remember about your text.

3. Open your book. Listen to your partner and make notes in the table about what he/she says. In pairs, compare your notes.

Robots and Work

Did you know that companies already use over 1 million robot workers? Most of these robots are used by car companies. These automated workers can build cars in the factories without getting tired or making mistakes. However, building robots is very expensive so not many companies can afford to use robots. Companies also need engineers and computer experts to tell the robots what to do. They also need people to fix them. But it is hard to find people to do these jobs because it is a new skill. In the future, many people will look after robots for their jobs. This means that people will have easier and safer jobs because robots can do difficult or dangerous tasks. Robots can go to dangerous places – for example, places that are very hot or very cold.

MEDIATION

2.3 Talk about specific information: Student A

1 **a** Ask Student B questions to find out about Person 1.

What's her name?
Could you repeat that, please?
How do you spell that?

b Read the text about Person 2. Answer Student B's questions about him.

2 Do you think Person 1 and Person 2 would be friends? Why / Why not?

	Person 1		Person 2
Name		\multicolumn{2}{l	}{Hi! My name is Marcus Morgan. I'm American and I live in Chicago. I'm 20 years old and I'm a university student. I live with two friends at university. Their names are Brad and Michael. We all study languages. Brad studies Spanish, Michael studies French, and I study Chinese. We like playing games and watching TV. And our favourite food is pizza. We eat it almost every day!}
Age			
Nationality			
Lives in			
Lives with			
Pets			
Studies			
Favourite food			

3.3 Write about specific information: Student A

1 You need to arrange a meeting with your partner in working hours (Monday-Friday 9 a.m. to 5 p.m.). Look at your calendar and write an email to him/her explaining when you are free and when you are busy.

> Hi ....
> Can we meet some time next month?
> I have a conference from 1 May to 3 May, but I am free on Thursday and Friday that week …

2 Read the email from your partner. Look at your calendar and the dates when your partner is free. When is the best day and time for the meeting?

May

Mon	Tue	Wed	Thu	Fri	Sat	Sun
1 Conference	2 Conference	3 Conference	4	5	6	7
8 Dentist (a.m.) Meeting (p.m.)	9 Business trip to Italy	10 Business trip to Italy	11	12	13	14
15 Meeting (a.m.)	16 Spanish lesson (p.m.)	17 Prepare for trip	18 Business trip to Spain	19 Business trip to Spain	20 Picnic	21
22	23	24 Visit customer (p.m.)	25 Sales Conference	26 Sales Conference	27	28 Holiday
29 Holiday	30 Holiday	31 Holiday				

6.3 Explain diagrams: Student A

1 Look at the picture. Explain to your partner what the weather is like in Canada.

In Vancouver it's sunny and it's warm. It's 28 degrees.

2 Listen to your partner. Complete the table with information about the weather in Australia.

City	Weather
Perth	
Darwin	
Alice Springs	
Cairns	
Brisbane	
Sydney	

126

MEDIATION

5.3 Work together: Student A

1. Look at the picture. Describe it to your partner and answer his/her questions. He/She will draw it.

   On the right, there is a man sitting at a table.
   He's wearing ...

2. Listen to your partner and complete the picture. Ask questions to help you.

   I don't understand. Can you say that again?
   Does the woman have long hair? Is she sitting down?

8.3 Talk about a text: Student A

1. Read the text. Tell your partner the life story of this person, but <u>don't</u> say his name. Can your partner guess who it is?

   He was born on ... Then he ...

2. Listen to your partner telling you about the life of another famous person. Guess who it is.

Stan Lee

Stan Lee was born in New York on 28 December 1922. His parents came to the USA from Romania before he was born. His parents were poor, so when Lee finished high school in 1939, he started work at Timely Comics as an office assistant. After a couple of years, he became an editor and the company changed its name to Atlas Comics. In 1961, the company changed its name again – this time to Marvel Comics, and Lee created his first big comic series: The Fantastic Four. The following year, he created Spiderman and soon after, he created other famous characters like Iron Man, Thor and the Hulk. In the 1980s, he went to Hollywood to try to create

TV shows and films about his characters. After several successful cartoons, the first big movies were *X-Men* in 2000 and *Spiderman* in 2002. Lee had a small acting role in both of these films and in all the other films made from his comics. He became very famous and often went to comic conventions to talk to fans of his comics. He died on 12 November 2018.

MEDIATION

2.3 Talk about specific information: Student B

1   a Read the text about Person 1. Answer Student A's questions about her.

   b Ask Student A questions to find out about Person 2.
   What's his name?
   Could you repeat that, please?
   How do you spell that?

2   Do you think Person 1 and Person 2 would be friends? Why / Why not?

Person 1

Hello! I'm Giuliana Balducci. I live in Melbourne in Australia, but I'm Italian. I live in a big house with my mother, father and sister. I'm 19 years old and my sister Claudia is 15 years old. We have two cats. Their names are Max and Sam. They're really cute! I'm a university student and I study photography. In my free time, I like surfing and eating strawberry ice cream!

Person 2

Name	
Age	
Nationality	
Lives in	
Lives with	
Pets	
Studies	
Favourite food	

3.3 Write about specific information: Student B

1   You need to arrange a meeting with your partner in working hours (Monday–Friday 9 a.m. to 5 p.m.). Look at your calendar and write an email to him/her explaining when you are free and when you are busy.

Hi ....
Can we meet some time next month?
I'm free from Monday 1 May to Wednesday 3 May, but I'm on holiday for the rest of that week.

2   Read the email from your partner. Look at your calendar and the dates when your partner is free. When is the best day and time for the meeting?

May

Mon	Tue	Wed	Thu	Fri	Sat	Sun
1	2	3	4 Holiday	5 Holiday	6 Holiday	7 Holiday
8	9	10 Training course	11 Training course	12 Training course	13	14
15 Meeting (p.m)	16 Presentation (a.m.)	17 Doctor's appointment (a.m.)	18	19	20	21
22 Visit customer	23 Meeting (a.m.)	24 Meeting (a.m.)	25	26	27 My birthday!	28
29	30 Meeting (p.m.)	31				

6.3 Explain diagrams: Student B

1   Listen to your partner. Complete the table with information about the weather in Canada.

City	Weather
Vancouver	
Calgary	
Winnipeg	
Toronto	
Montreal	
Halifax	

2   Look at the picture. Explain to your partner what the weather is like in Australia.
In Brisbane it's raining and it's cold. It's 2 degrees.

128

MEDIATION

5.3 Work together: Student B

1. Listen to your partner and complete the picture. Ask questions to help you.

   I don't understand. Can you say that again?
   Does the woman have long hair? Is she sitting down?

2. Look at the picture. Describe it to your partner and answer his/her questions. He/She will draw it.

   On the right, there is a man sitting at a table.
   He's wearing ...

8.3 Talk about a text: Student B

1. Listen to your partner telling you about the life of a famous person. Guess who it is.

2. Read the text. Tell your partner the life story of this person, but <u>don't</u> say her name. Can your partner guess who it is?

   She was born on ... Then she ...

Elizabeth Bowes-Lyon
(The Queen Mother)

Elizabeth Bowes-Lyon was born in London on 4 August, 1900. She had nine brothers and sisters and her parents were very rich. She grew up at a castle in Scotland and had lessons at home. When she was 8 years old, she moved to London and started school there. When she was 23 years old, Prince Albert, the King's second son, asked her to marry him. At first, she said no, but he asked again and she said yes. They were married in Westminster Abbey in London on 26 April, 1923. Three years later, they had their first child, who they called Elizabeth, too. In 1936, the King died and Prince Albert's brother, Prince Edward, became king. However, after ten months he decided he did not want to be king, so Prince Albert became the new king – and changed his name to King George VI. Sadly, King George died in 1952 and Princess Elizabeth became queen when she was very young. Elizabeth attended events and worked to help her daughter for more than fifty years. She died on 30 March, 2002.

129

MEDIATION

4.3 Take notes: All students

1 🔊 **4.10** You work for a marketing company. Look at the picture. Then listen to a presentation by a customer and complete the notes.

Company name	
About the tents	
About the campsite	
People per tent	
Price per person per night	
Months open	
Website	

7.3 Simplify a text: Student B

1 You are planning a journey from London to Paris. Look at comments about two ways to travel and <mark>highlight</mark> the important information.

2 Tell your partner the important information about these two ways to travel. Listen to your partner tell you about two more ways to travel.

 The taxi costs …
 The journey takes …

3 In pairs, decide how you would like to travel.

Taxi and plane

I took a taxi to the airport in London. It cost £50 and it took about an hour. I flew with a budget airline, so it was quite cheap. It cost about £70 and the flight took one hour and fifteen minutes. However, I needed to be at the airport two hours before. When I arrived in France, I took another taxi from the airport to Paris city centre and that cost another £40. That journey took another hour. So it wasn't a very expensive journey, but it wasn't very quick.

Car

We wanted to drive to Paris because we have two small children and we have a lot of things to carry. We hired a car, which cost £250. There was a lot of traffic in London, so the start of our journey was really slow. It took about two hours. However, the Channel Tunnel was great. We drove our car onto the train at Folkestone and it only took 35 minutes to get to France and cost £100. Then we were in the car again for three and a half hours to get to Paris. We stopped for a break, so the whole journey took about seven hours in total.

11.3 Explain in your own words: Student B

1 Read the text. Write notes on the good things and bad things about robots.

Good things about robots	Bad things about robots

2 Close your book. Tell your partner everything you can remember about your text.

3 Open your book. Listen to your partner and make notes in the table about what he/she says. In pairs, compare your notes.

Robots and Health

Would you like to be treated by a robot doctor? Scientists are trying to make a robot doctor because there may not be enough doctors to help people in the future. One way robots can help is by doing operations. Robots are very careful and do not get tired, so they are good at operations. Robots are also very strong. Lifting and carrying people is difficult for doctors and nurses, but robots can do it easily. However, robots are not very friendly, so people don't like talking to robots. They want to talk to a doctor or a nurse. Also, robots are not very good at making decisions. They need a person to tell them what to do. So at the moment, robots are just helping doctors – but they will probably get better, so in the future your doctor will probably be a robot.

MEDIATION

9.3 Help a friend: All students

1. Your friend Antonio needs some help. He received an email, but he can't understand it. In pairs, look at the email and discuss what the highlighted words mean.

2. In pairs, write a reply to Antonio to explain what Alison's message means.

Fw: About the dinner party

Hi,
I need help! I can't understand this email. Can you explain what it says? I highlighted words I do not understand.
Thanks,
Antonio

Hi Antonio, how are you?
Thanks for inviting me and my family to dinner next week. It was incredibly kind of you, and we are really looking forward to trying some traditional Italian dishes! However, some of the people in my family have special diets, so I want to tell you about that before you buy any ingredients and start preparing the food! First of all, my sister Charlotte is vegetarian, so it would be great if you could provide something that she can eat. Also, my father tries not to eat dairy products. It's OK if he eats a tiny amount, but he prefers to avoid it if he can. However, my mother has a seafood allergy, so please don't serve any of that. Sorry about that!
Please tell me if this makes it too difficult to cook something. We can always bring some traditional Irish dishes for you to try. Have you ever had Colcannon (mashed potatoes and cabbage)? I can give you the recipe if you like.
Alison

10.3 Write about a text: All students

1. Read the information about the fan. In pairs, create a simple list of instructions for how to use it.

How to use the fan

- Put the fan on a flat surface.

Instructions
Congratulations on your purchase of a brand-new MBC Electrics fan.
We are sure that you will find it easy to use and great for cooling down on hot summer days. Here's how to get set up: First of all, place the fan on a flat surface and plug it in. Make sure there is nothing too close to the device because it may stop the fan from working. When you want to use it, press the big green button to turn it on. The green light shows that the power is on. You can also press the blue button if you want the fan to turn while you are using it. The clock button allows you to set the timer. Press it once to make the fan turn off after 15 minutes or press it twice to make the fan turn off after 30 minutes. You can press it up to six times. Alternatively, you can press the big green button again to turn the fan off. Enjoy your new fan!

12.3 Discuss concepts: All students

1. You have to choose the cover for a book. Read the information about the book. In pairs, look at the pictures and discuss which one you want to use and why.

   What do you think of this image? I like it because … / I don't like it because …

2. Tell another pair about your choice.

Fear
This new book explains the reasons that people feel fear. It also gives advice on how to stop feeling afraid of things.

a
b
c
d

GRAMMAR REFERENCE   UNIT 1

1.1 to be

We use the verb *to be* to say who people are and to give other information about them, e.g. *nationality*, *job*, *age*. We usually use contractions when we speak or use informal language.

	Full form	Contracted form	
+	I am You/We/They are He/She/It is	I'm You/We/They're He/She/It's	French.
–	I am not You/We/They are not He/She/It is not	I'm not You/We/They aren't He/She/It isn't	Mexican.
?	Am I Are you/we/they Is he/she/it		Spanish?
Y/N	Yes, I am. Yes, you/we/they are. Yes, he/she/it is.	No, I'm not. No, you/we/they aren't. No, he/she/it isn't.	

NOTE: we also see the contraction *'s* in, for example, *that's*, *where's*, *here's*:

That's my sister. (= That is my sister.)
Where's the cat? (= Where is the cat?)

▶ 1.1

1.2 Possessive adjectives and possessive *'s*

We can show what belongs to people or things using a possessive adjective before a noun:
It's my car.
The possessive adjective agrees with the person or thing that the object belongs to.

It's her car.   *It's his car.*   *It's their car.*

There is no plural form:
They're my bags. **NOT** *They're mys bags.*
We also use possessive adjectives when we talk about relationships:
Sacha is my brother.
Do you know his wife?

Subject pronoun	I	you	he	she	it	we	they
Possessive adjective	my	your	his	her	its	our	their

NOTE: *its* (without ') is a possessive adjective, but *it's* (with ') = *it is*
This restaurant is famous for its pizza.
It's a great restaurant. (= It is a great restaurant.)
We can also show what belongs to people by writing possessive *'s* after names and other nouns:
Katie's bag (= the bag belongs to Katie)
Dad's keys (= the keys belong to Dad)
We write ' (NOT *'s*) after plural nouns ending in *s*:
the students' flat, my parents' house
NOT *the students's flat, my parents's house*
BUT we use *'s* after irregular plural nouns not ending in *s*:
children's toys, men's clothes

▶ 1.2

1.1 a Write the contracted forms of the verbs in **bold** where possible.

> Hi. My name **is** Yukiko.
> I **am** Japanese. I **am not** from Tokyo. I **am** from Kyoto.
> This **is** Lee. He **is** a good friend. He **is not** Japanese.
> He **is** Korean. He **is** from Seoul. We **are** students at the same English school.
> We **are not** very good at English – but we like it!

b Complete the questions using the correct form of the verb *to be*.
1 Where .... Lee from?
2 .... Lee and Yukiko friends?
3 .... you Japanese?
4 Where .... you from?
5 .... you a student?

c Answer the questions in b. Use full sentences.

d Choose the correct option to complete the sentences.
1 This *is* / *are* a very interesting book.
2 A Are you from Barcelona?
  B No, I *aren't* / *'m not*.
3 Lee *Japanese isn't* / *isn't Japanese*, he's Korean.
4 *Are* / *Is* those your keys over there?
5 We *am* / *are* students in the same class.

1.2 a Choose the correct possessive adjective.

> This is me and these are ⁽¹⁾*my* / *our* friends.
> We play in the same football team. This is ⁽²⁾*your* / *our* coach. ⁽³⁾*Your* / *Her* name's Jenny.
> She's great! This is ⁽⁴⁾*his* / *her* boyfriend, Tom.
> And this is ⁽⁵⁾*your* / *their* house. It's very near the park where we play football.

b Complete the sentences by adding *'s* or *'*.
1 This is Freya....... phone, I think.
2 Is that your parents....... new car?
3 A Where are you?
  B I'm at Pablo....... party!
4 Annabel is my brother....... wife.
5 My friends....... house is lovely, but their garden is very small.
6 Those are too small for you, Pete, I think they're women....... boots!

2.1 Present simple (I, you, we, they)

We use the present simple to talk about facts – things that are generally true.
I work as a waiter.
Waiters don't earn much money.
Do you finish work at 11 p.m.?

+	I/You/We/They	live	in Oxford.
−	I/You/We/They	don't live	in Oxford.
?	Do I/you/we/they	live	in Oxford?
Y/N	Yes, I/you/we/they do.	No, I/you/we/they don't.	

▶ 2.1

2.2 Present simple (he, she, it)

+	He/She/It	comes	from Mexico.
−	He/She/It	doesn't come	from Mexico.
?	Does	he/she/it come	from Mexico?
Y/N	Yes, he/she/it does.	No, he/she/it doesn't.	

For most verbs we add -s to make the he/she/it form of the present simple:
Louise lives in Scotland.
When the verb ends in -ch, -ss, -sh, -x or -z, we add -es:
It washes clothes really well.
He watches TV in the evening.
When the verb ends in a consonant + -y, we change y to i and add -es.
She studies Spanish in Salamanca.
The verbs *have*, *go* and *do* are irregular.
He has three children.
She goes to work on the bus.
Lex does her homework in the library.

▶ 2.2

2.3 Question words

We use *who, what, which, where, when, why, how many* and *how old* to ask questions.

Who	a person	When	a time
What	a thing or idea	Why	a reason
Where	a place	How many	a number
Which + noun	a choice	How old	age

How can also be used with other adjectives and adverbs:
How difficult is the exam?
How often do you visit your parents?
When we use prepositions in questions, they usually go at the end:
Who does this coat belong to?
What do you want to talk about?

 2.3

UNIT 2 GRAMMAR REFERENCE

2.1 a Write questions beginning *Do you …?* with the verbs in the box.

eat	live	pay	speak	walk

1 .... in the centre of town?
2 .... to work or college?
3 .... meat?
4 .... the bills?
5 .... two languages?

b In pairs, ask and answer the questions.

c Complete the sentences with the verbs so they are true for you. Add *don't* to make them negative.

have (x2)	earn	live	play	work

1 We .... a computer at home.
2 I .... a lot of money.
3 I .... with my parents.
4 We .... a pet cat.
5 I .... in an office.
6 We .... tennis every day.

2.2 a Choose the correct option to complete the sentences.

1 *She does / Does she* share a flat with friends?
2 Matt and Sue's baby *cries / cry* all day.
3 At the weekend, I *go / goes* to the gym.
4 My job doesn't *helps / help* me speak English.
5 My brother *teach / teaches* Japanese.
6 *Does / Do* Jamie pay the bills?

b Complete the text with the present simple form of the verbs in brackets.

Karen is a teacher. She (1) .... (come) from Shanghai. She (2) .... (teach) Chinese at a night school in Vancouver. She (3) .... (not have) a typical routine because she (4) .... (study) in the morning and (5) .... (work) in the evening. She (6) .... (not like) life in Canada much because she (7) .... (miss) China.

2.3 Match the questions to the answers.

1 How old is Abbie? .... a Pippa and Marco.
2 Which cake do you want? .... b In the garage.
3 Why does she go to bed so early? .... c She's 11.
4 What do you want to drink? .... d £110.
5 How much is that phone? .... e Because she's tired.
6 When does he go to bed? .... f Chocolate cake, please.
7 Who do you play tennis with? .... g Just a glass of water.
8 Where's your car? .... h At 11 p.m.

133

GRAMMAR REFERENCE UNIT 3

3.1 Adverbs and expressions of frequency

We use adverbs of frequency to say how often we do things.
I almost always eat lunch at my desk.
She never goes to a café at lunchtime.

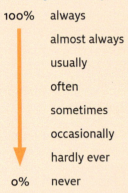

100% always
almost always
usually
often
sometimes
occasionally
hardly ever
0% never

Adverbs of frequency go before most verbs:
I usually work/I don't usually work on Saturdays.
But they come after the verb *to be*:
I'm usually/I'm not usually late for work.
We can also use expressions of frequency:
every + day / week / month / year.
once / twice / three times + a day / a week / a month / a year.
These expressions usually go at the end of a sentence:
I go shopping once a week.
They get up late every day.

▶ 3.1

3.2 Modifiers

We use modifiers to change the meaning of adjectives. They come before the adjectives:

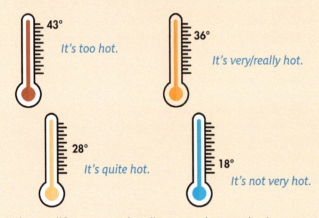

43° It's too hot.
36° It's very/really hot.
28° It's quite hot.
18° It's not very hot.

The modifiers *very* and *really* are used to emphasize an adjective (make it stronger):
That book is really interesting.
He has a very expensive car.
But if we use *not very*, this makes the adjective weaker:
I'm not very tired. (= I don't want to go to sleep at the moment.)
The modifier *too* can make an adjective negative:
My life is too busy. (= Sometimes I don't enjoy my life because I do a lot of things.)
The modifier *quite* can be used to make an adjective a little weaker than normal:
This film is quite good. (= The film isn't bad, but there are better films you can see.)

▶ 3.2

3.1 a Look at the information about Pedro's week. Complete the sentences with the adverbs of frequency in the box.

	Mon	Tue	Wed	Thur	Fri	Sat	Sun
start at 7 a.m.	✓	✓	✓	✓	✓	✓	
tennis				✓		✓	
restaurant							
social media	✓	✓	✓		✓	✓	
Mum and Dad							✓

almost always   never   often
once a week   sometimes

1 He ………………………… gets up early.
2 He ………………………… plays sport.
3 He ………………………… eats out.
4 He ………………………… chats with friends online.
5 He sees his parents ………………………… .

b Put the words in order to make sentences.

1 at / have / o'clock / usually / breakfast / I / eight
2 the / ever / go / to / hardly / cinema / I
3 I / occasionally / class / late / for / am
4 go / to / once / week / a / I / gym / the
5 bed / sometimes / very / I / to / late / go
6 I / read / before / I / to / sleep / always / go
7 a / cook / meal / evening / every / I

c Rewrite the sentences so they are true for you.

3.2 a Read the sentences. Underline the modifiers and the adjectives they change.

1 I'm sorry, I can't help right now, I'm really busy.
2 Don't try learning Japanese, it's too difficult.
3 That's a very interesting book. Why don't you read it?
4 We hardly ever go to the theatre because it's quite expensive.
5 I'm not very good at speaking English.

b Make the sentences true for you using modifiers.

1 I'm ………………………… tired right now.
2 It's ………………………… fun to speak English in class.
3 My mobile phone is ………………………… easy to use.
4 It's ………………………… cold today.
5 Our English teacher is ………………………… friendly.
6 Riding a bike in my town is ………………………… dangerous.

4.1 there is/are

We use *there is/are* to say that something exists. We use *there is* when we are talking about one thing:

+	There's a big sofa.
-	There's isn't a kitchen.
?	Is there a shower?
Y/N	Yes, there is./No, there isn't.

We use *there are* when we are talking about more than one thing:

+	There are some tables and chairs.
-	There aren't any pillows.
?	Are there any cushions?
Y/N	Yes, there are./No, there aren't.

NOTE: *there's* = *there is*. BUT we don't use this contraction when we give the short answer 'Yes':
A: *Is there a shower?*
B: *Yes, there is.* NOT *Yes, there's.*
We often use *a/an* with *There is/isn't …* and *Is there …?*
There isn't a computer. Is there an armchair?
We often use *some* with *There are …*
There are some blankets.
We use *any* with *There aren't …* and *Are there …?*
There aren't any chairs. Are there any mirrors?
If two nouns are joined by *and*, and the first noun is singular, we use *There's …*
There's a table and four chairs in the dining room. ▶ 4.1

4.2 Prepositions of place

We use prepositions of place before a noun to show where a thing or person is:
The bed is next to the window.
There's a pillow on the bed.

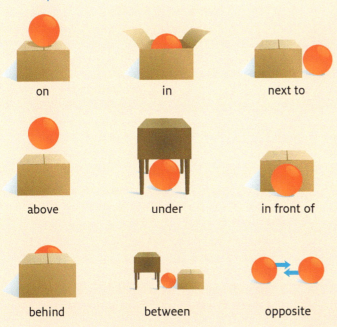

on · in · next to
above · under · in front of
behind · between · opposite

▶ 4.2

UNIT 4 GRAMMAR REFERENCE

4.1 a Look at the map of a beach resort. Correct the statements about it.

1 There are four car parks.
2 There isn't a swimming pool.
3 There are two banks.
4 There's a supermarket and two cinemas.
5 There's an art gallery.
6 There are a lot of hotels.

b Rewrite the sentences with *some*, *any* or *a/an* where necessary.

1 There isn't airport.
2 There are beaches.
3 There's train station.
4 There aren't bars.

c Look at the map again and write two new sentences with *there is/are …*

4.2 a Look around your classroom and answer the questions.

1 What's **on** the table?
2 Who or what's **in front of** you?
3 Who or what's **next to** you?
4 What's **above** your head?
5 Who or what's **behind** you?
6 What's **in** your pockets now?

b Look at the map in 4.1 again and choose the correct option, a or b.

1 a There's a bank next to the cinema.
   b There's a bank opposite the cinema.
2 a There's a beach behind the train station.
   b There's a beach in front of the train station.
3 a There are cars under the car parks.
   b There are cars in the car parks.
4 a There's a restaurant between the supermarket and the bank.
   b There's a restaurant opposite the supermarket.

c Write five more sentences about the map using the prepositions in the box.

| behind | between | in front of |
| opposite | next to | |

135

GRAMMAR REFERENCE UNIT 5

5.1 can/can't

We use *can/can't* + infinitive to talk about ...
1 ability: *I can ski. (= I know how to ski.)*
2 permission: *You can't talk in here.*
3 a general possibility: *Where can I buy a drink?*

+	I/You/He/She/It/We/They	can	swim.
–	I/You/He/She/It/We/They	can't	swim.
?	Can	I/you/he/she/it/we/they	swim?
Y/N	Yes, I/you/he/she/it/we/they can.	No, I/you/he/she/it/we/they can't.	

We use *can/can't* with the infinitive without *to*:
I can sing. NOT *I can to sing.*
We don't add *-s* for the third person singular:
He can sing. NOT *He cans sing.*

▶ 5.1

5.2 Present continuous

We use the present continuous to say what is happening **now**.

+	I'm You're/We're/They're He's/She's/It's	listening.
–	I'm not You/We/They aren't He/She/It isn't	listening.
?	Am I Are you/we/they Is he/she/it	listening?
Y/N	Yes, I am. Yes, you/we/they are. Yes, he/she/it is.	No, I'm not. No, you/we/they aren't. No, he/she/it isn't.

1 When a verb ends in *-e*, remove the *-e* and add *-ing*:
   dance → dancing
2 When a verb ends in consonant + vowel + consonant, double the final consonant and add *-ing*:
   shop → shopping
3 When a verb ends in *-ie*, change *-ie* to *-y* and add *-ing*:
   lie → lying

▶ 5.2

5.3 Present simple and continuous

We use the present simple to talk about:
1 things that are generally true: *I study Medicine.*
2 things that happen regularly: *He plays football on Fridays.*
We use the present continuous for actions happening now:
I'm studying for my final exams right now.
We don't use state verbs (*like, love, want, need*, etc.) in the present continuous:
I like your new dress. NOT *I'm liking your new dress.*
We use adverbs and expressions of frequency (e.g. *sometimes, never, once a week*) with the present simple:
I go on holiday twice a year. I never travel abroad.
We use time expressions like *at the moment, today* and *(right) now* with the present continuous:
I'm lying on a beach at the moment.

▶ 5.3

5.1 a Complete the sentences with *I*, or the name of someone you know, so that they are true.

1 .... can play a musical instrument.
2 .... can't ski.
3 .... can only speak one language.
4 .... can play lots of different sports.
5 .... can't swim.
6 .... can't ride a bike.

b Write sentences or questions with *can/can't* using the words.

1 Where / I / buy / a sandwich (?)
   Where can I buy a sandwich?
2 you / buy / them / online (✗)
3 they / pay / by card (✓)
4 he / get / a discount (?)
5 Where / we / find / the best price (?)

c Look at the airport signs. Use the words in the box to write what they mean.

| bus | car | ~~information~~ |
| liquids | luggage | mobile |

6 = You can ask for information here.

5.2 Complete the text with the present continuous form of the words in brackets.

The boss isn't here, so I can talk. We
(1) .... (not work) at the moment ... Craig (2) .... (read) a book, Petra (3) .... (write) an email to a friend, Guido and Antonio (4) .... (sit) outside and Laura (5) .... (listen) to music. Rhona (6) .... (not feel) well, so she (7) .... (lie) on the grass outside too! What (8) .... (you/do), Mary? (9) .... (you/study) now?

5.3 a Choose the correct tense to complete the questions.

1 What *are you doing / do you do* at the moment?
2 What *are you usually wearing / do you usually wear* for work/college?
3 *Are you studying / Do you study* anything right now?
4 *Are you having / Do you have* a good day today?
5 *Are you always doing / Do you always do* your English grammar exercises?

b Write answers to the questions.

6.1 *like, love, hate* + noun/*-ing* form

love	😍	don't like	😣
like	🙂	can't stand	😖
don't mind	😐	hate	😡

We use the *-ing* form of verbs after *like*, *love* and *hate*:
I love walking along the beach.
Do you like studying English?
She hates working on Sundays.
We can also use nouns after *like*, *love* and *hate*:
I love trips to the beach.
Do you like your course?
We hate bad weather.
The expressions *can't stand* and *don't/doesn't mind* are also followed by a noun or *-ing* form:
I can't stand going to the beach.
He doesn't mind the hot weather.
I don't mind getting up early.

▶ 6.1

6.2 Object pronouns

We can use personal pronouns instead of the names of people and things.
Subject pronouns tell us who, or what, the subject of the verb is. They usually come before the verb:
*Layla is kind. **She** helps other people every day.*
*My parents are teachers. **They** work at the same school.*
Object pronouns tell us who, or what, the object of the verb is. They come …
1 after the verb:
   *My grandmother lives near me. I visit **her** every day.*
2 after prepositions:
   *Julio is my boss, but I often work with **him**.*

| Subject pronoun | I | you | he | she | it | we | they |
| Object pronoun | me | you | him | her | it | us | them |

With some verbs, e.g. *give*, *tell*, we can use more than one object pronoun:
*What can you tell **us** about **it**?*
*I am giving **them** to **you**.*

▶ 6.2

UNIT 6 GRAMMAR REFERENCE

6.1 a Write sentences and questions in the present simple using the prompts.
1 Karl / can't stand / get up / early
2 she / love / play / tennis
3 you / like / Japanese food?
4 I / hate / clean / the flat
5 we / not mind / help / you
6 Mia / not like / her new job

b Write sentences that are true for you with *like*, *love*, *hate*, etc., using the words in the box and your own ideas.
I love making cakes.

| cold weather | do exercise | go to the beach |
| make cakes | my home town | watch TV |

6.2 a Choose the correct options to complete the sentences.
1 I can't find my keys. Can you help *me / I* look for *they / them*?
2 That's Phoebe. *She's / Her's* Antonia's younger sister. I really like *she / her*.
3 I don't buy newspapers anymore because *me / I* never read *them / it*.
4 Josef usually drives *we / us* to work and then *us / we* get the bus home.
5 Here's a letter for my brother. Would you give *it / I* to *him / her*?

b Complete the sentences with subject or object pronouns.

1 This is Annie Leibovitz.
   I like .... a lot. ....'s a great photographer.

2 This is my watch.
   ....'s an old Rolex but ....'s broken.
   I hope they can fix .... for ....

3 This is our son's bike.
   .... rides .... most days but it's too small.
   We're buying .... a new one and giving .... to .... on his birthday.

GRAMMAR REFERENCE UNIT 7

7.1 Past simple of *be, there was/were*

We use the past simple form of the verb *to be* to describe people or things in the past:
The hotel was very big.

+	I/He/She/It was You/We/They were	quiet.
−	I/He/She/It wasn't You/We/They weren't	quiet.
?	Was I/he/she/it Were you/we/they	quiet?
Y/N	Yes, I/he/she/it was. Yes, you/we/they were.	No, I/he/she/it wasn't. No, you/we/they weren't.

We use *there was/were* to say something existed in the past:
There was a swimming pool.   *There were lots of rooms.*

+	There was There were	a swimming pool. some shops.
−	There wasn't There weren't	a swimming pool. any shops.
?	Was there Were there	a swimming pool? any shops?
Y/N	Yes, there was. Yes, there were.	No, there wasn't. No, there weren't.

▶ 7.1

7.2 Past simple regular verbs

We use the past simple to talk about actions that happened at a particular time in the past:
I visited my grandparents a few days ago.

+	I/You/We/They/He/She/It	stayed		in Paris.
−	I/You/We/They/He/She/It	didn't	stay	in Paris.
?	Did	I/you/we/they/he/she/it	stay	in Paris?
Y/N	Yes, I/you/we/they/he/she/it did.		No, I/you/we/they/he/she/it didn't.	

We form the past simple of most regular verbs by adding *-ed* to the base form of the verb:
play → played, wait → waited
When a verb ends in *-e*, we add *-d*:
dance → danced, love → loved
When a verb ends in consonant–vowel–consonant, we double the final consonant and add *-ed*:
stop → stopped, plan → planned
When a verb ends in consonant + *y*, we remove *-y* and add *-ied*:
try → tried, study → studied
The verbs *go*, *do* and *have* are irregular and don't end in *-ed*:
go → went   We went skiing in the Alps.
do → did   We did a lot of practice.
have → had   We had some extra lessons.

▶ 7.2

7.1 a Choose the correct form of the verb. Then decide if the sentences are true (T) or false (F).
1. There *was* / *were* a wall between East Berlin and West Berlin before 1989.   T / F
2. Tokyo, Vienna and Sydney *was* / *were* all Olympic cities.   T / F
3. Rio de Janeiro *was* / *were* once the capital of Brazil.   T / F
4. The Vikings *wasn't* / *weren't* from Scandinavia.   T / F
5. Moscow *wasn't* / *weren't* the capital of Russia in 1900.   T / F

b Put the words in order to make questions. Then answer the questions.
1. born / you / were / where ?
2. a / was / town / your / there / in / park ?
3. name / the / what / of / your / primary / school / was ?
4. there / computers / primary / in / any / your / were / school ?
5. you / at / home / night / last / were ?

7.2 a Complete the text with the past simple form of the verbs in brackets.

My friend Carlos and I (1) _____ (go) on a trip to Edinburgh last weekend. We (2) _____ (book) our train tickets online – they (3) _____ (be) really cheap! We (4) _____ (stay) in a small hotel in Princes Street. When we (5) _____ (arrive), we (6) _____ (have) a coffee and then (7) _____ (go) sightseeing – the castle was awesome! In the evening, we (8) _____ (decide) to rest in the hotel – Carlos was tired so we (9) _____ (not watch) TV. The next day, we (10) _____ (do) some shopping and in the afternoon, we (11) _____ (visit) an art gallery. There (12) _____ (be) some wonderful pictures there. At about six o'clock we (13) _____ (return) to the station – we (14) _____ (not want) to leave!

b Write four sentences about what you did yesterday. Choose from the verbs in the box.

| chat | finish | go | have | play | try |

1. ....
2. ....
3. ....
4. ....

138

UNIT 8 GRAMMAR REFERENCE

8.1 Past simple irregular verbs

Some verbs have irregular past simple forms and don't end in -ed.

buy → bought,   feel → felt,   see → saw,   write → wrote

+	I/You/We/They/He/She/It	ate	a lot of food.
−	I/You/We/They/He/She/It	didn't eat	a lot of food.
?	Did	I/you/we/they/he/she/it	eat	a lot of food?
Y/N	Yes, I/you/we/they/he/she/it did.	No, I/you/we/they/he/she/it didn't.

See page 168 for a list of common irregular verbs

Question and negative forms follow the same rule as regular verbs – did/didn't followed by the verb in the infinitive form:

Did she write an email? NOT *Did she wrote an email?*
They didn't write to me. NOT *They didn't wrote to me.* ▶ 8.1

8.2 Verb + to + infinitive

Some verbs are always followed by to + infinitive:

decide: We **decided to go** to the festival.
hope: She's **hoping to study** music next year.
learn: I'm **learning to play** the piano.
need: We **don't need to pay** for the tickets.
plan: They're **planning to buy** a new house.
prefer: Do you **prefer to read** the news online?
want: He **doesn't want to come** to the concert.
would like: I'd **like to see** that painting. ▶ 8.2

8.3 Sequencers

We use sequencers to show the order of events and actions in a story. They often come at the beginning of a sentence, followed by a comma.

first or *at first*: introduces the initial event or action in a series:
At first, I felt happy.

then: introduces the events or actions that follow:
Then, there was some difficult news.

after that: introduces an event or action in relation to something that happened before it:
After that, everything went wrong.

after + time or time + *later*: show that an event or action happened some time after the others:
After a while/A year later, things began to improve.

finally: to talk about the end of the story:
Finally, we were together again.

in the end: to talk about the result of a problem or to give unexpected news:
I wanted to stay but in the end, I didn't. ▶ 8.3

8.1 a Complete the sentences with one negative and one positive past simple form of the verb in brackets.

1 Agatha Christie ____*didn't write*____ romances, she ____*wrote*____ crime novels. (write)
2 Hadrian _____ 'Veni, vidi, vici,' Caesar _____ it. (say)
3 We _____ products online in the past, we _____ them in shops. (buy)
4 People _____ emails in the past, they _____ letters. (send)
5 People _____ e-books in the past, they _____ paper books. (read)
6 People _____ a partner online in the past, they _____ in person. (meet)

b Complete the conversations with the past simple form of the verbs in brackets.

1 A _____ (you / see) Jo yesterday?
   B Yes, we _____ (have) lunch.
2 A _____ (they / go) to the party?
   B No, they _____ (know) about it.
3 A I _____ (speak) to Alice yesterday.
   B Really? What _____ (she / say) ?

8.2 a Order the words to make sentences. Are they true for you?

When I was a child …
1 hoped / famous / I / be / to / one day
2 make / a lot of money / planned / to / I

Now that I'm older …
3 happy / want / I / have / life / to / a
4 better / like / a / be / I'd / to / person

b Complete the sentences so they are true for you.

1 I'm planning _____
2 I don't want _____
3 I prefer _____

8.3 Complete the story using the words in the box.

| after that | at first | in the end | later | then |

I always wanted a large house and lots of money, so I got a job in a bank. I fell in love with my manager and we got married. (1) _____, we were very happy. (2) _____, my husband lost his job. (3) _____, we lost the car and all our savings, and two years (4) _____, we lost the house. But we still had each other. (5) _____, I understood that money isn't everything!

139

GRAMMAR REFERENCE UNIT 9

9.1 Countable and uncountable nouns

Countable nouns are nouns that you can count. They can be singular or plural:

This is an orange.   There are three oranges in the fridge.

We can use *some* with plural countable nouns:

There are some oranges in the fridge.

Uncountable nouns are nouns that you can't count. They are always singular and take a singular verb form:

The bread is on the table.   This coffee is very hot.

We can't use *a/an* or numbers with uncountable nouns, but we can use *some*:

I have some butter. NOT *I have a butter.*

We use *any* in questions and negatives with plural countable nouns and uncountable nouns:

I don't want any nuts.   There isn't any meat.   Is there any milk?

	uncountable	countable (singular)	countable (plural)
+	I'd like **some** cheese.	I'd like **an** egg.	I'd like **some** grapes.
−	I don't want **any** meat.	I don't want **a** banana.	I don't want **any** carrots.
?	Do you have **any** milk?	Do you have **a** tomato?	Do you have **any** olives?

▶ 9.1

9.2 Quantifiers

We use *How much/many ...?* to ask about quantity. *How much ...?* is for uncountable nouns, *How many ...?* is for countable nouns.

How much meat do you eat?   How many eggs do you have?

We use *a lot of* for large quantities of countable and uncountable nouns. We use *a little* (uncountable nouns) and *a few* (countable nouns) for a small quantity.

I have a lot of bowls and a lot of soup.
I have a little sugar in my tea, and a few biscuits!

We use *too much/too many* for quantities that are more than you need or want:

I have too much pasta.   He eats too many sweets.

uncountable	countable
How **much** tea do you drink?	How **many** eggs do you eat?
I drink **a lot of** coffee.	I eat **a lot of** vegetables.
She only wants **a little** milk.	We have **a few** apples.
We eat **too much** meat.	Don't eat **too many** biscuits!

▶ 9.2

9.3 should

We use *should/shouldn't* + infinitive (without *to*) to give advice or a recommendation:

You should see that film. It's great.
He shouldn't drink too much coffee.

To ask for advice or a recommendation, we use *should* + the subject of the sentence:

Should I eat less meat, Doctor Ali?
Which trainers should I buy, the red ones or the black ones?

▶ 9.3

9.1 Match the pictures to the sentences. Then choose the correct word to complete the sentences.

1 You need to add *a / some* water.   ....
2 Do we have *any / an* onions?   ....
3 Molly doesn't want *an / any* rice.   ....
4 Would you like *a / an* apple?   ....
5 There *'s / are* some delicious coffee in the cupboard.   ....
6 Can I have *a / a piece of* bread, please?   ....

9.2 Choose the correct options to complete the text.

(1)*How many/How much* salt and sugar do I eat? I don't use (2)*much/many* salt. But the problem is that I love sweet things. I know that I eat (3)*too many/too much* biscuits! I really like fruit though, so I eat (4)*a little/a lot of* apples, and I try to eat (5)*a few/a little* fresh vegetables every day. At the weekend, I often cook some pasta with (6)*a little/a lot* meat or fish.

9.3 Match the advice with the problems and complete the advice with *should* or *shouldn't*.

1 Janice feels cold.   ....   a They .... try that new restaurant.
2 I'm really tired today.   ....   b You .... ask for help.
3 They'd like a nice meal.   ....   c She .... wear a sweater.
4 He wants to save money.   ....   d You .... go to bed so late.
5 I don't understand this.   ....   e He .... buy so many clothes.

140

UNIT 10 GRAMMAR REFERENCE

10.1 Comparatives

We use comparatives to compare two things and talk about the difference between them. We use *than* after comparative adjectives.

This laptop is faster than my old computer.

The comparative depends on how long the adjective is. We usually add *-er* to short adjectives:

old → older, fast → faster

But we add *-r* to short adjectives ending in *-e*:

safe → safer, large → larger

We double the final consonant and add *-er* to short adjectives ending in consonant + vowel + consonant:

hot → hotter, thin → thinner

With short adjectives ending in *-y*, we remove the *-y* and add *-ier*:

busy → busier, happy → happier

We use *more* before longer adjectives. The adjective doesn't change:

beautiful → more beautiful, difficult → more difficult

Some adjectives are irregular in the comparative form:

good → better, bad → worse

▶ 10.1

10.2 *going to*

We use *be + going to +* infinitive to talk about future plans:

I'm going to buy a new phone next month.

+	I'm You're/We're/They're He's/She's/It's	going to	fix the car.
−	I'm not You/We/They aren't He/She/It isn't	going to	fix the car.
?	Am I Are you/we/they Is he/she/it	going to	fix the car?
Y/N	Yes, I am. Yes, you/we/they are. Yes, he/she/it is.	No, I'm not. No, you/we/they aren't. No, he/she/it isn't.	

▶ 10.2

10.1 a Write the comparative form of the adjective in brackets.
1 Shopping online is _____ (cheap) than going to the supermarket.
2 Coffee is _____ (nice) than tea.
3 English is _____ (easy) than Chinese.
4 Snow is _____ (bad) than rain.
5 A desktop computer is _____ (good) than a laptop.
6 Trains are _____ (comfortable) than planes.

b Do you agree with the sentences? If not, change them so they are true for you.

c Look at the pictures. Write sentences to compare the classic car with the sports car. Use the adjectives in the box.

| big | expensive | heavy | new | slow |

CLASSIC £30,000   SPORTS £49,995

10.2 a Put the words in the correct order to make questions with *going to*.
1 what / you / to / going / do / are / tomorrow ?
2 going / you / are / to / when / study ?
3 what / you / to / are / going / study ?
4 see / your / when / going / to / are / you / friends ?
5 you / watch / going / tonight / are / to / TV ?
6 are / what / you / to / going / watch ?

b Write true answers to the questions. You can use positive and negative sentences.

No, I'm not going to watch TV tonight. I'm going to play tennis.

c Complete the sentences with the correct form of *going to/not going to* and the verbs in the box.

| come | do | eat | send | wash | wear |

1 These trousers are dirty. I _____ them.
2 It's very hot outside. I _____ a coat.
3 Kit doesn't know you're here, so we _____ her a message.
4 I'm really hungry. I _____ this cake.
5 Paul's ill. He _____ to the cinema.
6 What _____ Ciara _____ after she finishes college?

141

GRAMMAR REFERENCE UNIT 11

11.1 (don't) have to

We use *have to* + infinitive to say that it is necessary or important to do something:
Pippa has to wear a uniform.
We use *don't have to* + infinitive to say that it is not necessary to do something:
I'm not working today. I don't have to get up early!

+	I/You/We/They He/She/It	have to has to	get up.
−	I/You/We/They He/She/It	don't have to doesn't have to	get up.
?	Do I/you/we/they Does he/she/it	have to	get up?
Y/N	Yes, I/you/we/they do. Yes, he/she/it does.	No, I/you/we/they don't. No, he/she/it doesn't.	

▶ 11.1

11.2 Superlatives

We use superlative adjectives to compare a thing or person with all the other things or people in that group:
Hairdressers are the happiest profession in the list.
(= Hairdressers are happier than all the other professions.)
We often use *the* or possessive adjectives (*my, your, his*) with superlative adjectives:
It's the nicest job.   She's my oldest friend.
We usually add *-est* to short adjectives:
tall → tallest, cheap → cheapest
But we add *-st* to short adjectives ending in *-e*:
safe → safest, nice → nicest
We double the final consonant and add *-est* to short adjectives ending in consonant + vowel + consonant:
big → biggest, fat → fattest
With short adjectives ending in *-y*, we remove *-y* and add *-iest*:
heavy → heaviest, busy → busiest
We use *most* before longer adjectives:
difficult → most difficult, comfortable → most comfortable
Some adjectives are irregular in the superlative form:
good → best, bad → worst

▶ 11.2

11.3 will for predictions

We use *will/won't* + infinitive to talk about predictions:
It will rain tomorrow.   I won't fail my exam next week.

+	I/You/We/They/He/She/It	will/'ll	change.
−	I/You/We/They/He/She/It	won't	change.
?	Will	I/you/we/they/ he/she/it	change?
Y/N	Yes, I/you/we/they/he/she/ it will.	No, I/you/we/they/he/ she/it won't.	

We use *definitely/probably* after *will* and before *won't* to say how sure we are about a prediction:
Robots definitely won't do some jobs.
Robots will probably take some of our jobs.
Alice will definitely come. NOT ~~Alice definitely will come.~~
I probably won't come. NOT ~~I won't probably come.~~

▶ 11.3

11.1 Complete the conversation with the correct form of *(don't) have to* and the verbs in brackets.

A My sister Elena has a new job at Café Luxe.
B I love that place, the waiters look so smart – (1) _____ she _____ (wear) the uniform?
A Yes, she does, and she (2) _____ (speak) English because there are so many tourists.
B (3) _____ she _____ (work) at weekends?
A She (4) _____ (work) on Sundays, but she works every Saturday.
B That's too bad.
A She doesn't mind. And she (5) _____ (pay) for any drinks or food – they're free for people who work there.
B That sounds much better than my job. I (6) _____ (sit) at a desk all day and I hardly speak to anyone!

11.2 a Complete the questions with the superlative form of the adjective in brackets.

1 What's the _____ thing about learning English? (easy)
2 What's the _____ thing about learning English? (difficult)
3 What's the _____ café you know? (good)
4 What's the _____ city you know? (interesting)
5 What's the _____ thing about travelling? (bad)
6 What's your _____ electronic device? (new)

b Answer the questions and explain your answers.

The easiest thing about learning English is the grammar. The grammar in my language is more difficult!

11.3 a Put the words in the correct order to make sentences with *will/won't*.

1 robots / replace / teachers / will / by 2030 / probably
2 won't / it / probably / snow / at Christmas
3 I / visit / another country / next year / will
4 will / I / definitely / pass / next exam / my
5 my / see / won't / parents / I / this weekend

b Do you agree with the sentences in a? If not, change them so they are true for you.

142

12.1 Present perfect

We use the present perfect to talk about experiences in our lives. We form the present perfect with *have/has* + a past participle of the main verb:
I have visited the Great Wall of China.
The past participle of regular verbs is the same as the past simple of the verb:
visit → visited
Some past participles are irregular:
see → seen, take → taken, win → won

+	I/You/We/They He/She/It	've/have 's/has	made	a cake.
−	I/You/We/They He/She/It	haven't hasn't	made	a cake.
?	Have Has	I/you/we/they he/she/it	made	a cake?
Y/N	Yes, I/you/we/ they have. Yes, he/she/it has.	No, I/you/we/they haven't. No, he/she/it hasn't.		

We often use *ever* with questions to ask about experiences in our lives.
Have you ever eaten Japanese food?
We often use *never* to say we haven't had experiences.
I've never eaten Moroccan food.
NOTE: the verb *go* has two past participles, *been* and *gone*:
He's been to Lima. (= He went and came back.)
He's gone to Lima. (= He went and he's still there.)

▶ 12.1

12.2 Present perfect and past simple

We use the present perfect when we don't give a specific time in the past:
I've been to Rome. (= at some time in the past, I'm not saying when)
We use the past simple if we say when something happened:
I went to Zurich a few years ago.
We use the present perfect to ask an initial question about past experiences:
What's the most interesting place you've ever visited?
We use the past simple to ask for or give more information:
A: When did you go to Bangkok?
B: I went with my brother in 2016.

▶ 12.2

12.3 Tense review

The present simple describes things we do regularly:
I go to English class twice a week.
The present continuous describes what we are doing now:
I'm walking to English class.
The past simple describes what happened at a specific time in the past:
I didn't go to English class last week.
The present perfect describes past experiences:
Have you ever studied English?
We use *will* for what we know or think about the future:
English will probably be easier than Japanese.
We use *going to* for future plans:
I'm going to speak English in Australia next year.

▶ 12.3

UNIT 12 GRAMMAR REFERENCE

12.1 a Put the letters in order to make irregular past participles. Then write the infinitive form of the verb.

1 neeb   *been*   *be*
2 konpes   ....
3 tenrwit   ....
4 nlwof   ....
5 nteea   ....
6 tugaht   ....

b Put the words in order to make questions.

1 you / Have / Thai / eaten / ever / food ?
2 father / Has / a letter / ever / your / written / to you ?
3 you / flown / Atlantic / the / Have / across / ever ?
4 spoken / Has / your / ever / mother / English ?
5 taught / you / ever / Have / something ?
6 of / been / your / family / a member / to / ever / Australia / Has ?

c In pairs, ask and answer the questions in b. Use short answers.

12.2 a Choose the correct options to complete the conversation.

A Have you ever (1)*play / played* any unusual sports?
B Yes, I (2)*have / played*. I (3)*tried / have tried* a sport called Jorkyball when I was on holiday. I (4)*have liked / liked* it. It (5)*was / has been* fun.
A And (6)*did / have* you ever met a famous person?
B No, I (7)*'ve never met / never met* anyone famous – what about you?
A Yes, I (8)*met / meet* Barack Obama in 2016.
B Really? That's amazing! What (9)*was / were* he like?
A Very friendly. But I only (10)*have talked / talked* to him for a few seconds.

b In pairs, ask and answer two more *Have you ever ...?* questions. Use the questions in 12.2a or your own ideas. Tell your partner about your experiences.

12.3 Look at the pictures. Write two or three sentences for each to talk about the past, the present and the future. Make the sentences true for you.

I had a dog when I was young, but I don't have one now. I'm not going to get a dog because my flat is very small.

143

WRITING BANK   UNIT 1

Filling in forms

1 Look at the pictures and forms a and b. In pairs, answer the questions.
   1 Where are the forms from?
   2 Which person is filling in which form?
   3 Do you ever fill in forms in English?

2 Look at the instructions. Did Ana follow the instructions correctly in answer A or answer B?

> ❶ **Tick the correct box.**
> A male ☐ female ✓
> B male ☐ female ⊙
>
> ❷ **Please use BLOCK CAPITALS.**
> A *Ana Pérez Rodríguez*
> B ANA PÉREZ RODRÍGUEZ
>
> ❸ **Delete as applicable.**
> A single / ~~married~~
> B <u>single</u> / married
>
> ❹ **Date of birth (DD/MM/YYYY)**
> A Jan / 18 / 1995
> B 18 / 01 / 1995

3 Read the Writing box. Then complete forms a and b with your details.

> ✎ **filling in forms**
>
> Always read the instructions carefully before you complete a form.
> - There are different names for the same information:
>   *Family name = Surname, Sex = Gender*
> - Forms often use abbreviations:
>   *Mr* = man, *Mrs* = married woman, *Ms* = woman
>   *M* = male, *F* = female, *No* = number, *Tel* = telephone

a

RH   Regency Hotel   ☰

Date check in	18 ▼	Jan ▼
Date check out	24 ▼	Jan ▼
No of people	2 ▼ adults	0 ▼ children
Title	Mr / Mrs / Ms ▼	

First name _____
Surname _____
Email _____
Passport / ID No _____
Tel No _____
Time of arrival _____

b

LANDING CARD

Please complete clearly in English and in BLOCK CAPITALS, using a black pen.

Family name _____
First name(s) _____
Sex (tick the correct box)   M ☐   F ☐
Marital status (delete as applicable) single/married
Date of birth (DD/MM/YYYY) __ __ / __ __ / __ __ __ __
Town and country of birth _____
Nationality _____
Occupation _____
Passport No _____
Signature _____

144

UNIT 2 WRITING BANK

A personal profile

1 In pairs, discuss the questions.
   1 Which social media sites do you use?
   2 Do you have a profile page?
   3 What's your photo like?
   4 What information do you include?

2 a Look at the pictures on Florian's social media profile. In pairs, guess the answers to the questions.
   1 Where is he from?
   2 Where does he live?
   3 What is his job?
   4 What activities does he do?

   b Read Florian's profile and check.

3 Tick (✓) the things Florian writes about in his profile.
   1 his age
   2 his job
   3 his education
   4 his family
   5 his religion
   6 his hometown
   7 his hobbies
   8 his pets

4 Complete the sentences with *and* or *but*. Check your answers in the text.
   1 My name's Florian _____ I'm a doctor.
   2 I love my job _____ it's difficult at times.
   3 I'm from Galicia in the north of Spain _____ my girlfriend is Moroccan.
   4 We don't have any children, _____ we have a pet cat called Coco.

5 Read the Writing box. Then write a personal profile about you.

   ✎ **a personal profile**

   When you write a personal profile, give information about yourself.

   - You can include information that you think is important, e.g. your job, where you're from, where you live, your family and hobbies.
   - Try to connect ideas using linkers *and* and *but* to add and contrast information:

   I'm a teacher and I work in a primary school.
   I'm from Brazil, but I live in the USA.

Florian Alonso

Timeline | About | Friends | More ▼

- Work
- Education
- Contact
- Family
- 12 Jan, 1990
- in a relationship

Hi, my name's Florian and I'm a doctor at University College hospital in London. I work in the emergency department. I love my job, but it's difficult at times. I live with my girlfriend in a flat in Brixton. We don't have any children, but we have a pet cat called Coco. I'm from Galicia in the north of Spain and my girlfriend is Moroccan. My hobbies are running, fishing and collecting records.

WRITING BANK — UNIT 3

A blog post

1. Look at the picture and the title of the blog post. What activities do you think the writer does on Sunday? Read the text and check.

2. In pairs, discuss the questions.
   1. Is your typical Sunday similar to Sara's? Why/Why not?
   2. What's your favourite day of the week? Why?
   3. What do you do if you have a 'lazy' day?

3. Match the ideas with the paragraphs.
   Paragraph 1 ....   a Bedtime
   Paragraph 2 ....   b Introduction
   Paragraph 3 ....   c The afternoon
   Paragraph 4 ....   d After I wake up
   Paragraph 5 ....   e Breakfast

4. Complete the sentences from the text with *so* or *because*. Check your answers in the text.
   1. On Saturday I go shopping and do the housework, ... **on Sunday I like to be lazy!**
   2. I don't have time for a long breakfast during the week .... **I start work really early.**

5. Look at the phrases in bold after *so* and *because* in exercise 4. Which one is a *reason* to do something and which is the *result* of a situation?

6. Read the Writing box. Write a blog post called 'My typical day'.

✏️ **a blog post**

When you write a blog post, write informally about your personal experiences.

- Start with a short introduction saying what the blog post is about. Then write a paragraph about each of your ideas.
- Try to give information about why you do things. Use:
  so to explain the result: *I'm tired, so I stay in bed.*
  because to give a reason: *I stay in bed because I'm tired.*

LAZY SUNDAYS

Posted by Sara Andersen   22 July 2020

I love Sundays. I'm really busy all week and on Saturday I go shopping and do the housework, so on Sunday I like to be lazy!

I usually wake up around 9 a.m., but I don't get up. I read a book or I sometimes listen to the radio in bed. I always make a cup of tea and take it easy. I like to wake up slowly on Sunday!

Then I make breakfast: coffee, fruit and toast. I sometimes have an egg for breakfast, or I occasionally make pancakes! I don't have time for a long breakfast during the week because I start work really early in the morning.

After breakfast, I like to get out of the house, so I go for a walk in the park, or I sometimes ride my bike. And in the afternoon, I spend time with friends. We don't do anything special. We just have a coffee and chat, or maybe go to see a movie.

When I get home in the evening, I usually have a bath because I want to feel really relaxed. I go to bed quite early and sleep well … and then I'm ready for another busy week!

146

UNIT 4 WRITING BANK

Asking for information

1. Look at the pictures. In pairs, say which you room you prefer. Why?

2. Read the message. In pairs, answer the questions.
   1. Which room does Kim want to rent?
   2. What extra information does she ask about?
   3. When does she want to visit the room?

3. Read the message again. Put the information in the correct order.
   a. ☐ Ask for information about the neighbourhood
   b. ☐ Ask for more information about the room
   c. ☐ Explain why she is writing
   d. ☐ Ask to visit the room
   e. ☐ Introduce herself

4. Put the words in the correct order. Check your answers in the text.
   1. interested / I'm / in / Burnaby / renting / the / in / room
   ....
   2. I / about / have / questions / it / some
   ....
   3. see / come / I / one / could / and / afternoon / it
   ....?

5. Read the Writing box. Write a message asking for information about one of the rooms. Think about:
   1. which room you want to rent.
   2. why you want to rent it.
   3. how long you are in Vancouver.
   4. what information you want to know.

asking for information

When you write to ask for information, introduce yourself and say why you are writing, then ask questions.

- Use *I'm interested in* + *-ing* form of the verb to say why you're writing:
  I'm interested in renting the flat.
- Use *About* + topic and then ask specific questions:
  About the price: Does it include Wi-Fi?
- Use *Could I …?* to make polite requests.
  Could I visit the flat next week?

Roomfinder

Vancouver: rooms available

Mount Pleasant
$190 per week   Contact

Burnaby
$280 per week   Contact

Langley
$250 per week   Contact

Hi,

My name's Kim and I'm a medical student. I'm in Vancouver for three months and I need a large bedroom with a desk so I can study. I'm interested in renting the room in Burnaby. It looks nice and comfortable, but I have some questions about it.

About the room: Does it have a bathroom? Is Wi-Fi included in the price? Is there good Wi-Fi access in the bedroom?

About the neighbourhood: Is there a bus stop near the flat? Is it easy to get to the General Hospital?

I'd also like to see the room. Could I come one afternoon and see it?

Thanks for your help,

Kim

WRITING BANK — UNIT 5

Describing a photo

1 Look at the picture. In pairs, answer the questions. Read the text and check.
   1 Where are the people?
   2 What are they doing?
   3 What other things can you see?

2 Complete the sentences with the present simple or present continuous forms of the verbs in the box. Check your answers in the text.

come	look	want (x2)	wear

   1 I always .... here when I .... to buy presents.
   2 They .... sunglasses because it's a lovely day.
   3 Sandra .... at some necklaces because she .... a present for her mother.

3 Match the people and things with the positions in the picture.
   1 Sandra ....   a at the top
   2 Carlos ....   b on the left
   3 earrings ....   c in the middle
   4 baby hats .... d on the right

4 Read the Writing box. Find a photo of some of your friends and write a description. Think about:
   1 Where are they?
   2 Who are they?
   3 What are they doing?
   4 What other things can you see in the picture?
   5 What is the position of these things?

describing a photo

When you describe a photo, use the present simple and present continuous tenses.

- Say who the people are and what they're doing:
  That's Michael, my brother. He's trying on a hat.
- Use *there is/are* to talk about other things in the photo:
  There are some great second-hand clothes.
- Describe position: *on the right/left, at the top/bottom, in the middle*:
  Can you see the jackets on the left (of the picture)?

 Photoshare Sign out   Profile

Babi W Follow
200 posts   98 followers

This is a photo of my friends at the street market in the town centre. I always come here when I want to buy presents. That's Sandra on the right. She's an old university friend. And in the middle is her boyfriend, Carlos. They're wearing sunglasses because it's a lovely day. Sandra's looking at some necklaces because she wants a present for her mother. There are some really pretty earrings on the left, too. And can you see the baby hats at the top of the picture? They're so cute!

 Share   Like   Comment

UNIT 6 WRITING BANK

Messaging

1 In pairs, answer the questions.
   1 How many messages do you send each day?
   2 How many people do you call each day?
   3 Why is it easier to send a message?
   4 When is it better to call someone?

2 a Look at the messages in a. In pairs, order them to make a conversation.

b Look at the conversation below and check your answers to exercise 2a.

c <u>Underline</u> the words that aren't included in the messages.

Me I'm going to the town centre. Do you want to meet for a coffee?
Ethan That's a great idea! I'm studying for my exams and I really need a break! Where shall we meet?
Me Why don't we go to Dream Bean? It's on Marshall Street.
Ethan That sounds great. Shall we meet at 2.00? Is that OK?
Me Yes, that's cool. See you later.
Ethan The traffic is really bad. I'm late. I'm sorry!
Me That's no problem. I'm waiting at a table near the window now.

messaging

When we write short text messages we can include only the important information. We don't always include words that the reader can easily guess.

- *I* in the present simple: *I love it!* > *Love it!*
- *I am* in the present continuous: *I'm working today.* → *Working today.*
- Articles (*a, an, the*): *Get a taxi to the cinema* → *Get taxi to cinema*
- *is/are* to describe people and things: *The restaurant is busy.* → *Restaurant busy. David is at home* → *David at home.*
- *Do you* in Y/N questions: *Do you want to meet up?* → *Want to meet up?*
- Question phrases when the meaning is clear: *Where shall we meet?* → *Where? Shall we meet at 2.00?* → *meet at 2.00?*

3 Read the Writing box. In pairs, read the conversation in b and cross out words to make short text messages.

> Hi Pablo! It's raining a lot. Shall we cancel the football match? Carla and Gary are at the gym. Do you want to play tennis instead? What time shall we meet?

> Yes, the weather is horrible today! I'm sitting on the sofa watching TV right now! A game of tennis sounds great. Why don't we meet at the gym at 10.30? How about lunch at the new Italian restaurant?

> That's a great idea! The food is really good there! See you later.

4 In pairs, have a conversation using short messages. Think about:
   1 What are you doing now?
   2 What do you want to do?
   3 Where and when do you want to meet?

WRITING BANK UNIT 7

An informal email

1 a Read the email messages. In pairs, put them in the correct order.

   1 .... 2 .... 3 .... 4 ....

   b Look at the picture. Which email was it sent with?

2 Read the emails again. In pairs, answer the questions.
   1 What was Jon's birthday present?
   2 Who had the idea?
   3 Why didn't Ulrike go on the trip?
   4 Did they have a good time?

3 In pairs, find phrases to:
   1 start an email
   2 ask how people are
   3 start a reply
   4 say why you're writing
   5 end an email

4 a Read the Writing box. Write an informal email to your partner about a trip you went on recently.

   b In pairs, swap emails and write a short reply.

an informal email

We write informal emails to friends and people we know well.

- Start an email in a friendly way: *Hi ..., Hello ...*
- Ask about the person: *How are you? How are things? I hope you're well.*
- Mention earlier emails in replies: *Great to hear from you, Thanks for writing.*
- Say why you are writing: *I (just) wanted to tell/ask/ thank you ...*
- Finish the email in a friendly way: *See you soon, Bye for now, Take care.*

a

Hi Carola, how are things?
I just wanted to ask about Jon's birthday present. Are you still looking for an idea? What about this? It's a special offer for hot air balloon trips. I think he'd love it! You can book tickets on the website.
Bye for now,
Ulrike

b

Hello Ulrike, it's great to hear from you!
I just wanted to thank you for your fantastic idea. I'm booking tickets for the balloon trip today. Can you come too? Jon and I want to see you again.
Take care
Carola

c

Hi Ulrike, I hope you're well.
I wanted to tell you about the balloon trip. Jon loved his birthday present. The views were so beautiful up there. The trip took three hours and when we got back we had a picnic in the park. The weather was perfect – it was warm, sunny and not windy at all. Here's a photo of us in the balloon.
All the best,
Carola

d

Hello Carola, thanks for writing.
And thanks for inviting me, but I can't come. I have a big project to finish next week. I hope you have a great time. Send me some photos, please!
Speak soon,
Ulrike

UNIT 8 WRITING BANK

A biography

1. **a** Look at the pictures. In pairs, answer the questions.
   1. Do you know the film? What is it about?
   2. What is the relationship between the film and the man?

   b Read the biography and check your answers.

2. Read the biography again and answer the questions.
   1. Where was Stieg Larsson born?
   2. What did his parents give him as a present?
   3. What was his main job?
   4. Why didn't he see his books in the shops?
   5. Which actors were in *The Girl with the Dragon Tattoo*?
   6. Who wrote *The Girl in the Spider's Web*?

3. In pairs, underline all the past simple verbs in the biography. In pairs, answer the questions.
   1. Which verbs are regular and which are irregular?
   2. What is the purpose of the first paragraph?
   3. Are the events in the order that they happened?

4. Read the Writing box. Choose a famous person who isn't alive. Write a biography, using this information:
   1. Why is he/she famous?
   2. When was he/she born?
   3. What were the most important events in his/her life?
   4. Where did he/she live?
   5. Did he/she get married and have children? When?
   6. When did he/she die?

> ### a biography
>
> A biography is a short summary about someone's life.
> - The first paragraph is short and explains who the person is, where they are from and why they are famous.
> - The next paragraphs explain the most important events in the person's life in the order that they happened.
> - If the person isn't alive we use the past simple for all of the events.

Stieg Larsson was a writer and journalist. He was born in 1954 in Sweden. He is famous for the *Millennium Trilogy* of books.

On his 12th birthday, Larsson's parents gave Stieg a typewriter as a gift and he knew he wanted to write. He worked as a journalist for many years, but in his free time, he began writing a series of novels about Lisbeth Salander, a woman with a photographic memory, and Mikael Blomkvist, a journalist.

He didn't get married and he didn't have children, but he lived with his partner Eva Gabrielsson in Stockholm. Unfortunately, he never saw his books in the shops because he died in 2004 at the age of 50. His books came out after his death and were very successful around the world. In 2011, Daniel Craig and Rooney Mara appeared in a film version of the books called *The Girl with the Dragon Tattoo*.

In 2013, another Swedish writer, David Lagercrantz, decided to continue the *Millennium* series with the same characters. They made a film based on his first book, *The Girl in the Spider's Web*, in 2018.

WRITING BANK UNIT 9

A review

1. Look at the pictures of the restaurants. In pairs, answer the questions.
   1. What type of food can you eat?
   2. Which would you prefer? Why?

2. Read the reviews. Complete them by adding 'rate your restaurant' stars.

3. Read the reviews again. Tick (✓) the things that the reviews mention.

	Al Toke Pez	La Lucha Sanguchería
1 the food	☐	☐
2 the drinks	☐	☐
3 the menu options	☐	☐
4 the restaurant size	☐	☐
5 the service	☐	☐
6 the price	☐	☐
7 the waiting time	☐	☐

4. Order the paragraphs in the reviews.
   a ☐ positive points   c ☐ advice for customers
   b ☐ negative points   d ☐ description of restaurant

5. Read the Writing box. Think of a restaurant you went to recently. Write a review of it.

a review

When you write a review, you give useful information to other customers.

- Start with a quick description of the restaurant and say when you went there.
- Talk about the positive points: *I like it because …, The … are/is great/delicious/friendly*
- Talk about the negative points: *The only problem is that …, However there isn't/aren't …*
- Finish the review with advice for other customers: *If you eat here, you should …, I recommend …*

Restaurants in Lima, Peru

Al Toke Pez

Some friends told me about this place, so I came here last Sunday for lunch. It's a tiny restaurant near Miraflores. They cook the food right in front of you. It's like you're eating in somebody's kitchen! We got the 'combinado' taster dish which included ceviche, fried fish, rice and chicha morada (a purple corn drink). The food was delicious and the waiters were really friendly. It only cost 17 soles – that's around $5, which is really cheap for this area.
The only problem is that only ten people can eat at the same time … and lots of people want to eat here. We waited about 40 minutes to get a table, but I think it was worth it!
I recommend this restaurant if you are in Lima and you're looking for local food at a good price, but you should get here early.

 rate your restaurant

La Lucha Sanguchería

I come to this snack bar near Kennedy Park about once a week. Lots of people come here to get sandwiches and chips for lunch. You pay for your food, then you find a seat and the waiters bring it to you.
I like it because the food is simple and all the ingredients are fresh. I usually get a smoothie too – they make them with lots of fresh fruit and they're delicious. The waiters are great and they serve the food really quickly, so you don't have to wait long.
However, it isn't great for vegetarians. Most of the sandwiches have meat in them. They have some salads on the menu, but there isn't much choice.
If you go to this restaurant, you should sit outside on the street. It's a great place to watch the people in Kennedy Park.

 rate your restaurant

UNIT 10 WRITING BANK

An online post

1 Look at the pictures. In pairs, answer the questions.
1 Do you have a PC or a laptop?
2 What do you use it for?
3 Which is better? Why?

2 Compare laptops and PCs using the comparatives of the adjectives in the box.

> big   cheap   comfortable   easy to use
> heavy   powerful

3 Read the online posts. Tick (✓) the best summary of Sam's reply.
a Laptops are better because you can use them anywhere. ☐
b PCs are better because they are more powerful. ☐
c There are advantages and disadvantages of PCs and laptops. ☐

4 a Match the halves to make sentences. Check your answers in the text.
1 It's a difficult question,
2 You can buy cheap laptops,
3 You can only use a PC at home.

a However, a PC is more comfortable to use.
b although they aren't very powerful.
c but I'll try to answer it!

b How do you say the words in **bold** in your language?

✎ an online post

When you write an online post, try to be objective and talk about the advantages and disadvantages so people can make a decision.

- Use comparatives to compare different options: *PCs are heavier than laptops.*
- Qualify your opinions: *I think a PC is better if you need/ want to …,*
- Use **but**, **although** and **however** to contrast information:
  Laptops are light, **but** tablets are lighter.
  This laptop is cheap, **although** it isn't very powerful.
  I prefer PCs. **However**, I know lots of people with laptops.

5 Read the Writing box. Choose one of the questions and reply with an online post.
1 I'm looking for a new flat to rent. Should I live in the city centre or out of town?
2 What's the best way to get fit? Should I join a gym or get a personal trainer?
3 I have two weeks of holiday. Should I go abroad or stay in the country?

StudentBUZZ

Laptop or PC for uni?

Laura G (11 June)

Hi, I'm going to start university in September and I need a computer. Is it better to buy a laptop or a PC? Please can someone help me?
Thanks!

Replies (1)

Sam Wilcox (12 June)

Hi Laura, it's a difficult question, but I'll try to answer it! A laptop is more portable than a PC. That means you can take a laptop to class, to the library, or use it at friend's house, but you can only use a PC at home. However, a PC is more comfortable to use. The keyboard is bigger and the mouse is easier to use. So I think a PC is better if you need to write lots of long reports.

The next thing to think about is price. Laptops are generally more expensive than PCs. You can buy cheap laptops, although they aren't very powerful. If you want to edit videos and photos or play computer games, then you need a powerful machine – and a powerful PC is cheaper than a powerful laptop. However, a cheap laptop is probably OK just to check the internet or do some university work.

Good luck with your course!

WRITING BANK UNIT 11

A formal email

1 Look at the job adverts. In pairs, which job do you think is the most interesting? Why?

Jobsquest

Junior office worker needed. A local online newspaper is looking for a young person with computer skills and good phone manner. Must have own car.

Airport information officer. Applicant should have excellent inter-personal skills, be good at teamwork, speak three languages, and be able to work flexible hours.

Monitor at summer camp. We're looking for a young person who loves working with children aged 8–14. You should like playing sports and play a musical instrument.

---

2 Read Serge's job application email. In pairs, answer the questions.
1 Which job is he applying for?
2 In what ways is he a good candidate for the job?
3 In what way isn't he a good candidate?
4 Do you think he will get the job?

3 Read the email again and answer the questions.
1 Does Serge know who he is writing to?
2 How does he start the email?
3 When does he explain why he is writing the email?
4 What information does he give in the other paragraphs?
5 How does he finish the email?

4 How does Serge make these sentences more formal?
1 I think I'm the right person for the job.
2 I can speak English and German, too.
3 I'm sorry but I can only work in the evenings.
4 You can send me an email if you have any questions.

a formal email

We write formal emails to people we don't know for important or official reasons, e.g. job applications.

- Start the email politely: *Dear Mr Jones, Dear Sir/Madam*
- Explain who you are and why you're writing: *My name is … and I am writing to …*
- Don't use contractions: *My name is …* NOT ~~My name's …~~
- Try to use more formal language: *Please contact me …* NOT ~~You can send me an email …~~
- End the email formally: *Kind regards, Best wishes*

5 Choose one of the other jobs and write an application email.

To: info@LHRservices.com
From: serge.bernard@x-mail.com
Subject: job application

📎 serge_bernard_cv.doc

Dear Sir/Madam,

My name is Serge Bernard and I am writing to apply for the information officer job advertised on the Jobsquest website.

I am 23 years old and I am a student at Central University. I believe I am the right person for the job because I speak four languages. I am half French and half Spanish and I can also speak English and German. I am very sociable, friendly and patient, which I think is important in this job. I also like working in a team and I play in the university basketball team every week.

I am afraid I can only work in the evenings and at the weekend because I have to study during the week. I hope this is not a problem.

My CV is attached. Please contact me if you have any questions.

Kind regards,

Serge Bernard

UNIT 12 | WRITING BANK

An information leaflet

1 Look at the pictures of language learners. In pairs, answer the questions.
  1 What are the people doing?
  2 Do you want/need to do these activities?
  3 What's the best way to do these things well?

2 Read the leaflet about learning English. In pairs, answer the questions.
  1 Do you agree with the tips? Why/Why not?
  2 Which tip do you think is most useful?

3 In pairs, answer the questions.
  1 Is the leaflet easy to read?
  2 Who is 'you' in the leaflet?
  3 Why does the writer ask questions?
  4 Do the headings help you?

4 Put the words in the correct order to make sentences from the text. Who is the subject of the sentences?
  1 five / just / simple / these / steps / follow
  _____!
  2 think / don't / what / people / worry / other
  _____.
  3 something / about / video / talking / yourself
  _____.

5 Choose a different topic and write an information leaflet with five steps.

  Get fit   Avoid stress   Sleep well
  Make money   Be happy   Find love

an information leaflet

Information leaflets should be easy to read.
- Use headings to break up the text and say what each section is about.
- Write to the readers as 'you' so it's more personal.
- Ask questions so readers think about the topic.
- Use the imperative to give general advice:
  *Always **listen** to the teacher.*
  ***Don't forget** to do your homework.*

FIVE STEPS TO FLUENCY!

Do you want to speak English fluently? It isn't as difficult as you think. Just follow these five simple steps!

1 Make mistakes
Are you sometimes afraid to speak because you don't want to make a mistake? That's not good! Don't worry what other people think. Everyone makes mistakes – it's normal … in fact it's the best way to learn!

2 Be confident
Maybe you've failed English tests before, but exams are all about grammar. Speaking is different. Forget about your tests. Relax and say what you want to say.

3 Listen and learn
You can learn a lot from other English speakers. Listen to how they say things and copy them. If you don't have English-speaking friends, watch your heroes on YouTube!

4 Video yourself
Have you ever recorded yourself speaking? It's a great way to improve. First, video yourself talking about something. After that, watch it and think about what you can do better. Then video yourself again talking about the same thing. The second time will be better, I promise!

5 Travel
The best way to practise English is when you *have to* speak English. That means you should be with people who don't speak your language! You don't have to go to the USA or the UK. English is the world's international language, so go to any country – it's easy to find somebody to talk to.

155

EXAM PRACTICE UNIT 1

Talking about yourself

✓ exam information

In this part of the exam you work in pairs, or sometimes in a group of three. You answer simple questions about yourself and talk about everyday topics.

1 🔊 **1.13** Listen to the conversation. In pairs, answer the questions.
   1 What three questions does the examiner ask?
   2 Do Jorge and Laura give long or short answers?

💡 tip

At the beginning of the exam, the questions are easy and you only need to give short answers.

2 Read the tip box. In pairs, ask and answer the questions.
   1 What's your name?
   2 Where do you live?
   3 Do you work or are you a student?

3 🔊 **1.14** Listen to the conversation. In pairs, answer the questions.
   1 How many topics do Jorge and Laura talk about?
   2 Do they answer the same questions or different ones?
   3 What is important about the *Tell me something about …* question?

💡 tip

Next, the examiner asks you about **two** topics related to your daily life (food, shopping, free time, etc.).

For each topic, you have two short-answer questions.

For one topic you also have a *Tell me something about …* question.

Answer with three sentences or more.

4 a Read the tip box. In groups of three, decide who is an examiner and who are Students A and B. Ask and answer the ten exam task questions.

   b Swap roles and repeat the task.

exam task

Now, let's talk about shopping.
_____

(Short questions for Student A)
1 What's your favourite place to go shopping?
2 How do you travel when you go shopping?

(Short questions for Student B)
3 What sort of things do you enjoy buying?
4 How often do you go shopping?

(Long question for Student A)
5 Please tell me something about the last thing you bought.

Now, let's talk about holidays.
_____

(Short questions for Student B)
6 What activities do you like doing on holiday?
7 Who do you usually go on holiday with?

(Short questions for Student A)
8 Where do you stay when you go away on holiday?
9 What things do you take with you when you go on holiday?

(Long question for Student B)
10 Please tell me something about a good holiday you had.

UNIT 2 EXAM PRACTICE

Completing a short text

✓ **exam information**

In this part of the exam you complete a short text by writing words in gaps. The text is an email or a blog post.

1 Look at the exam task. In pairs, answer the questions.
  1 How many gaps do you have to complete?
  2 What kind of words are they?
  3 Can you write more than one word in a gap?

💡 **tip**

Read the whole text first to get an idea of what it is about.
When you complete a gap, look carefully at the language around it. What type of word do you need?
When you have finished, read the whole text again to check it makes sense.

2 Read the tip box. In pairs, match the types of words with the gaps in the exam task in exercise 3.
  1 .... a a verb we use before adjectives
  2 .... b a preposition (*on, at, in*, etc.)
  3 .... c a word we use when we compare two things
  4 .... d a word used to talk about regular actions
  5 .... e a linker to join ideas (*and, or, because, but*, etc.)
  6 .... f an article (*a, an, the*, etc.)

3 Complete the exam task. Check your answers in pairs.

exam task

For each question, write the correct answer.
Write **ONE** word for each gap.
Example: **0 old**

A Malaysian student in Edinburgh

My name's Matthew and I'm from Malaysia. I'm 19 years (0)............... . At the moment, I'm studying (1)............... Edinburgh University in the UK. I love Edinburgh, (2)............... there are some things from Malaysia that I miss. For example, (3)............... weather is very cold here! In Malaysia it's always hot. We swim almost (4)............... day, and during the holidays we go hiking in the rainforest. The shops (5)............... different, too. In my city in Malaysia the shops stay open much later (6)............... they do here. However, Edinburgh is a beautiful city and everyone is so friendly. I'm very happy here!

Writing a message

✓ **exam information**

In this part of the exam you write a short email or a note to a friend. You have to write 25 words or more.

1 Look at the exam task. In pairs, answer the questions.
  1 Who do you write to?
  2 What do you write about?
  3 How many pieces of information must you include?

2 Read a student's answer. Underline the three pieces of information from the task.

Hi Ali,
I live in an apartment in a quiet part of Milan, in Italy. I live with my parents and my brother. I like my home because it's close to my university.
Best wishes
Marco

💡 **tip**

Read the instructions carefully to understand why you are writing the message and what information to include.
Write between 25–35 words.

3 Read the tip box. Complete the exam task in exercise 1. Then swap with a partner and answer the questions.
  1 Did he/she include all the information?
  2 Is the word count OK?
  3 Are there any mistakes with the spelling or grammar?

exam task

Your English penfriend, Ali, wants to know something about your home.
Write an email to Ali.
Tell Ali:
- where you live
- who you live with
- why you like your home.

Write **25 words** or more.

EXAM PRACTICE   UNIT 3

Listening to a long conversation

exam information

In this part of the exam you listen to a long conversation and complete a matching task.

1 Look at the exam task. In pairs, answer the questions.
   1 Who are the speakers?
   2 What is the topic of this conversation?
   3 Look at the list on the left. How many people are there?
   4 Look at the list on the right. How many activities are there?

tip

You won't always hear the words exactly as they appear in the list on the right. For example, if the answer is 'clothes', you may hear 'shirts and trousers.'

You often hear words related to two of the options for a question, but only one is correct.

You hear the conversation twice. If you miss an answer the first time, don't worry. Move to the next question.

2 Read the tip box and the beginning of the conversation. Then answer the questions.

   Dad   Are you going out again this evening, Holly? Aren't you really tired?
   Holly I *am* quite tired, Dad, but meeting up with people always makes me feel better. It's my favourite way to relax. I prefer it to watching TV.

   1 Underline the words that match F.
   2 Why isn't H the right answer?

3 Look at the list of activities in the exam task. In pairs, guess which words the speakers might say if they talk about each of the topics.

4 🔊 3.8 Listen and complete the exam task. Compare your answers in pairs. Do you remember which words and phrases gave you the answers?

exam task

For each question, choose the correct answer.

You will hear Holly talking to her dad about her friends. What is each friend's favourite way to relax?

Example

0 Holly   [F]

People

1 Jessica ☐

2 Liam   ☐

3 Poppy   ☐

4 Josh   ☐

5 Daniel   ☐

Favourite way to relax

A cooking

B photography

C playing an instrument

D playing video games

E riding a bike

F seeing friends

G walking

H watching TV

UNIT 4 EXAM PRACTICE

Reading three short texts

✓ **exam information**

In this part of the exam you read three short texts and match them to questions.

💡 **tip**

Read the texts to understand the general idea of what they are about.

For each question, underline the information you need to find.

1 Look at the exam task. In pairs, answer the questions.
  1 How many questions are there?
  2 What is the topic of the texts?
  3 What do you have to do?

2 Read the tip box. Then look at the underlined words in question 1. Find the text that has this information.

3 Underline the information you need to find in questions 2–7. Then complete the task.

exam task

For each question, choose the correct answer.

		Lotte	Anna	Emily
1	Who says guests are <u>not allowed to cook</u> in her home?	A	B	C
2	Who explains what kinds of transport are available near her home?	A	B	C
3	Who says she is happy to spend time with her guests?	A	B	C
4	Who describes what you can see from one of the rooms?	A	B	C
5	Who gives information about a good place to go shopping?	A	B	C
6	Who explains why guests must use the stairs to get to her home?	A	B	C
7	Who says that her home can be noisy?	A	B	C

Three wonderful city centre homes to rent

Lotte – Amsterdam

My apartment is in a beautiful 17th century house on the canal in Amsterdam. It has a small kitchen, a sitting room, an outdoor terrace, a bathroom and two bedrooms. You may use the whole apartment during your stay, but there's one important thing you need to know – it's on the fourth floor and, because of the age of the building, there's no lift! I'm always available if you have any questions, and you're very welcome to join me if I am going out in the evening.

Anna – Melbourne

My bright and modern apartment is right in the centre of Melbourne. The kitchen is big enough for the whole family, and there's a comfortable living room that has a fantastic view of the city centre. Because it's so central, you may want to close the windows at night as the traffic is sometimes quite loud. You can catch trains and trams to all the famous sights from just outside the front door and there are maps and guidebooks to help you plan your stay.

Emily – York

My traditional townhouse is 140 years old and is just a short walk from York's beautiful medieval city centre. I live here with my husband and children and rent out a large double bedroom on the second floor. At the moment the kitchen is not available for guests, but there are many lovely cafés nearby. Across the road is a beautiful park with a Saturday morning market. People come from all over Europe to visit this! Let me know if you are coming by car, as parking is difficult.

159

EXAM PRACTICE UNIT 5

Answering questions about a conversation

✓ exam information

In this part of the exam you listen to a long conversation and answer questions about it. Most of the questions are about facts and details, but some are about feelings or opinions.

1 Look at the exam task. In pairs, answer the questions.
  1 What is the topic of the conversation?
  2 Which questions are about facts, and which are about feelings or opinions?
  3 How many options are there for each question?

💡 tip

You have 20 seconds to read through the questions before the conversation starts. As you read, think about what the speakers might say.

You usually hear things related to all three options, but only one is the correct answer.

2 Read the tip box and the first part of the conversation. Which option in question 1 is the correct answer? Why are the other two wrong?

Steven Ollie, can you come shopping with me this weekend? I really need some new clothes and you're great at giving advice.
Ollie Sure! Is Saturday afternoon OK? I'm playing football on Saturday morning, and I want to sleep late on Sunday.
Steven No problem!

3 🔊 5.8 Read the other questions. In pairs, think about what words you might hear if the options are correct. Complete the exam task.

4 Compare your answers in pairs. Try to remember the words that match the correct options.

exam task

For each question, choose the correct answer.

You will hear Steven talking to his friend Ollie about going shopping.

1 When will Steven and Ollie go shopping?
  A Saturday morning
  B Saturday afternoon
  C Sunday morning

2 What does Steven want to buy?
  A clothes for going out
  B clothes for doing sport
  C clothes for every day

3 Why does Ollie suggest going to Westlake Shopping Centre?
  A It's closer than the city.
  B He may get some discounts there.
  C It's his favourite place to shop.

4 Steven is happy to go to Westlake Shopping Centre because
  A it's never crowded.
  B the shops are indoors.
  C it stays open late.

5 How will they travel to the shopping centre?
  A by bus
  B by car
  C by train

6 What time will they meet?
  A 4 p.m.
  B 4.15
  C 4.30

UNIT 6 EXAM PRACTICE

Discussing a topic

✓ **exam information**

In this part of the exam you look at some pictures and discuss the topic with your partner. Then you answer some of the examiner's questions about the topic.

1 🔊 6.9 Look at the pictures and listen to two students doing the task. Then answer the questions.
   1 What is the topic of the task?
   2 Do the students talk about every picture?
   3 What questions does the examiner ask Anthi and Nicolas?

💡 **tip**

The examiner will let you speak together about the pictures for 1–2 minutes. Try to talk about all the pictures.

Ask your partner questions and respond to what he/she says.

2 Read the tip box. Are the phrases asking questions (Q) or responding to what someone says (R)?
   1 What about you?   ☐
   2 Me too!   ☐
   3 Do you like cycling?   ☐
   4 Really?   ☐
   5 What do you think of cycling? ☐
   6 Oh, that's great.   ☐

3 In pairs, do the task. Remember to ask questions and respond to what your partner says.

4 🔊 6.10 Listen to the next section of the exam and answer the questions.
   1 What are the questions about?
   2 Do Nicholas and Anthi answer the same questions?
   3 Why does the examiner ask *Why*?

💡 **tip**

Try to give reasons for your answers. If you don't, the examiner can ask you *Why*?

If you don't understand the examiner, you can ask him/her to repeat what they said.

5 Read the tip box. In pairs, ask and answer the questions. Remember to give reasons for your answers.
   1 Do you prefer to do sports alone or with other people? Why?
   2 Which sport do you want to try in the future? Why?
   3 Do you prefer watching sports on TV or playing them? Why?
   4 Which sports are best for relaxing? Why?

exam task

Do you like these different sports?

161

EXAM PRACTICE UNIT 7

Reading a long article

✓ exam information

In this part of the exam you read a long article about one topic and answer questions about it.

1 Look at the exam task. In pairs, answer the questions.
   1 What is the article about?
   2 How many options are there for each question?

tip

Read the text first to get the general idea.

Look at the questions carefully. For each question find the paragraph which has the answers.

Read the paragraph carefully and find the sentence(s) which matches one of the options exactly.

2 Read the tip box. Then read the text once. Tick (✓) the best description of the article.
   A Advice for swimmers in Mexico ☐
   B A description of a swimming holiday ☐
   C An advert for swimming lessons ☐

3 Look at question 1 and read the underlined sentences in the first paragraph carefully. In pairs, answer the questions.
   1 Which is the correct answer?
   2 Why aren't the other options correct?
   3 Do you think it was difficult to answer? Why?

4 Complete the exam task and underline the sentences that match the correct options.

5 Compare your answers in pairs. Did you underline the same sentences?

exam task

For each question, choose the correct answer.

A Mexican swimming adventure

By Helen Knowles

I <u>always liked the idea of 'wild swimming'</u> in rivers or lakes, but <u>I was too afraid of deep, cold water to actually leave my nice, safe pool and try it</u>. Then I saw an advert for a swimming holiday in Mexico. <u>The price</u> <u>looked OK</u> and the pictures of clear, warm seas made me think <u>this was a kind of wild swimming I might enjoy</u>.

I booked my place and travelled to the island of Espiritu Santo in the Sea of Cortez, where I met the ten other swimmers on the trip. We stayed in a campsite right by the beach, and every day after breakfast we met our guide at the harbour and sailed out to beautiful little bays for our swims.

Some of the swimmers in the group talked a lot about times and who was the fastest, but most were like me, and were there just to swim slowly and enjoy ourselves. Luckily, we were put into groups by the guide so we always swam with people who were the same level as us. In the mornings we swam around 3 km. Then we returned to camp for a break and a delicious lunch prepared by our team chef. After that we got back on the boat for another shorter swim of around 2 km.

It was a fantastic holiday. Over the week I swam 25 kilometres, explored a beautiful island and got a lot fitter. And the best thing is – I'm not scared of deep water anymore. I can't wait to join a wild swimming club near me and start exploring.

1 Why did Helen choose the holiday in Mexico?
   A It looked cheaper than other swimming holidays.
   B She was bored of swimming in a pool.
   C She wanted to try wild swimming.

2 What do we learn about Helen's holiday from the second paragraph?
   A She went with friends from home.
   B Every morning there was a boat trip.
   C She slept in a different campsite every night.

3 Helen was happy because
   A she didn't have to swim with the fast swimmers.
   B she was better than most of the other swimmers.
   C she was able to choose who to swim with each day.

4 What does Helen say about lunch?
   A She sometimes stayed on the boat to eat it.
   B The food was better on some days than others.
   C The group had it between the two swims of the day.

5 What was Helen most pleased about after her holiday?
   A She has become very fit.
   B She is able to swim in new places.
   C She can swim further than before.

162

UNIT 8 EXAM PRACTICE

Completing a factual text

✓ exam information

In this part of the exam you read a short news article or information text and complete gaps by choosing the correct words.

1 Look at exam task. In pairs, answer the questions.
   1 What kind of text is it?
   2 What is the text about?
   3 What types of words are tested in this task?

💡 tip

Read the whole text first to understand the main ideas in the text.

Read the sentences before and after the gap carefully. Sometimes other sentences help you to choose the correct answer.

Sometimes the three options have similar meanings, but not all are grammatically correct. For example, you may need an uncountable or countable noun.

2 Read the tip box. Read the text once. In pairs, answer the questions.
   1 What does Inés Dawson do?
   2 Why did she decide to do it?

3 a Look at the three options for question 1. In pairs write a short sentence for each one.

   b Answer the questions.
   1 What does the first paragraph say about YouTube?
   2 Which of the three options matches the meaning of the paragraph best?
   3 Which of the three options goes best with 'most' in this sentence?

4 Complete the exam task. Compare your answers with a partner. Explain why you chose each one.

exam task

For each question, choose the correct answer.

A science star of the internet

YouTube is the world's most (1) .... video-sharing website. More than a billion hours of video are watched on it daily, on almost every topic you can (2) .... of, including science.

Inés Dawson is one of YouTube's best-known science 'vloggers'. She started her channel while she was still a university student. At the time she was bored with her studies and (3) .... that making videos might help her enjoy her subject again. It did. It also gave her the idea for her future career – science communication.

Inés posts videos in two (4) .... languages, Spanish and English. Each one (5) .... her a day to write, a few hours to film, and half a day to edit. In her videos, she works hard to share with her fans the pleasure she gets from (6) .... exciting new things about the world of science.

	A	B	C
1	favourite	special	popular
2	think	learn	understand
3	wanted	hoped	preferred
4	different	various	possible
5	has	lets	takes
6	getting on	finding out	taking off

EXAM PRACTICE UNIT 9

Understanding details in short dialogues

✔ **exam information**

In this part of the exam you listen to some short dialogues and answer a question for each one by choosing the correct picture.

1 Look at the exam task and answer the questions.
  1 Are the same people in all the conversations?
  2 How many pictures are there for each question?
  3 Are the questions about the main idea or specific information?

☼ **tip**

Read the questions very carefully and underline what information you need to listen for.

Look at the pictures and guess which words the speakers might say.

Listen carefully because the speakers mention all the options in the conversation but only one is the correct answer.

2 Read the tip box. Look at the underlined information in question 1 and read the first conversation. Which is the correct answer? Why are the others incorrect?

Woman Shall we meet for lunch tomorrow, Sonya?
Sonya Yes, sure. I'm doing some clothes shopping in the morning, but I'm free after that.
Woman Great! Well, I have to go to the library at 1 p.m., so why don't I wait for you there?
Sonya Perfect! Then we can walk down to James Street.

3 a In pairs, read the other questions and underline the information you need to listen for.

  b Look at the options and guess which words you might hear.

4 🔊 9.10 Listen and complete the exam task. Compare your answers in pairs. Explain why you chose the options.

exam task

For each question, choose the correct answer.

1 <u>Where</u> do the friends decide to <u>meet</u>?

A

B

C

2 What does the man decide to order?

A

B

C

3 What is the weather like at the moment?

A

B

C

UNIT 10 EXAM PRACTICE

Understanding short texts

✓ exam information

In this part of the exam you read some notices, signs and messages.

You answer a multiple choice question about each one.

💡 tip

Read the questions and options carefully.

Don't worry if you don't understand all the words in the texts.

Sometimes the options contain words or ideas from the text, but they aren't the correct answer.

1 Look at the exam task. In pairs, answer the questions.
   1 What kind of texts can you see?
   2 How many options are there under each text?
   3 Which have a question to answer?
   4 Which have a sentence to complete?

2 Read the tip box. In pairs, look at the text in question 1 and answer the questions below.
   1 How many of the words in the text don't you know?
   2 Read the question and the options and decide which is correct.
   3 Why are the other two options wrong?

3 Complete the exam task. Compare your answers in pairs.

exam task

For each question, choose the correct answer.

Put clothes into drum and close door. Insert coins, add soap and press start.

1 Where might you see these instructions?
   A on a box of soap
   B on a pair of trousers
   C on a washing machine

Sammy, I'm not coming to football practice tonight. I went for a run yesterday and I've done something to my knee. See you next week. Tom

2 Why did Tom write this email?
   A to ask Sammy for some help
   B to give Sammy some advice
   C to tell Sammy about a problem

We buy and recycle unwanted computers and laptops, and repair phone and tablet screens

3 What does this notice mean?
   A Mobiles are cheaper here than in other shops.
   B You may get some cash for your old equipment here.
   C You can learn how to look after your computer here.

From: Ali
To: Grace

Do you fancy going to the cinema tonight, or are you too busy? I'm happy to check what's on. We could get dinner afterwards.

4 Ali is asking Grace
   A if she's free to go out tonight.
   B if she prefers to have dinner or see a film.
   C if she can suggest a good film to see tonight.

Today is the last day to upload geography projects – several are still missing. If you're having problems using the new website, ask Mr Yip for help.

5 This notice says that students
   A should tell Mr Yip how he can improve the website.
   B who haven't uploaded their work yet need to do it today.
   C can't use the website to upload work at the moment.

From: Musicapp.com
To: Rick Prentice

You only have two days left to continue using Musicapp for free. Join today and get 50% off our usual price!

6 Why did Musicapp send this message?
   A to offer Rick Prentice a discount
   B to tell Rick Prentice about a change
   C to ask for Rick Prentice's opinion

EXAM PRACTICE UNIT 11

Listening and completing notes

✓ **exam information**

In this part of the exam you listen to one person speaking about a topic and you complete some notes.

1 Look at the exam task and answer the questions.
   1 What is the topic of the monologue?
   2 What kind of information must you listen for?

💡 **tip**

The information you need to write down will be specific details such as days, dates, times, places or spellings.
Sometimes the speaker will say, e.g. two dates or prices. Listen carefully. Which makes sense in the notes?

2 Read the tip box and question 1 in the task. What type of word do you need to complete the notes?

3 Read the first part of the message. Underline the two days mentioned. Which is correct?

> Oh, hello. This is a message for Imelda Finn. I'm calling from Tech Dreams. Thanks so much for meeting us last Tuesday. We're really pleased you've agreed to work here, and we're looking forward to your first day with us on Monday.

4 In pairs, match the other gaps with the types of words.
   a spelling ......
   b time ......
   c place ......
   d object ......

5 🔊 **11.9** Listen and complete the exam task. Compare your answers in pairs. Listen again and check.

exam task

For each question, write the correct answer in the gap. Write one word or a number or a date or a time.

You will hear a woman leaving a message about a new job.

First day of new job
Company: Tech Dreams
Start day: (1) ....
Time to arrive: (2) .... a.m.
Person to meet: (3) Jon ....
What to bring: (4) ....
Where to have lunch: (5) ....

Understanding the general idea of conversations

✓ **exam information**

In this part of the exam you listen to some short dialogues or monologues and answer a question for each one.

1 Look at the exam task and answer the questions.
   1 Are the same people in all the conversations?
   2 Are the questions about specific information?

💡 **tip**

Read the sentence so you know who is talking.
Read the question and options carefully so you know what information to listen for.
Don't worry if there are some words you don't understand.

2 Read the tip and the conversation for question 1. Which words show that A is the correct answer?

Jon Look at this, Eva. It's written by the police officer on that TV show you like.
Eva Show me. How much is it?
Jon It's only £7.50. It's got some great pictures in it.
Eva I don't think I'll get it. I actually read his blog every week on the internet. I'll probably never read this.
Jon OK then.

3 🔊 **11.10** Listen and complete the exam task. Write the words you heard that told you each answer.

4 Compare your answers with your partner.

exam task

For each question, choose the correct answer.

1 You will hear two friends talking together. What are they talking about?
   A buying a book
   B writing a blog
   C choosing a job

2 You will hear an advertisement on the radio. What is the advertisement for?
   A a food festival
   B a supermarket
   C a restaurant

3 You will hear a couple talking to each other. Who are they unhappy with?
   A the dentist
   B the pilot
   C the hairdresser

4 You will hear two friends talking about a painting. Where are the friends?
   A in a shop
   B in a museum
   C in someone's home

UNIT 12 EXAM PRACTICE

Writing a short story

✓ **exam information**

In this part of the exam you write a short story based on pictures. You have to write 35 words or more.

1 Look at the exam task. In pairs, answer the questions below. Then read the tip box.
   1 How many pictures are there?
   2 What do the pictures show?
   3 How many words should you write?

 tip

Look at the pictures. Think about where the people are, what they are doing and how they are feeling.

Include information about all three pictures.

Connect your ideas using linking words (*so/but/next/after that*) and reference words (*it/there/this/that/them*).

a Last year Sandy was feeling very bored with his life, so he started looking at websites about exciting places to visit. He found some great ones about the mountains of Patagonia and decided to go there. He had a fantastic time, hiking and taking photos of the beautiful views.

2 Look at the pictures on the right and read three stories about them (a–c). Does each story:
   1 have information about all the pictures?
   2 have the correct number of words?
   3 include linking and reference words?

3 In pairs, improve story c and include some linking words and reference words.

4 Complete the exam task. In pairs, swap stories and answer the questions from exercise 2.

b In my last summer holiday I was bored because all my friends were working. Then, one day I decided to go hiking in the mountains. They were really beautiful, and I took lots of photos of them. It was a great trip!

c Tom was very bored one day. He looked on his computer. He found some mountains. He went to the mountains. He took a lot of photos.

exam task

Look at the three pictures.
Write the story shown in the pictures.
Write **35 words** or more.

167

IRREGULAR VERBS

Infinitive	Past simple	Past participle
be	was, were	been
become	became	become
begin	began	begun
break	broke	broken
bring	brought	brought
build	built	built
buy	bought	bought
choose	chose	chosen
come	came	come
cost	cost	cost
do	did	done
drink	drank	drunk
eat	ate	eaten
fall	fell	fallen
feel	felt	felt
find	found	found
fly	flew	flown
forget	forgot	forgotten
get	got	got
give	gave	given
go	went	gone, been
have	had	had
hear	heard	heard
hold	held	held
keep	kept	kept
know	knew	known
leave	left	left
let	let	let
lose	lost	lost

Infinitive	Past simple	Past participle
make	made	made
meet	met	met
pay	paid	paid
put	put	put
read /riːd/	read /red/	read /red/
ride	rode	ridden
ring	rang	rung
run	ran	run
say	said	said
see	saw	seen
sell	sold	sold
send	sent	sent
show	showed	shown
sing	sang	sung
sit	sat	sat
sleep	slept	slept
speak	spoke	spoken
spend	spent	spent
stand	stood	stood
swim	swam	swum
take	took	taken
teach	taught	taught
tell	told	told
think	thought	thought
throw	threw	thrown
wake	woke	woken
wear	wore	worn
win	won	won
write	wrote	written